James S. Stewart
WALKING WITH GOD

Edited by
THE REVD GORDON GRANT

With an Introductory Memoir by
THE VERY REVD W. J. G. McDONALD DD

SAINT ANDREW PRESS
— • EDINBURGH • —

First published in 1996 by
SAINT ANDREW PRESS
121 George Street, Edinburgh EH2 4YN

Copyright of original sermons © James S. Stewart 1996
Copyright of publication © J. Gordon Grant (editor) 1996

ISBN 0 7152 0722 9

British Library Cataloguing in Publication Data
A catalogue record for this book
is available from the British Library.

ISBN 0715207229

Cover and **design concept** by Mark Blackadder.
Cover photographs of James S Stewart used with permission.
Typeset in 10.5/12 pt Bembo by Lesley A Taylor.
Printed and **bound** by BPC Wheatons Ltd, Exeter

Contents

James S. Stewart
SELECTED SERMONS

Acknowledgments

ONE of the outstanding characteristics of Professor Stewart's sermons is – like the Gospel itself – their timelessness. Some of them were first preached in Beechgrove Church, Aberdeen in the 1930s; most of them in North Morningside Church, Edinburgh during the 1940s, although many were amended and preached over the next forty years in locations as diverse as Daliburgh, South Uist and Melbourne, Australia.

The occasional reference dates a sermon's composition as having been during the Second World War, and this also accounts for some of the forms of expression used. For example, inclusive language was not yet in vogue. The sermons are now published exactly as Dr Stewart preached them – so that readers who remember his voice can still hear the vibrant accents of his passionate delivery sounding forth through the printed page.

The selection and publication of these sermons has been for me an inspiring privilege, particularly as the sermons were written in Dr Stewart's clear and legible handwriting. The sermon titles are his own, apart from sermons 1, 2, 15, 18, 22, 23 and 26 for which he left no titles. In these cases I have chosen the titles myself. The main title for the book is taken from the first sermon and seems appropriate for one whose own walk was so close with God.

I would finally like to record my grateful appreciation for the helpful co-operation of Dr Murray Simpson, who was at that time Librarian of New College Library, and to Lesley Taylor of Saint Andrew Press.

Gordon Grant
EDINBURGH 1996

Foreword

WHEN I asked my friend the Revd J. Gordon Grant BD whether he would consider making a selection of my father's sermons not already published in book form, he immediately agreed. This book is the result. It seemed a happy idea to include in the volume a personal memoir by one who had known my father for many years. This has been undertaken by the Very Revd Bill McDonald DD, his friend and parish minister. I wish to express my profound thanks to both Gordon and Bill, without whose labours this book could not have been published.

In these addresses my father gave the very best a man can give – heart, soul, mind and strength – for the kingdom's sake. For those who read them now, may they continue to be what they were for so many of those who first heard them – a means of grace.

Robin Stewart
MURTHLY 1996

Memoir

ONE evening in April 1975, some hundreds of people gathered at the Assembly Rooms in Edinburgh at the invitation of the publishers of an American magazine with a world-wide circulation. They were gathered to do honour to two of the greatest figures in the field of New Testament scholarship of their day.

One of these was Professor James S. Stewart.

He arrived by car at the appointed time. The doorkeeper told him that the limited parking space was for VIPs only. Professor Stewart apologised, drove his car a further half mile to a parking place, left it there and walked back (with his wife) to the hall. There are two things to be said about that. First is that James S. Stewart was regarded as a figure of international stature, whose name was revered throughout the English-speaking world. Second, of course, is that it simply did not occur to him that at that time, or at any other, he could possibly have been a VIP. These facts taken together may help to explain why the name of J. S. Stewart still rings bells.

The years pass by. Future generations may hardly comprehend the frisson of excitement that his preaching generated, or the response that it evinced; the generation that knew him, sat at his feet, felt moved by his preaching, nourished by his writing, is already moving into the elderly period of life. His may become a historic memory, a legend of a more spacious era of church life when men and women went on Sundays to 'hear' the preachers of their day; a day when books of sermons were printed and published. He was perhaps the last of an era: could the name 'prince of preachers' ever possibly be applied to any successor? But for those who knew him best, it was the nature of the man himself that will abide.

It was inevitable that among those who cherished his memory and his words spoken and written, there should be a desire for a volume of his hitherto unpublished sermons to be prepared, and that some kind of personal reminiscence should accompany it. It was altogether proper that his elder son, the Revd Robin Stewart, should set this in motion and determine the limits of it. His father's papers, lodged in the library of New College, Edinburgh, were placed (by J.S.S. himself) under a twelve-year embargo. Permission was granted for this embargo to be lifted and the material to be made available, on the responsibility of Robin Stewart as his father's executor, acting in consultation with Professor J. C. O'Neill. The Revd Gordon Grant then undertook to make a selection of sermons that would represent most characteristically the quality of the preaching.

It was evident that a public appeal for contributions would have produced an unmanageable mass of material, most of it along the same lines, *ie* reactions to his preaching and teaching and appreciations of what his life meant to so many. So Robin Stewart himself approached a representative number of people who, in different capacities, had known his father. He invited them to contribute their own personal reflections. The response to this personal appeal was immediate and Robin received a great deal of material. He asked me, as someone who had sat under James S. Stewart as a student, had subsequently been his parish minister for more than thirty years, and had become a personal friend and increasingly a confidante, to write a short memoir and to incorporate within it some of these reminiscences. I agreed to do this — well aware that few readers would be content with what would be offered, the half would not have been told.

These memories are deliberately selective — a few representative names — because their memories may speak to us all. Other memories of a multitude of people who would have wanted to contribute must be left, not unsaid, but recollected and exchanged and spoken anew in the right context, so that we will say — 'Of course the thing that I remember about him was ... ', or 'I don't suppose he would have wanted this published, but ... ', or 'He would have hated to think that what he wrote to us or spoke in private conversation was going to be broadcast, for we would want even still to respect his privacy.' But if these reflections unseal memories and encourage us to share with others what once meant so much to us, then its purpose will have been served.

A number of people on both sides of the Atlantic have prepared theses and papers on aspects of James S. Stewart's theology and of his teaching. Others are in preparation. This essay is more of a cartoon, a sketch, rather than any formal portrait, in order that particular aspects of him may be recognised and other generations may begin to understand why this most unassuming of men was regarded as a giant in his own day and was honoured and above all loved by so many.

So what do we recall? For some whose memory is longest it is quite simply the voice: that vibrant, essentially Scottish, splendidly romantic clarion voice, strained sometimes when he was tired, but clearly audible with no mechanical aids, often imitated by young ministers of his day but in the end inimitable. It was not a different voice when used in private conversation: then it was used diffidently and yet with the same bell-like quality, with a sensitivity to the hearer, a modesty, and with hesitancies that did not appear in the pulpit speech. But in public speech it was the clarion call of the Gospel that was heard, commanding, beseeching, comforting, caressing. It broke through the defences of many who heard and impelled them to respond. In his lectures too, from the opening prayer that put teaching into the context of affirmation and witness, the voice reflected the inner passion and conviction and could quite unexpectedly break through the lecturing format into a word of Gospel.

Reflect on the memories of others:

My own personal commitment to Christ came at the end of a sermon when we were asked: 'He does so much for you, what can you do in return?'
~ Dr Audrey E. Evans, paediatrician, Philadelphia ~

I came to faith as a student, during the War, in North Morningside Church, solely through sitting through Jim's faithful preaching of the mighty act of God and the good news of Jesus, preaching that was spirit-filled, always inviting his hearers to share in adoration of his Lord and Saviour.
~ Mrs Joyce Billett ~

And this recollection of student days from the Very Revd Professor James A. Whyte:

There was something deeply impressive, compelling, about that slim, passionate figure in the pulpit. His was not a strong voice – somewhat nasal, and from the head rather than the chest – yet it could compel our attention because the preacher himself was so clearly under the compulsion of the Gospel that he preached. Here was preaching that met our enquiring minds, but challenged us always to a response. The very vocabulary of J.S.S. was full of words like vibrating, pulsating, vital, dynamic, expressing a sense of the excitement of the Gospel. 'Christianity boring? – never!' he would say. And he never was either.

But for others too it was the quiet discussions in small groups for which he prepared material so carefully. Much of that material is extant also. We know he was aware that his papers would be assembled and find their way into library archives. It was also known that he would not likely want some of his *obiter dicta,* some of his occasional papers, Bible study material and communicants' class addresses to be perpetuated in a memorial volume. It was his set piece sermons on which he bestowed such labour, which he honed and polished, that he would wish to be recalled and through which his voice might be heard. We might wish that the recording machines of a later age had been available to those who heard his sermons delivered, for often one suspected that the most telling passages were spontaneous additions and amendments to the written text.

But the text as written is what we have to recognise. There was no question of abandoning the material after it had been used. Some of the sermons printed in this volume were delivered upwards of forty times over a period of more than forty years, and with them in some cases are the large print boldly-written synopses which he also took into the pulpit as immediate guidelines for the freedom of his thought and expression.

Do the memories become more golden with the passage of years? J.S.S. lived in an age of great preachers and preaching was the hallmark of the Church's life. The Very Revd Dr Ronald Selby Wright has written:

> *Of course there have always been 'giants in those days', but never more than in the years when J.S.S. not only taught and lived the faith, but inspired a countless number to live it too.*

J.S.S. may have spoken to some of what it meant to him to move from the central field of the parish pulpit to the academic world, but there is no record of this. His movement from the one to the other was, I am certain, directed by the fact that thereby his role and destiny would be to claim further generations of ministers for the work of teaching, persuading, commending, converting, and that this would prove to be a greater and more enduring influence than the building up of a single congregation; for the impact of one minister on a congregation can seem, perplexingly, to be of limited duration, however effective and enduring it may have been on the lives of individuals within it.

Indeed it might seem that the impact of James S. Stewart's own life work was essentially upon those whose lives individually were changed, rather than in the building up of a congregation which would not, despite the excellence of successive ministries, create a unified body of Christ within the community. And he may have been less gratified than some at the number of those who seem rather to have been his followers than sharers in the life of the congregation that he was ministering to.

Was he a popular preacher? The sermons must speak for themselves. Those who will read a volume like this will most likely come from a Christian background, and perhaps to some extent from the kind of social background to which the sermons of J.S.S. were essentially directed.

Literary allusions could be dropped in, an acquaintance with the text of the Scripture and the content of the Gospel could be assumed, and yet there was never any self-conscious literary skill. People did not say, for example, 'how well read he is in the Victorian poets' – though he was. And yet Dr Hans Maurer of the Swiss Evangelical Church at Zurich remembers sitting in St Cuthbert's, Edinburgh, under his preaching, when at the end of the service a fellow student said in amazement: 'This man has now underlined his thoughts with 13 quotations from works by famous thinkers and philosophers across the ages. I counted them.'

It is not easy to imagine J.S.S.'s kind of ministry as being repeatable, for the great preaching ministries of a particular literate quality belong to a period that already may have passed away. One recalls the balanced cadences, the controlled yet passionate expression of feeling, the absence of anything slovenly or careless, or of apparent improvisation – these may seem to belong to a more structured and secure age. How far his preaching would speak to our age is an open question. So many of the sermons printed here were given in times of turbulence, of international foreboding and fear and of social turmoil, when concerned people would not have been content with merely emotional or sentimental escapism. After all, 'the young Prince of Glory' whom he lived to proclaim had not been a distant religious figure speaking words of easy inspiration.

Some might wish that James had made more immediate reference to the events of the 1930s and 40s when his preaching was in its heyday. But he did not weary us with analysis of what the world's newspapers were representing – he dealt with the larger issues; and though we may wish he had spoken more about the shadows over the western world of these days, and about the impact of events of the War years, his sermons would then have been historical documents that would have helped us to see how a Christian mind reflected upon the secular events, but they would yet have been of their period. Instead, the fact that they are less than specific in offering the context of their delivery may give them a timelessness that provides a relevance for a generation beyond his own.

So, at least, believes the Very Revd Dr Roy Sanderson:

He did not rely to any great extent on contemporary events to make his preaching relevant; he rather used, and quite delightfully, poetry and literature to illustrate and supplement the Biblical text. He directed his message to the changeless needs of people and confronted them with the Christ, who is the same yesterday, today and forever. As someone once remarked to me – and I agreed with him – 'James Stewart's preaching would have been contemporary a hundred years ago and it would still be the same a hundred years hence.' That was essentially the strength of its power.

Was James S. Stewart popular then? *Yes!* The sheer humanity of him shone through, but there was no folksiness, no pulpit humour that I can recall, except that gentle humour that is part of our humanity – the wonder of what love is, the absurdity of unmerited love, the unlikeliness of total forgiveness and yet the joy that it should be so.

Would he have adapted his preaching to the changed medium of our day? Perhaps so. A television age would have responded to that quiet steady gaze and to the words of power that came from his lips. As his sole passion was to present Christ in His beauty, he would have mastered the forms of presentation that would have made that Christ attractive and contemporary, and yet retained that austerity of approach, for he was taking us on to holy ground.

To read what others have written of him presents one over and over again with the paradox of his humility and strength. Herrick Bunney writes:

> *I must add my memory of his amazing self-depreciation and humility, as if he could hardly believe what people thought about him and his preaching. But he became a lion in the pulpit!*

★   ★   ★

What are the particular points of reference other than the preaching, which this volume is chiefly concerned with, that we have continually to return to? Let us now gather up one or two.

The scholar

James S. Stewart's colleagues in the academic field have borne ample testimony to the quality of his scholarship. Published tributes from the Very Revd Professor Robin Barbour and from the Very Revd Professor T. F. Torrance reflect the regard felt for him in this area, as does the address given by Professor Barbour at the Memorial service for him in the Kirk of the Greyfriars. It is Professor Torrance who, in a notable paper on the influence of J.S.S., remarks:

> *I think it might be said that if any one truth or emphasis predominated in Professor Stewart's outlook, it was the resurrection of the Lord Jesus from the grave and of our resurrection in Him .... When my mother died at the age of 97, Jim Stewart took the funeral and it was the happiest funeral I have ever been at.*

The Very Revd Professor John McIntyre has analysed the theological content of J.S.S.'s preaching in terms which must be recorded at some length. He writes:

At a conference in the Pollock Halls, attended by members of the Presbytery of San Francisco, he gave an address on Jesus' use of imagination in his life and teaching as we encounter them in the Gospels. Here for me was the clue to his own preaching and teaching that I had missed all these years. For I have known expository preaching which was dull in excess, being little more than flat commentary; as I have known pastorally-oriented preaching which did not rise above counselling. But, by the use of imagination, Dr Stewart gave exposition and pastoral perception new power and relevance. As he described so graphically the situation of the biblical passage, he gradually incorporated his hearers in the situation. They so became part of it that they identified with the persons of whom, or to whom, Jesus was speaking. The nearest analogy I know is the ability of a great artist to draw the viewer into the action he is portraying.

But there was more. It was not merely an exercise in empathy. Embodied in the situation, the hearers could not escape the urgency of the words of Jesus directed to them. The Gospel appeal, or challenge, or invitation, was not a codicil to the descriptive passages going before. Each one of them was an integral – an inescapable – part of the whole presentation, directed at each listener.

And Lord Coggan, former Archbishop of Canterbury, has written:

I think I can say that he was one of my heroes. His writings influenced me – his books of sermons (always fresh) and especially A Man in Christ. *I must have bought this book soon after it came out in 1935 and I still have my copy heavily marked.*

From 1937 to 1944 I was lecturing in the New Testament in Canada and I believe this lively and scholarly book affected my lectures very considerably. I laughingly told him that he owed me a lot of money, that I had recommended so many people to read his books! .... By his writing and his own preaching, he magnified the office of the preacher. How sorely that magnifying is needed today.

And the comment of his senior colleague in New College is significant:

As one who was involved in the life of the college for many years, I would like to testify that Stewart never allowed his outstanding success as a teacher to make it difficult for his colleagues. He was the soul of generosity to others and appreciative of what they were doing.

~ Revd Professor N W Porteous ~

The family

J.S.S. came himself from a remarkable family of Christian commitment and service. A man of eminence – as he, despite himself, became – can have a place of loneliness and sometimes remoteness from his own family circle. It was not so with him: James and his beloved Rosamund were as one to the end. But one wondered how far she, who had so much hidden strength and who so readily it seemed subjected her own life to his, felt sometimes constrained by the demands his calling made upon her. Was he always so easy to live with as others assumed him to be?

There was a humanity about Rosamund, a deep lively understanding of people at least the match of his, and an approachability too. The upbringing of the children, Robin and Jack, fell often upon her, and children of a distinguished father are subjected to particular stresses and may even be oppressed by the stature of the father they care so much for. But the love of James for his family, and his pride in them, were always deep and unquestioned.

The public figure

J.S.S. was a very private man who inevitably had a public role. His involvement in public life was less than that of other key figures in the Church of his generation, but his sensitivity to what was happening in Scotland was clear. He saw in the Iona Community of the early days much of the social and spiritual concern that the Church needed. He was Chaplain to the Queen in Scotland and had the right to be present and to be involved in national events. He added his signature to a number of letters to the press which some might have thought alien to his own interests. Like others of his generation who had had first hand experience of war, he hated it and passionately sought to retain attitudes which would make war less likely.

He was uncompromising in his care for social righteousness and outspoken where he believed it was required to be so. It was seldom that he was heard to be critical of other people, yet one knew that there were situations in the life of the church and of society that not only dismayed him but also distressed him, and his social and political attitude was more radical than was sometimes recognised. There was a curiously austere strength about him. There was nothing of the softness that too often seems to accompany people who are clearly on the side of the angels. His was a generation that had known discipline in wartime and seen austerity in the society around it and had faced many realities. This is why ingratiating, sycophantic speech was an embarrassment to him – and how often he must have encountered it.

He was not a General Assembly figure, though his Moderatorship was a memorable one. But he was not afraid to take sides, and therefore what he said was heard the more responsibly and carefully.

Friendship

His commitment to his friends was a touching thing. J.S.S. was always courteous and would welcome his friends whenever they came to visit him.

Even on days when he was weary, many have commented on his readiness to lay down his fountain pen and give himself wholeheartedly to unexpected callers. Even those who perhaps taxed his courtesy beyond what was reasonable, or those from overseas who appeared unheralded with recording machines and microphones to take home some words from this figure of legend – to all, he was never less than gracious.

His correspondence was immense. There was a time when his handwriting lost something of its firmness, but that had recovered long before the end. And the strength of the writing and the graciousness and positiveness of what was written made his letters a delight to receive and a treasure to cherish. He knew how to express thanks without apology or qualification. He knew how to convey in writing a warmth that his shyness made less easy for him to show in personal meeting. To the end he sat at his desk and replied to the letters that came to him, and the requests too that he couldn't hope to satisfy. But the courtesy and the profound sympathy were always there.

It was perhaps difficult for J.S.S. to fulfil the duties friendship asked of him in his years of retirement from the work of the parish. It was the duty of those near him, who had a sense of responsibility for him, to protect James from requests for services that could have been beyond his power to meet. There was anxiety sometimes in allowing him to continue to preach eight times, morning and evening, for two months in summer in a pulpit where he was most at home – but it may have been unnecessary solicitude, for he put his heart and soul as ever into his preparation for such work.

As the years went by, the patterns of his preaching may have changed. One recognised more the mellow fruit of his reflection and his insight, but the passion was undimmed. He preached sparingly in the church to which in the last decade he belonged. His final sermon was delivered there one Good Friday evening and it was one that those who heard it will always remember.

Worship

He was a 'twicer' (as those who attended worship twice on Sundays used to be described) as long as he could be within his own church, and wherever he happened to be – not as a necessary duty for I don't believe duty in this sense played too much a part in his life, but simply because he enjoyed it and because it was part of what being a full, rounded Christian required of him. He would have been impoverished without it. His presence in any church improved the singing and the sense of worship. He was profoundly Scottish, unquestionably a member of the Church of Scotland, but he was also cosmopolitan and catholic in his tastes. Living in a city with a variety of options, he was quite prepared to find strength from other forms of worship, and he was particularly at home with the Episcopal Church, for he approved of order in worship and the liturgical order was a strength and comfort to him. His own prayers reflected the debt he owed to the great Catholic tradition of public prayer.

It was good that Robin Barbour could conclude his great address at J.S.S.'s Memorial Service with the words:

> *For me the final and most cherished picture of all is not that of the great preacher swaying the multitude; but that of the worshipper in the ranks of the people gathered in college or church singing God's praise as if his heart could burst for joy. And that, I dare to think, is how he would want it to be.*

Devotional life

Upon this his life was founded. Professor Torrance has referred to

> *... the inner saintliness and divine sensitivity of Jim Stewart's life and thought which we, his academic colleagues, felt as much in the senate room as his students felt in the classroom. I will never forget particularly the day when, after some bitter words by one of our colleagues in criticism of others, we saw the tears rolling down Jim Stewart's cheeks, the silent, gentle, but powerful rebuke of a saintly man of God.*

But was he a saint? Of course we are all called to be saints and we are not encouraged to believe there will be a particular batting order in the world to come. J.S.S. would no doubt have deserved the title more than some who have been saddled with it. But sanctity may not always be recognised as it should be. The more we knew him, the less remote he was, the less formidable, the less forbidding. And as he grew older, and smaller, and weaker, more fragile, more vulnerable, the more we loved him. There was nothing of the distortion of character that sometimes attends old age, when people become more inward-centred as their world grows smaller – so that we pity them the indignity that they should be reduced to this. His own quiet dignity never slipped; nor his courtesy. We could not patronise him – only trust that the end would be consistent with all that had gone before, as it was; that he would not suffer the fears of the character changes that even the greatest ones have shown; that we would not have to fear that our last memory would be of someone different from what we had known.

To pray with him, and to be prayed for *by* him, were experiences not to be forgotten, for he walked with his God. James Whyte has put it as well as anyone:

> *When I was Moderator designate, Elizabeth and I appeared in the visitors' room at St Raphael's Hospital and we encouraged him to talk about his experiences as Moderator. Before we left, I said: 'James, I would greatly appreciate it if you would give me your blessing.' He stood up and it was like the spirit of Ezekiel coming into the dry bones. His voice became stronger, the vibrant, passionate voice of the old J.S.S. and he prayed with confidence, assurance and strength, and I felt blessed indeed.*

And when he saw a visitor to the door or to the gate as he invariably sought to do, his words of encouragement were words to cherish – and to be believed. When he said, 'You know that I pray for you every day', you believed that and you went away lighter than you came.

Towards the end the other world was very close. Many have remarked on the difficulty he found in recognising that his dear Ros was no longer in this world. He knew that she was not far away, but he could not quite accept that she belonged to that other world where shortly he would join her. He still wrote his letters with sincere greetings 'from Ros and me'.

And so he slipped from us, with those he loved beside him – no cold river to cross, no dark valley to traverse – but in that radiant world which he had gazed upon for so long and where his heart and love already were, there now he was seen to be.

More than the rest of us he lived in the sense that the curtain between those two worlds is a thin one and at the last will be resolved. Both worlds were his world and now he has entered into those things which he knew and which he now beholds.

A last word from Dr J. S. S. Armour of the Church of St Paul, Quebec:

It was his transparent goodness that lingers longest. I remember once in New York after one of his many preaching marathons, picking him up at the hotel, and with another former student driving him to the airport. Small talk was never easy with Professor Stewart unless you were a football fan ... and we stood around rather awkwardly trying to find things to say. At length, the plane was called – to the relief of us all, I'm sure. After the formal goodbyes, I blurted out 'journeying mercies', hardly thinking what I was saying. He immediately turned and grasped my hand. 'Oh thank you, thank you. I'm so grateful for that.' What was for me a trite and much parroted phrase was for J. S. Stewart, the expression of a deep and abiding faith.

The Very Revd W. J. G. McDonald DD
EDINBURGH 1996

James S. Stewart
SELECTED SERMONS

CHAPTER 1

Walking with God

And Enoch walked with God: and he was not; for God took him.
~ Genesis 5: 24 ~

HERE in this dull chapter that no one reads because it is all genealogy, here is this gem of spiritual biography – 'And Enoch walked with God: and he was not; for God took him.'

Suppose yourself, one day, going through an art gallery, full of portraits of a rather dull and conventional type, competent enough in artistic technique, but flat and blurred and uninspired, and then suddenly coming upon one picture there, one face gazing out at you from its canvas, vivid and unforgettable and tremendously alive.

Or, suppose yourself turning the pages of an anthology of Elizabethan verse, wading through a mass of material, much of it formal and stereotyped and stilted and artificial, and then encountering one perfect lyric of Shakespeare's, a poised and winged thing.

Or, suppose yourself listening to the groping and pedestrian melodies of some of the more sentimental eighteenth and early nineteenth century composers, and then being suddenly startled and overwhelmed by the magnificent, shattering rhythm of a movement of a symphony by Beethoven.

Something like that is the feeling you get when, in the midst of this drab page of prehistoric genealogy, there flashes out upon you, moving and memorable and sublime, this gem of spiritual biography. You feel like the man in Jesus' parable who was ploughing in his dusty, stony field, and the plough knocked against something, and there – at his very feet – was treasure, and the gleam of gold.

Here is this dull catalogue of names, without any individuality, any personal characterisation, and as each name in the list follows the one before, we are told monotonously that he was born and lived and died. What do we care? Names and nothing more! But suddenly at one point the monotony is broken. Suddenly a real face looks out at you from the canvas, the lyric note at last escapes from the anthology, the pedestrian strumming on one dull theme is shattered by the rhythm of a life. All these others 'lived and died' – and that is all. But Enoch – lived? No, 'walked with God'. Died? No, 'he was not; for God took him'. How noble and sublime, this briefest of all biographies.

I daresay it would be possible, when all is said and done, to sum up a man's life in a single sentence. It would be possible to write any man's epitaph in half a dozen words:

'He amassed a fortune.'
'He built a dazzling reputation.'
'He carved out a career.'
'He never got a chance.'
'He got his chance and took it.'
'He missed the mark completely.'
'He rode roughshod to his goal.'
'He won the world's applause.'

But what brief, concentrated summary of a life could be more expressive or more moving than this? *'He walked with God.'*

Let us take this word and interrogate it. Let us ask some questions.

I

And first, this. *How did it become known that Enoch was walking with God?* How did that news get about? How did his contemporaries discover it? I don't suppose the man told them. The saints don't. They don't go about boasting – 'God and I are walking together every day.' Well, what made these people arrive at that conclusion?

It must have been this. They must have noticed something about the man, something which in that dim and barbarous age was quite unusual, something so distinctive and arresting that they could not account for it in any natural or ordinary way.

I wonder what that something was? Was it perhaps a quality of serenity, a dignity and composure in the man's face, a sense of settled peace in those strong eyes? They looked at him and they saw that; and they knew that that was nothing accidental. 'There is a man,' they said, 'who is walking with God!'

We turn from that and think of ourselves – ourselves who get so worried, so hectic with life's load of care; who carry our fever with us, and wince at pin-pricks, and get flurried and fussy and nervous, and can't relax; who feel that everything is getting on top of us, and life is too much for us, and quite lose our interior peace. There is no real remedy for that condition but this – a closer walk with God. But that *is* the healing secret: that is the Christian therapy. You must not start that difficult day, that overcrowded programme that sets you working against time, that worrying task, that trying interview, that fretting, nervy bit of the road so full of stress and strain – you mustn't start it without taking first some moments to remember God, who is the abiding, central peace of the great universe, and the only giver of a quiet, untroubled heart.

But perhaps what struck those people here about Enoch was not so much this inward peace as a certain quality of moral decisiveness. Here was a man living amid the corruption of that dark, evil age where right and wrong and good and evil were so blurred and terribly confused, moving amid rank temptations whose foul touch would contaminate and rot the soul, yet walking there unspotted from the world. And so they looked and drew their own conclusion: 'He walks with God.'

'Can two walk together, except they be agreed?' asks Amos. And so we turn again, and think of our divided loyalties, our blurred and blundering compromises with temptation, our oscillating between the high things of our holy religion and the miserable earthbound tyranny of self, our weak subservient acceptance of the monotony of defeat. And in our heart of hearts, in our dead honest moods, we know the remedy – if we would but take it: a stronger grasp of Christ's all-conquering hand, a deeper reconciliation to the will divine, a truer, daily walk with God.

> *The dearest idol I have known,*
> *Whate'er that idol be;*
> *Help me to tear it from thy throne,*
> *And worship only thee.*
> ~ Hymn 663: *Church Hymnary (third edition) (CH3)* ~

II

Let us come back to Enoch. Let us take this noble scrap of biography and interrogate it further. Our first question was: How did they know he was walking with God? We have seen the answer to that. Well, here is the next: *When did that walk with God begin?* Look back a couple of verses and you will find it. 'Enoch walked with God after he begat Methuselah' – after his first child was born. That is worth underlining. For it does suggest that until then he had lived an ordinary, more or less unspiritual existence.

Until then he had not been greatly concerned to get God into his life. He had not felt any particular urge towards religious dedication and self-commitment. But when *this* happened, when his first child appeared, then there was a change: then religion got its chance: then he suddenly found himself taking vows he had never made before. 'Enoch walked with God after he begat' the child who was to bear his name!

But we can understand. It happens still so often. When a new and precious life is born into a home; when the next generation appears, and a helpless babe is cradled there; when that immense responsibility is given as a high and holy trust – where is the man, the parent, who will not be visited with some strong impulse of self-dedication; some new resolve to walk henceforth with God? A little child has led him!

But isn't there a wider truth suggested here? 'Enoch walked with God, after' – this high moment of his life. The great experience in his case was the coming of his child. That was his day of the Lord. But any great experience, any high moment of joy or sorrow, may have that decisive effect.

'He walked with God, after' – that crisis in his life. Thus Jacob walked with God, after the terrible midnight wrestle with the angel at Peniel. So Samuel walked with God, after the voice that called his name rang through the silence of the shrine. So Hezekiah walked with God, after he had gone down to the gates of death, and had then recovered from his sickness. So Charles Kingsley walked with God, after a night of magic on the shore beside the sea. So Henry Martyn walked with God, after a disappointment in love that broke his heart. So Tennyson walked with God, after his wedding-day that brought – he tells us – the peace divine into his soul. So William Cowper walked with God, after an illness that – as he says – 'scourged him' into religion. God uses the great hours of life to draw men to Himself.

'He walked with God, after … ' – can you not finish the sentence for yourself? Can you not take out Enoch's name, and put in your own? 'You walked with God, after … ' – was it after your first Communion? Was it after that shattering bereavement? Was it after the coming of a great love had constrained you to say – 'I'm not worthy of this, but God helping me, I'll try to be'? Was it after some trial that made you cry – 'I can't face this alone: I must break or else find God'? Was it after you received a loved one back from the very gates of death? 'He walked with God, she walked with God, after … ' – that unforgettable experience, after that decisive hour. For no personal event that happens to us in this world – whether of great sorrow or of great joy – no such event is a mere natural occurrence or accident; it is a spiritual constraint; it is life itself putting pressure upon us to be done with our irreligious self-sufficiency, and to walk henceforth with God.

III

We have been interrogating this man's biography in Genesis. Our first question was: How did they know he was walking with God? Our second was: When did that walk begin? There is one final question now to ask: *Where did it end?* To that, the answer is, 'It didn't. It never ended. Enoch walked with God: and he was not; for God took him'.

Mystery, they said, had shrouded the close of that noble career. One day he had slipped from sight. One day his place was empty. They missed him from the familiar scenes. He disappeared from human ken. But those who knew him best had their own theory as to what had happened. Enoch, they said, walked with God – and that walk went right on, without any transition or interruption. He did not have to begin, when 'the mortal coil was shuffled off', to learn the ways of immortality. He did not have to acquire, at death's dark portal, the language of fellowship with God and the speech of heaven. He knew it all already. A life so intimate with God on earth, so knit here below to the unseen and eternal, could manifestly not have stopped short, or disintegrated, or been destroyed. The mystery of his going was really, they felt, no mystery at all. God and Enoch, from the first day of that walk together, had been friends right through the man's life: and in death they were certainly not divided. 'He was not; for God took him.'

Is it not wonderful to meet, out of this dim age so long ago and far away, to meet almost on the first page of the Bible, such a sublime fore-shadowing of the Christian revelation, such a deep, magnificent insight into the true doctrine of life eternal? I do want you to get this clear, for there has been – even amongst Christians – so much hazy and mistaken thinking about it.

The New Testament never speaks of eternal life as something that begins only at death, something new into which death suddenly ushers us: that is quite unscriptural. On the contrary, the New Testament always speaks of eternal life as something that begins here and now, on this side of the grave, something that exists as a present possession of those who are in fellowship with God. Eternal life simply means God's quality of life; and therefore those who have entered into fellowship with God have entered into that new eternal, quality of being; and for those who have entered into eternity, death is simply an irrelevance.

I do want you to see that this – nothing less – is the characteristic New Testament emphasis about the life eternal: it is *not* that when we are finished with this world, and the fever of life is over and our work done, that then there will come the great essential transition from temporality to eternity. *That* is not it – that is definitely not the New Testament teaching nor Christ's teaching: but this that for those who are making the present life a walk with God, the great essential transition *has happened already.* 'We have passed from death into life,' they say. For us, eternity has projected itself out of the remote future into the actual present. The new eternal order has begun. We are tasting *now* the power of the age to come. 'This *is* life eternal,' said Jesus, 'to know Thee, the one true God.' We are living *now* by the power of the world to come. And again: 'He that liveth and believeth in Me shall never die' – not, mark you, shall have eternity handed out to him as a reward or as a new faculty on the other side of death, but actually 'shall never die'! He is living eternally already – living in a realm where death has ceased to count. He is possessed of something which death can't touch!

I am sure that many of us Christians have never yet realised the really revolutionary thing our faith is saying. We imagine that what Christianity is concerned with is simply ethical advice, moral values and decent behaviour. Nothing of the kind! It is far more explosive than that. It is the offer – here and now – of life of a new quality, a super-human divine quality, the very life of God Himself.

I wonder if I could put it like this? We know even from science that there are different levels or dimensions of existence. There is the level of inorganic matter. Above that, there is the level of organic life, in plants and flowers. Above that again, there is the level of sentient life, in animals. Above that again, there is the level of human life, with intelligence, emotion and will. That is our natural life – our *nature* as human beings. But the whole force of Christianity is concentrated on this – that above that, there is something more than nature, there is super-nature, there is God's kind of life, life eternal, and that we can share in it.

And if you ask: How? – Christianity answers *that*. It is not that we have to climb up to that higher level by some process of emergent evolution or by painful efforts of our own. No, if we are to share this supernatural eternal quality of life, it must come down to us. And that, says Christianity, is precisely what has happened.

When God became man in Christ, the unbridgeable gulf was bridged. Right down in our midst, the supernatural life has appeared. So that, in so far as we lay ourselves open to Christ, He shares His life – which is God's life – with us, imparts it to us just as the vine injects its life into the branch.

Come Almighty to deliver,
Let us all Thy life receive.

~ Hymn 437: *CH3* ~

That is the great discovery. And it means, you see, that once you have said of any man, 'he walks with God', he is eternal already, the sequel is not really surprising or mysterious: it is inevitable. 'Enoch walked with God: and he was not; for God took him.' There could be no other ending. There can never be any other ending of a life which has made its earthly dwelling in the secret place of the Most High, and under the shadow of the Almighty. Did you think a man could learn to walk with God, and only have this poor earth to do it in? Did you think God would train a man and discipline a soul in the spiritual, imperishable values, only to snuff him out like a guttering candle at the last? When the writer to the Hebrews says, 'God is not ashamed to be called their God', he is at least suggesting that if God lifted souls up into fellowship with the spiritual realities, and then allowed them, *having tasted that,* to be cast as rubbish to the void, He *would* have reason to be ashamed: He would have reason to resign His Godhead, and to abdicate His throne of the universe. The life that is rooted in God's eternity is abiding and indestructible. The vital force within it is actually – here and now – the force of eternity. Therefore it goes right through death, and out at the other side. And therefore 'God is not ashamed to be called their God'.

I leave with you a question which I do not attempt to answer now. If we have *not* walked with God on earth, if no union of our nature with His nature has taken place, if we have *not* cared to seek His fellowship here, are we likely to be ready for that fellowship hereafter? Jesus said, 'I go to prepare a place for you'. The place may be prepared for us – but what if we are not prepared for the place?

Will it be any kind of bliss to be 'forever with the Lord' if we have had no liking for that companionship on earth? Will Heaven be Heaven to us, if we are not learning *now* to share God's interests, to love the things that God loves, and to seek the things that God seeks? I leave you to answer that question in the secret place of your own souls. Here is the answer that a poet gave:

> Some day or other I shall surely come
> Where true hearts wait for me;
> Then let me learn the language of that home
> While here on earth I be,
> Lest my poor lips for want of words be dumb
> In that high company.

CHAPTER 2

The God of the Hills and the God of the Valleys

And the servants of the king of Syria said unto him, 'Their gods are gods of the hills; therefore they were stronger than we; but let us fight against them in the plain, and surely we shall be stronger than they'.

And they pitched one over against the other seven days. And so it was, that in the seventh day the battle was joined: and the children of Israel slew of the Syrians an hundred thousand footmen in one day.

~ I Kings 20: 23,29 ~

AGAIN and again in reading the Old Testament you are made to feel that this is the Book of a Highland people. Prophet, psalmist and seer were born and bred with the skyline of the mountains before them, and it was Highland blood that flowed in their veins. Jerusalem itself lay 4000 feet above the sea – the height of Cairngorm or Braeriach. That is why the Old Testament has a special appeal for Highland peoples today. That is why the Switzerland of John Calvin and the Scotland of John Knox have both in a special sense made this Book their own. It was not so much 'deep calling unto deep' as 'height calling unto height', mountain top answering to rugged mountain top. Through this Old Testament from first to last you feel – bracing, strong and invigorating – the breath of the high hills. You feel, throbbing through it all like an undertone, that wild, indomitable passion for freedom which the breath of the hills always creates: for a Highland people, whether in the heights of Lebanon, or in the Alpine snows, or in the Grampian fastnesses, must be free or die. You feel, too, on every page of this old Book, that wide, open spaciousness, that sense of dignity and settled composure, that utter absence of triviality and pettiness and littleness and meanness, that instinct for the big things of life, which long contact with the mountain silences and the rugged solitudes inevitably breeds in the souls of men. This is the Book of the hills of God.

Turn its pages and see how they come back to that again and again. Here, for example, is a psalmist, seeking to answer for his people the old question that has always hung about the human heart, and is still hanging about the human heart today: What is God like? Is He the kind of God a man can trust?

And here is how he answers it: 'Thy mercy, O Lord, is in the heavens; Thy righteousness is like the great mountains!' – as much as to say to those people, 'It is no stuff of dreams we are founding on in our religion, no thin, tenuous mists blown across the threshold of consciousness for a moment and then gone, no far airy mirage that vanishes into the empty blue when you try to grasp it – but something solid and massive and rock-like and rivetted in the very foundations of the universe. That, says this man, is the mercy and righteousness of God – 'like the great mountains!'

Or, turning the pages, you come to this: 'As the mountains are round about Jerusalem, so the Lord is round about His people forever' – and you see the picture there, Zion's walls lined with watchers peering away to the horizon where the terror of invasion was rumbling, gazing away to the circling hills that stood like sentinels against the skyline, and wondering – 'Will they get through? Will our outposts hold?' And so they waited, tense and anxious; and the enemy flung themselves at that bastion of rock, fell back spent and broken, came to the onset again, and once again the mountains beat them, rolled them back at last defeated! Even so, says this psalmist, when life grows grim and threatening, why should you be afraid? For as the mountains are round about Jerusalem, so God is round your soul forever!

But turning the pages again, you find that it was in the time of the Exile that the passion for the hills grew strongest. There they were in Babylon, those Israelites. And Babylon was a land of mudflats and plains and monotonous levels stretching away for hundreds of miles unbroken with never a hill in sight – great cities and highways and canals and brick-fields and towering buildings to bear witness to man's genius and man's work, but never a mountain top in sight to bear witness to the work of God. So that again and again the cry that you hear breaking out of the exile is a cry for the hills of home. 'I will lift up mine eyes unto the hills,' exclaimed one of them, for if they weren't there for him to look at, they were there in his heart at least for him to dream about. 'How beautiful on the mountain-top,' cried another exiled soul, 'are the feet of him that bringeth good tidings.' 'It shall come to pass in the last days,' said another, 'that the mountain of the Lord shall be exalted above the hills!' So it was that in those drab, hopeless Babylonian plains, the longing for the hills became a passion. It was the Highland heart crying out for its Highland home.

All through this old Book then, from first to last, there breathes the spirit of the hills. So much so, indeed, that it might have been natural to suppose that the God of Israel must have been pre-eminently or even exclusively a God of the hills. Now that is precisely what Benhadad of Syria in this story in the Book of Kings *was* saying.

See what had happened. Benhadad of Syria, leaving his cavalry in the plains, had sent his infantry up to attack Israel on the heights, and the attack had disastrously failed. And when he thought to renew it, his officers had come to him protesting.

'No,' they said. 'The God of the Israelites is a mountain-God; and as long as they stay up there among their native mountains, obviously they are under His protection, and we can't do anything against them. It is just wasting men, throwing away lives, to try to fight those wild Highlanders on their own ground – the God of the mountains will thwart us every time we try it. No, here's what we must do! We must get them down out of the hills into the plain, entice them out of their mountain-fastnesses into the valleys, and then – why, then, we'll be able to do what we like with them, no mountain-God will avail them down here, and we'll crush them at our leisure.'

Well, it looked like sound strategy; and when a few days later the Syrian captains, scanning the mountainside, saw something moving, something like a thin line of men beginning to defile from the rocky gorge and come down towards the valley, 'Why,' they cried, 'Look yonder! Can it be? Yes! Their God has delivered them into our hands! We've got them now!'

And they ran and told Benhadad their king.

'Sire!' they said. 'Now is your day of vengeance. Now we'll sweep those pestilential brigands of the hills off the face of the earth!'

And down the hill the Israelite battalions came, chanting their wild, rugged psalms, marching into the jaws of death, hopelessly, pitifully outnumbered, every man of them going straight to his doom; and Benhadad of Syria, waiting, waiting, gloating over their fate, exulting in the smashing victory that he saw coming, hearing already in anticipation the trumpets blaring out his triumph!

It never came. Why? Because all through Benhadad's strategy there was one possibility he had forgotten to reckon with, one weak link he had never seen in his chain of calculation; and it was there that the chain suddenly snapped, and by snapping ruined him. For here was the lesson he had to learn, had to learn in the bitterness of defeat and disaster, when he saw his vast army melting away before the Israelite handful like snow before the sun – here was the lesson: that Israel's mountain-God was God of the plains as well; that the Unseen Power that marches on the mountain peaks and treads on the high places of the earth, is lurking also where shadows deepest lie on glen and valley; that the Lord of life's high altitudes is also Lord of life's low levels; that the men who can cry 'Praise to the Holiest in the height!', can follow that up with 'And in the depths be praise!' For the God of the hills is the God of the valleys too.

Now then friends, has that discovery ever gripped us as it should, gripped us with the full splendour and glory and meaning and romance of it? The God of life's hilltops – that is easy to believe. But the God of life's valleys – have we got that into our Creed? God of the sunlit peaks, fired with the red glow of the onrushing morning – it doesn't take any heroics of faith to be sure of that. But God of the low, shadowed places – the same God down there as we had known up above – have we faith enough for that? Is yours a local or a universal God? Let us drop the metaphor and get this into the language of human experience.

I

This, for one thing – *That the God of our joys is the God of our sorrows too.* That the God who was so near you that day when the world was radiant and your heart was singing and it was good to be alive, is the God at your right hand – the same God – when the foundations of things have been knocked to pieces. That the God whose mercy and Providence have been in all the happy and lovely things that have ever come to you is the God whose mercy and Providence are the surest fact when your eyes are blind with tears. Oh, it's easy touching the hem of God's garment when your feet are planted on the hills, easy in the day of joy to stand and say – 'Bless the Lord, O my soul, and forget not all his benefits! Bless Him for His goodness, bless Him for His wonderful love!' Ah, but it is down in the valleys, it is in the deeps of sorrow, that God gets hidden. 'He's not here!' the heart cries. 'Yonder He is, where men walk happily in the sunshine; but here – no God, no God!'

Let us take one look at the Israelites on those mud-flats of Babylon again. The real bitterness of it all was that they had lost God or thought they had.

'How shall we sing the Lord's song in a strange land? He isn't here to hear it – we'd be singing it to the brazen, unheeding skies and to the stars! Yonder, 1000 miles across the desert to the west, yonder in the Jerusalem we'll never set eyes upon again, yonder is God, and we've lost Him.'

And it took all the fire and passion of a Jeremiah to shake them out of that, to get their eyes open to see that God's territory was not de-limited to Him, that by the rivers of Babylon where they sat and wept, yes, even by those so God-forsaken streams, there was a God – and oh, the comfort of it, when they discovered it! – the same God there in their black tragedy, controlling it, working through it, turning it to blessing; the same God who in the old happy days had called the daughter of Zion, His Bride and His Queen!

But it's hard, hard to believe it, and men were never really sure of it till Jesus came. But they saw Jesus not only travelling on the hills of the morning, but walking also where the mists and shadows still trailed along the valleys – and then they knew. They met Him on the road in their happy hours, and His smile was a benediction. But they met Him again in the Gethsemane of pain, and ...

'Are you here too, Jesus?' they would cry.

'Yes,' he would answer, 'here too: My son, My daughter, I've come!'

And then the road of pain became a glory.

In every pang that rends the heart,
The Man of sorrows has a part.

Not far from Nazareth where Jesus was brought up, there were two other villages: one was Cana, and the other was Nain, lying quite close together. In one of them, you remember, there was a wedding; and in the other there was a funeral – but Jesus was there at *both,* which meant that *God* was in both. And, friends, God is in both Cana and Nain still today, the Cana and Nain of our tangled human experience, God in laughter and God in tears and God in all the lights and shadows of those hearts where the springs of laughter and of tears lie so close together. And it is Jesus of Nazareth who has made us so sure of it. The God of the hills is the God of the valleys too.

II

Well, there is one thing that great discovery means – that the God of our joys is also God of our sorrows.

But besides that I think it means, for a second thing, this – *that the God of our great religious experiences is the God of our common days as well.* That the God of the hill of Transfiguration is the God of the common plain where we have to tackle and wrestle and just try to be faithful all our ordinary days. That the God of those flashing hours that have burnt themselves forever into your memory, and that still as you look back are standing there like beacons, landmarks on the road you have travelled, is the God also of those weary, toilsome, plodding days when your heart has never a thrill in it, and the road runs straight and monotonous to the horizon, and the angels have ceased to sing. Oh, it's easy in the big moments grasping God – easy when you sit down for the first time in your life with Jesus at His Table, or when some great blessing that you have dreamed about is put at last into your hands, or when in some great gathering where 1000 voices are singing the glories of Christ a door suddenly swings open in your heart and there is Jesus Himself and the next five minutes are worth a lifetime – it is easy, I say, in those big moments grasping God and being very sure of Him. Ah, but it is down on the common levels of life, it is in the whirl and the clatter of the toilsome days, it is in that groove where life confines us, it is in all the littleness and ordinariness of things that so often make us sick at heart – it is there that the Divine gets lost. No morning stars are heard singing together there, no sons of God shouting for joy. And the dust of that weary road gets into a man's very soul.

But stay! Yonder down the dusty road, coming towards us, is another traveller. And look! as He draws near, isn't there something familiar about Him, something about His walk, something about His bearing, that we seem to know?

'Why,' the heart cries out, 'are you here too, Jesus, here on the dreary, drudging way? Is it really *you?*'

'Yes, My son, My daughter, it is I! And this road you are on is the king's highway.'

Blessed be Christ for this – that He has shown us that Heaven bends down on the commonest lot to hallow it; that no soul – not even the poorest and loneliest – can ever be lost in the crowd; that the day's mechanical monotony can be a perpetual Sacrament; and that all through the grey fabric of life there has been woven the golden thread of God. For the God of the hills is the God of the valleys too.

III

I have spoken of two things this great discovery means. Let me add this for a third and last – *It means that the God of life's sunlit heights is also the God of the last and deepest and darkest valley of all, a valley so narrow only one can pass at a time, the valley of the shadow of death.* That when on our day of life the night is falling, and all the old familiar scenes we have lived among begin to slip away, and one after another life's kindly lights go out, and at last we feel ourselves sinking, sinking, sinking down into the dark, and everything seems gone – that then one thing, whether we feel it or not, will be absolutely sure and certain, the everlasting arms of God beneath us!

How sure our Christian faith has always been of that! St Francis, in that great Canticle of his, after praising God for his brother, the sun, and his sister, water, and his mother, the earth, suddenly looks the last darkness in the face and cries, 'Praised be my Lord for our sister the death of the body!' Is it an echo of that, I wonder, that we have in Walt Whitman's great serenade to Death?

Praised be the fathomless universe,
For life and joy ....
For love, sweet love – but praise! O praise and praise,
For the sure-unwinding arms of cool-enfolding death.
Death, I bring thee a say.

~ 'When Lilacs last in the Dooryard bloomed' ~

'This,' cried Perpetua, one of the loveliest, fairest souls of the Early Church, just in her twenty-second year, when they led her out to die in the Carthaginian arena – 'This is my day of coronation!'

And there was that great shout the Grassmarket in Edinburgh heard when James Guthrie had climbed the scaffold – 'This is the day the Lord hath made: I will rejoice and be glad in it!'

Or what of the ringing exultation of one who was greater than them all, the cry that has come echoing down the centuries – 'To me to die is gain! O Death, where is thy sting?'

How sure our Christian faith has always been, facing out to the last dark valley, that the God of love and mercy would be there!

Why has it been so sure? It is because yonder down the valley, down where the way is darkest and the shadows thickest, it has seen something, Someone moving, Someone dimly, vaguely familiar going on before! And the heart of Christianity has leapt out at that in a great hope. And 'Is that you in front, Jesus?' it has cried out. 'Are you here, here in this last valley too?'

And back the answer has come through the dark: 'Yes, my son, my daughter, it is I! Follow Me close – I know the way!'

Jesus, still lead on!
And although the way be cheerless,
We will follow calm and fearless.

~ Hymn 567: *Revised Church Hymnary* ~

'Yea, though I walk through the valley of the shadow of death, I will fear no evil – for Thou art there.' For the God of all the hills and valleys is the God of that valley too. And it leads right on to the rising sun.

CHAPTER 3

The Rejuvenation of the Church

Where is the Lord God of Elijah? ~ II Kings 2: 14 ~

THAT sudden cry athwart the centuries goes right to the heart of the Church's deepest need today. We wish so often that the great days of Christendom would come again. Fourteen hundred years ago Saint Columba landed on these shores. Four hundred years ago John Knox was carrying the Reformation flame across the land. One hundred and fifty years ago there was born the man whose vision of a new Continent for Christ thrilled the soul of this people – David Livingstone. And perhaps we think – those were better days for the Church than this. In other words, we say – 'Where is Elijah?' Where are Columba and Knox and Livingstone and Thomas Chalmers and all the giants of the Church's fame?

But here is this old story telling us that is the wrong question altogether. Not 'Where is Elijah?', but 'Where is the *Lord God of* Elijah?' Not 'Where are Columba and Knox and Chalmers?', but 'Where is the Lord who clothed their weakness with His strength?' This, I say, goes right to the heart of the Church's need today.

What a moving, memorable narrative this is! Look how it opens. It opens with the words, 'When the Lord would take up Elijah into heaven'. When God had decided to take His servant home to Himself, what did Elijah do?

He set out on a round of visits – Gilgal, Bethel, Jericho, the Jordan: one last look at the old familiar haunts, one last lingering look. We can understand it, for there are places in this world which will always mean more to us than any others, because of their personal memories.

I think of Sir Walter Scott, hurrying home from Italy on his last journey, urging the carriage on – 'Quicker! Quicker! I must see the Borderland again and Tweed and Abbotsford, before I die!'

I think of the old man in Neil Munro's *Doom Castle*, found sitting at the door while the gloaming deepened into darkness. 'For think,' said he, 'if I were to die in the night, with never another sight of the hills and the heather and the loch.' We understand that ...

> God gave all men all earth to love,
> But since our hearts are small,
> Ordained for each one spot should prove
> Beloved over all.

So it was with Elijah, longing to see just once again Bethel and Jericho and the Jordan.

And when they came to the river at last, suddenly Elijah turned and faced his young companion. 'Ask what I shall do for thee,' he said. 'Name any legacy you want!' Why, to hear him you would think this were some rich magnate or monarch with vast possessions to dispose of, instead of being, as in fact he was, poor as the poorest beggar on any street in Israel, with no possessions whatever but the mantle he wore. 'Ask what I shall do for thee!'

Mark well the answer: 'I pray thee, let a double portion of thy spirit be on me.' That was the request.

Elisha might have asked something totally different – some eternal keepsake. He might have asked for Elijah's prophet staff. But no. Only this: 'a double portion of your spirit.'

Now we are thinking about the Church. Here we are with our membership in the Church of Knox and Columba and Henry Drummond. What are we asking from the centuries that have gone before us? What sort of keepsake or tradition are we most concerned about today? Is it some external possession – a venerable Reformation tradition perhaps, a time-worn order of worship from the Celtic Church? Is that what we want – a Church rooted in the past, a Church in which you can always be secure against any disturbing new methods? 'This is the way we have always done things here, and this is the way we will do them to the end.' Is that our major emphasis – Scottish democratic Presbyterianism, a Covenanting ancestry, and a Reformed theology? If it is, then here is the question we have to face – What are John Knox's traditions worth, without John Knox's spirit? Or Calvin's theology, without Calvin's God? What is the worth of a Covenanting ancestry, without the Covenanters' flaming hearts for Christ?

Our Anglican friends talk to us about 'apostolic succession'. We Presbyterians retort about our spiritual ancestry – tracing our descent back through Chalmers and Rutherford and Knox and Kentigern and Columba and Ninian, back through the Celtic Church to the age of the apostles. That is the line of *our* religious descent, we say, perhaps with a touch of pride, our Scottish 'apostolic succession'.

But wait! As if that could guarantee our continuance for one day, or keep a twentieth century Church alive! As if that kind of argument would impress a generation brought up on and indoctrinated with Darwin and Marx and Freud and Russell! I sometimes wonder – are we Church folk awake to the kind of world we are living in? Are we alive to the challenge our faith is up against today – with secularism rampant, and sub-Christian standards of value and culture in literature, press, television keeping such a perpetual daily bombardment that being a Christian, an active, witnessing Christian, takes real grace and courage and independence?

The fact is – the challenge to faith today is so acute that any Church which is content to rest on the past is finished. It is a redundant anachronism, destined to rot and wither and die. What is the worth of any succession or descent – Livingstone, Knox, Columba – if the Spirit who was in these men has not descended to their successors? Indeed Elisha knew what he was doing when he refused to ask for any external, visible token, but said – 'I pray thee, let a double portion of thy spirit be on me!'

But the climax of the story makes this even clearer. There comes that mysterious, unearthly scene in which we are given Elijah's welcome home to heaven, with all the trumpets sounding for him on the other side. What shall we say about it? Let me tell you this. When Mozart was dying, he asked for the 'Requiem' he had himself composed. He said to his daughter Emily, 'Play that to me'. And while his daughter was playing it, his soul, wafted on his own glorious music, passed away. So here. Elijah's death was like the music of his life – mysterious, dramatic, swift as the lightnings of God. The rest is silence. 'He walked with God: and he was not; for God took him.'

But think of Elisha, left lonely and desolate there by the Jordan. How could he face the future? How could his people, Israel, continue to exist, with no Elijah to direct their destiny? He gazed up into the darkening heavens that had seemed to snatch his master from him. 'O my father,' he cried, 'my father, the chariots of Israel and the horsemen thereof!'

And then suddenly he knew it. This was the decisive moment of his life. 'Here am I, Elisha, standing alone for God and for the Kingdom, with no Elijah to lean on any longer. I have to face the hatred of Ahab, the curse of Jezebel, the venom of a paganised society. How to do it?' He looked around. There was Elijah's mantle lying where it had fallen, the mantle with which – so it was said – Elijah had split the Jordan.

He lifted it up. He looked at it, fingered it lovingly. Was the prophetic power in this – this mantle, this keepsake from the past? 'Perhaps with this I could divide the Jordan too! Perhaps this memory from the past is all I need for miracles in the present.' Many a man, many a Church, would have said that – and would have gone down to mediocrity and failure. But not Elisha! He was not trusting to past tradition and dead memory. No! One thing was needful. Suddenly the silence was shattered by a shout: '*Where is the Lord God of Elijah?*'

I am sure that sudden cry from long ago and far away tracks down our deepest problem as a Church today. For indeed, in our Churches we have got the mantle of Elijah – and we have tried doing Elijah's work with that. But the Church needs more than a dead man's mantle if it is going to divide the Jordan. We need more than venerable tradition, more even than tried and tested methods of efficient organisation and elaborate machinery, if we are ever to drive a clear path through the futility and agnosticism of this bewildered age, and redeem the world to God. You, yourself, you need more than the Church's creed and the faith of your fathers if there is going to happen for you the miracle of being able from your heart to say 'All for Jesus', the miracle of the Church's frozen creed thawed out for you and throbbing with vitality. You need God the Holy Spirit for that.

'*The little more, and how much it is; the little less, and what world's away.*'
'*My heart and my flesh cry out for the living God.*'
'*Where is the Lord God of Elijah?*'

Now do mark this – it is terribly important. In that decisive hour by the Jordan, when Elisha's future was in the balance, *he was being watched*. Did you notice that in the story? It says fifty men, sons of the prophets – a kind of critical intelligentsia – were standing there on the hillside, watching everything that happened. Of course they were! They always are. They wanted to see whether this new man were the real thing or not, whether the new generation could do the mighty works of the old.

It is like that today. You don't need me to tell you that Christianity in this generation is being watched. There are a million critical eyes on the Church. They are watching the Church's worship, watching the Church's mission, watching the Church's integrity – in life and action and personal relationship. The secular world wants to know whether this is the real thing or not; and if not – 'Away with it! Why cumbereth it the ground?' In other words, if we don't have that life of God which the New Testament calls the power of Pentecost; if we are not that kind of fellowship, if within the Church are found class distinctions, racial barriers, social cliques; if my life and yours don't radiate the Master's courage and confidence and compassion; if, as St John puts it, the love of God is not 'shed abroad in our hearts' so as to take in its sweep all the folk with whom we have to do – then nothing else that we may say or do or organise is going to matter one iota, and nothing will save Christendom in our generation from the taunting cry: 'How art thou fallen from heaven, O daystar, son of the morning!'

If Karl Marx had been a Christian, how different the history of the world might have been. But Marx was watching Christianity. And various things put him off. One of them was this. When Marx was a boy, his parents, his Jewish parents, became Christians; but young Marx noticed that as Jewish Christians they were apt to be cold-shouldered, were not welcome in certain Christian circles. And the hatred began to smoulder.

If Gandhi had been a Christian, how different the history of the world might have been! It could have happened. But Gandhi was watching Christianity. And various things put Gandhi off. One was this. He went to a Church in South Africa and was told he could not enter: no Asiatics were allowed. And again the anger kindled.

The world is constantly watching Christianity – watching to see whether this generation of Christians have the power of God in them or not, to see whether they reflect or don't reflect the integrity and the compassion of Jesus. And the consequences can be dreadful when the Church or Christians let Christ down.

Can't you imagine the mocking laughter pealing down from those fifty sons of the prophets on the hill, if Elisha had taken up the mantle of Elijah and waved it in the air – and nothing had happened? That would have been the end of Elisha as a prophet. And in this day of watching sceptics and muddled morals – well, it won't be the end of the Church, but it will certainly be the end of *our* Christian impact, *unless* we are clear-sighted enough to see the resources of the supernatural available for every one of us in our holy faith, and humble enough to cast our insufficiency upon the sufficiency of Christ.

I wish I could put it to you so that this great cry of our text would get through the defences of the Church in Scotland and come right home to us. 'Where is' – not Elijah, not that – 'Where is the Lord God of Elijah?' *Not* 'Where is St Paul? Where is St Columba? Where are Luther and Wesley?', as though to say, 'If only *they* were here, things might really begin to happen. We should know then how to evangelise Scotland and the world'. As if the risen Christ were somehow there in those great days of the past, but not here! As if those mighty days had monopolised the Spirit of God, and the grace of Christ were somehow more available to the first century or the sixteenth than the twentieth! Men and women, we may wait for a Luther or a Wesley for a hundred or a thousand years: but we don't need to wait five minutes for the God of Luther and Wesley. God is waiting for us.

This is the crux of everything. And surely the old mystic had put his finger on the root of the trouble when he said – 'Till thou art emptied of thyself, God cannot fill thee.'

That applies to the Church. Till the Church is emptied of itself, God cannot fill it. And the Church is not emptied of itself. The Church has not – like Jesus – been content to be made of no reputation. It has been too respectable to attract, as Jesus did, the disreputable and the disinherited. It has been too concerned to maintain its own life, forgetting that Jesus said – 'Whoever tries to save his life in this world shall lose it; but whoever is prepared to lose his life for My sake shall find it.' It applies to the Church.

And it applies to you and me. 'Till *thou* art emptied of thyself, God cannot fill thee.' And you and I know we are not emptied of self. We still want our own way in so many things. We still sit at the centre of our little universe. We still evince sometimes towards the outsider or the fallen brother a censorious righteousness which is a blasphemy upon the love of Jesus. 'Till thou art emptied of thyself.' This is what the breath from heaven is tarrying for today.

But give God this and see what will happen. Once again, as here in the story, the watching world will say – 'The spirit of Elijah doth rest upon Elisha.' Once again the Jordan will be split asunder. Once again the going of the Lord God will be heard throughout the land, across the world the jubilant Hosannas – 'Blessed is He that cometh in the name of the Lord, Hosanna in the highest!' Churches that had lost heart and hope standing up throbbing with vitality; Christian lives that were standardised and conventionalised blossoming with the fruit of love and joy and gratitude and conviction; your own life – why, no one can measure what might happen there, the new purposefulness, the new poise and power, the new ineffable serenity!

'Where is the Lord God of Elijah?' For us, for the whole Church, that shout still rings athwart the centuries. Only – today it has become this: 'Where is the Lord God of Jesus and the Resurrection?' And the answer is – Here for the asking. Here, in this moment, for the claiming.

If the Church would realise this, how quickened its worship! I can't understand anyone not being thrilled by our Lord's description of what happens in worship: 'Where two or three are met in My name, there am I in the midst of them.' An ordinary Sunday morning service, we say, treating rather cavalierly our citizenship in Zion. Ordinary? How could it ever be that, with the risen Christ quite certainly there? How eagerly we should welcome every returning Lord's Day, like those excited folk of Galilee lining the roads where they knew Jesus was to pass; and with what heartfelt sincerity we should echo the psalmist's cry ...

I joy'd when to the house of God,
  Go up, they said to me.
Jerusalem, within thy gates
  Our feet shall standing be.

~ Hymn 489: *CH3* (Psalm 122) ~

How quickened the Church's worship when God is in the midst!

Yes, and how energised its work for the Kingdom! What a new passion to get out into the world and share that life of God for lack of which the world is dying! Don't imagine they are not wanting that life – the multitudes in this land and beyond the seas to whom the Church means nothing. They certainly don't want a Church that is just a religious club, a purveyor of hail-fellow-well-met camaraderie. They don't want from the Church the one hundred and one things they can in any case get elsewhere and probably get much better. They do want (whether they acknowledge it or not) the one thing they can get nowhere else – a sense of purpose, the secret of life's meaning, the kindling contact of the flame of heaven. 'I am come to send fire upon the earth,' said Jesus, the fire of a mission that can have no end; and you, this Christian community, are to be the torch that is to carry the flame!

We are just going to sing one of Charles Wesley's greatest hymns, about how the very life of God can enter the Church and the souls of men. It has two lines that sum up everything I have tried to say:

Come, almighty to deliver;
  Let us all Thy life receive ...

I have been a minister now for well-nigh forty years, and I have seen this miracle happening – lives that once went their own unthinking, not very satisfying way; and then the life of God got hold of them, not making them religiously priggish or aggressive, but flooding their whole personality with something of the loveliness and attractiveness and unselfishness that I have seen in the Lord Jesus Christ. It is still liable to happen, does happen regularly, the transfiguring miracle. Why should it not happen now and here while we are singing of it?

Come, almighty to deliver;
  Let us all Thy life receive;
Suddenly return, and never,
  Never more Thy temples leave.

~ Hymn 437: *CH3* ~

This is the rejuvenation of the Church.

CHAPTER 4

The Waves of Time

AN EVENING SERMON FOR THE LAST DAY OF THE YEAR

The times that went over him.   ~ I Chronicles 29: 30 ~

WITH that singular phrase the Chronicler closes his book and brings the story of King David to an end. 'There,' he says in effect, writing the Epilogue to his history, 'there is the record of this man's life, from the sheepfold to the throne, from the cradle to the grave, all he did and suffered and achieved, all the times that went over him: there is the total record, which whoso wills may read.'

It is an arresting phrase – 'the times that went over him' – suggesting wave after wave breaking on a rock, and rolling towards the shore. And tonight, when an old year is dying, and we are all conscious of 'time like an ever-rolling stream bearing all its sons away', this word is worth our pondering. We'll find it sets before us certain decisively important facts. It is to these I would call your attention now.

I

It speaks to us, first, of *the vicissitudes of experience*. 'The times that went over him.' That refers to the different, clearly-marked stages in David's life. The Chronicler is thinking not just of the passing from childhood to youth, and from youth to manhood, and from manhood to age: he is thinking not merely of the kind of sequence Shakespeare described in his 'seven ages of man'. He is thinking of the different, distinctive periods in David's fortunes, each with its characteristic light or shade. He is thinking of the dramatic alternations of that chequered career – shepherd lad, prince, outlaw, guerrilla leader, king, sinner, penitent, saint. These were the diverse stages of David's history. These were 'the times that went over him'.

So our life, too, has its times, its distinguishable stages, its contrasting chapters, its vicissitudes. Turn back the pages of the story tonight, your own story, I mean, and what do you find? Here's a chapter full of eager anticipation and high resolve: that was when you first found and followed your vocation. Here's another throbbing with a queer strain and tension: that was when you wrestled with religious doubt. Here's one chapter drenched in sunshine and written in letters of gold: that was where the great desire of your heart came true. Here's another shadowed with clouds and blotted with tears: that was when bereavement came, and you had to make your peace with death. Here's one chapter breathing the spirit of adventure: that was when you made your big decision, and launched out into the deep. Here's another suffused with an ineffable serenity: that was when you had discovered the reality of the companionship of Christ. These are the stages, the epochs, that the record marks, the experiences through which you have passed. These are 'the times that have gone over you'.

II

Now here immediately the question arises: What lies behind this strange, incalculable element of vicissitude in life? What determines the diversity of the experiences that come to us? What force controls events? These times that go over us like waves – what power directs and rules them?

Is it chance? Is it blind fate? Is it sheer mechanical cause and effect? Do these waves roll on dead and meaningless forever? What a dismal, dreary, paralysing philosophy of life that would be!

David had a different answer. For, writing in one of his psalms, he looked up into the face of God and cried – 'My times are in Thy hand!'

That was the great discovery. Looking back across the whole course of his life, David saw this tremendous fact – that even when things had gone desperately wrong, even when he had transgressed and bungled hopelessly the intended pattern of his life, God had come in there, and compelled the very mistakes to serve His ultimate purpose. The times like waves had gone over him; but there was a God who ruled the waves!

Is that your faith tonight? Have you seen the terrific twist that can be given to circumstance by the compulsion of an unseen hand? 'The things that happened unto me,' cried St Paul, referring to the shattering vicissitudes of his own career, 'have turned to the furtherance of the Gospel!' That's God's hand twisting evil, recalcitrant circumstance to glorious gain.

So if our text tonight speaks first of the vicissitudes of experience, it speaks, second, of the *sovereignty of providence*. The times that have gone over us like waves have not been chance or fate: God rules them. 'Thy way, O God, is in the sea, and Thy path in the great waters.'

Do you remember that vivid touch in Matthew? 'In the fourth watch of the night,' writes the evangelist, 'Jesus went to them, walking on the waves.' And there are tens of thousands who could say tonight, 'I know that is true: for it has happened to me. I've gone across stormy Galilee, but Christ had his foot on the neck of the storm, and trampled the proud waves level!'

There was a day when Luther, at the crisis of his career, was taunted by the Papal ambassador. 'Listen! renegade monk,' blustered the ambassador, 'where do you think *you'll* be when princes, pope and people turn against you? Where will you be *then?*'

Luther's magnificent answer had a thousand trumpets in it. 'Where shall I be then? Then, as now, in the hands of Almighty God.'

Yes, 'the times that go over' you – the best and the worst – are God-ruled, Christ-controlled.

John Bunyan was flung into gaol, and his preaching silenced: but that dark time that went over him in prison was the genesis of his book, *Pilgrim's Progress.*

The Pilgrim Fathers were exiled for their faith, driven to the desperate expedient of emigrating to a far-off, alien land; but that bleak, wintry time that went over them became the marshalling of a new continent for the Christianisation of the world.

But for ourselves – our faith is so feeble often! We see the vicissitudes, but not the victory; the waves, but not the God who rules them. What a difference it would make if we entered this New Year, not in the dubious timidity of a vague half-belief, but in what Kingsley called 'an absolute enthusiastic confidence in God!' And why shouldn't we?

> *Your harps, ye trembling saints,*
> *Down from the willows take;*
> *Loud to the praise of love divine,*
> *Bid every string awake!*   ~ Hymn 561: *Revised Church Hymnary* ~

III

The vicissitudes of experience, the sovereignty of providence what else does our text speak of? It speaks, third, of the *permanence of the spiritual life*, the continuity of character. For mark well the verb the Chronicler uses. The times, he says, *went over* David. The waves went over the rock. The experiences and vicissitudes loomed up, they came, they rolled on; but what David was in his own soul – that survived them all.

Have you ever pondered that phrase so familiar in the Bible – 'It came to pass'? It is the regular phrase with which the Bible introduces some fresh incident or event in a man's life. But have you tried putting the accent on the second verb there? 'It came *to pass.*'

It came, it existed, it was left behind. It had its hour, it was present fact, it went forever into the category of things that *had been.* It came – only to pass. But the man who goes through the experience remains. He literally 'goes through it' ... out the other side ... and leaves it behind.

Not that some experiences don't leave their mark on you. They do indelibly – right on to the journey's end. They leave you different for ever. You'll carry the marks of them with you up to the gates of heaven. You'll still be wearing the sign of them when you stand before the face of the Son of Man.

But the point is – the man who has found God (please underline that: the man *who has found God*) is not the helpless slave of circumstances and events. His true life is not at the mercy of the ravages of time. The times go over him: the man *remains.*

But it must be a life *rooted in God.* That's essential. Without that, time can and does ravage and destroy. Without that, time can and does play the tyrant terribly. The attrition of the years can be a grim reality when a life lacks a spiritual basis. For then it is not only youth that is consumed and corroded by the years. There are other more serious things that happen: the hardening of the arteries of the spirit, the quenching of enthusiasm, the lapse into cynicism, the 'freezing of the genial current of the soul', the filching away of faith and generosity and tenderness and hope. 'The years,' cries W. B. Yeats in 'The Countess Cathleen' ...

> The years like great black oxen tread the world
> And God the herdsman goads them on behind,
> And I am broken by their passing feet.

It is the sorrowfully familiar tragedy: the destruction wrought in countless lives by the passing of the years, the havoc of the waves of time.

But it needn't happen. In the mercy of God it doesn't happen where the spiritual basis is secure. 'Our outward man perishes' – so much the years can do – 'but our inward man is renewed day by day' – they can't touch that. The vicissitudes of life and the waves of time can't steal anything that really matters from the man who daily is being renewed within by wonder, love and adoration. And in this coming year, you – if you will – can prove that true.

IV

But tonight, within a few hours of the final exit of the dying year, I'd be failing in my duty to this text and to you if I did not point to a fourth, perhaps sombre, truth that is written here. It speaks — this text — of the vicissitudes of experience, of the sovereignty of providence, and of the permanence of spirituality. But there is no denying that it speaks also of the *transitoriness of life.* 'The times went over him,' says the Chronicler, summing up the story of King David: for those incredible waves of time no man can stop or retard — no, not even a King. Not the wisest or the greatest among men!'

'Give me life!' cries Bishop Nicholas in Ibsen's play 'The Pretenders', imploring the physician at his death-bed. 'I tell you — give me life! One more hour of life! Anything for life.' And then, when the physician shakes his head and confesses it is beyond his power to arrest those resistless waves, 'Miserable hound!' cries the dying man, 'what boots all your learning if you cannot give me one more hour of life?' That is the fact to be faced — not bypassed or thrust uncomfortably out of sight, but *faced:* the transitoriness of all existence here.

It does come home to us at an hour like this, when the year is dying in the night. 'We all do fade like a leaf,' says Isaiah. 'Our life,' declares the apostle, 'is but a vapour that appears for a little, and then vanishes away.' 'Our days on the earth,' cries King David, 'are as a shadow, and there is none abiding.'

What are we to say to these things? When we reflect on the transience of existence, and the uncertain lease on which we occupy as tenants this house of life — so that we may be here today and done with it tomorrow — what are we to say? This from St Paul: *'Redeem the time.'* And this from Jesus: *'Seek first the kingdom and righteousness!'* And this from every page of the Gospels: *'Be ye reconciled to God!'*

For if the New Testament does not speak to us with an off-hand, dilettante casualness, as one who should say, 'Take it or leave it, it doesn't vitally matter' (and emphatically it doesn't speak like that); if on the contrary it thrusts its message upon us urgently and even violently; if it reiterates that there is something genuinely at stake at every moment of our life — it is because it has heard the hurrying of the waves of time, 'the mighty waters rolling evermore'. And the man who won't see the force of that insistence is blind or frivolous or both. The waves move on inexorably. Don't say 'Tomorrow'. Behold, NOW is the accepted time!

V

One final word. This text has spoken to us tonight of the vicissitudes of experience, of the sovereignty of providence, of the permanence of spirituality, of the transitoriness of life. But its ultimate word is of the *assurance of immortality*. 'The times went over David' – yes; but beyond all the times that ever were, stretch the infinite horizons of eternity. 'Time?' cries Browning, 'What's time? *Man has for ever!*'

Have your times robbed you of someone who was dearer to you than life itself? Robbed you? Never again let time deceive you with that lie! He lives in God for ever – that dear one; and you won't grudge him one atom or one moment of the splendours of the glory yonder.

I ask you – which is the more impressive: that sad, almost truculent, dirge of Henley ... 'Beyond this place of wrath and tears, Looms but the horror of the shade', or Ralph Erskine, dying with the sudden shout upon his lips, 'Victory! Victory! Victory!'

No, I don't ask which is the more impressive, but which is the more true – which is the authentic truth of God? Which represents the mind of Christ?

I wonder if we have ever really grasped Christ's teaching on this matter. He doesn't say that after death begins eternity. He does say that if we belong to Him we are eternal already. It is not postponed till after death. He says that, if we are dwelling in God, then eternal life is a present possession here and now – so that the physical incident we call death, when it comes to us one day is, well, an incident, ultimately an irrelevance. The waves of time go over us, and death is just the last of the waves: it can't touch your essential being, for that – in fellowship with God – is eternal now, tonight. That is what our Lord meant when He said – 'Whoso liveth and believeth on Me *shall never die.*' And again – 'Fear not them that kill the body, and after that have no more that they can do.' The last wave goes over you, 'the swellings of Jordan' roll past and are forgotten: you – who are eternal now – live on. Fear death? There is no death: only life, and victory.

Yes, *if* you have found eternity here by fellowship with Christ. *If* you are sharing His imperishable quality of life. That is the crucial condition. That – in this solemn hour of a dying year – is the urgent question. If you haven't ever quite settled it, will you not, before this year is gone, look into Christ's eyes and settle it – now?

'That which is born of the flesh is flesh' and therefore perishes: 'that which is born of the Spirit is Spirit' and lives for ever. You have your choice. 'O friend,' cried Augustine, 'join thy heart to the immortality of God.'

CHAPTER 5

How to make our Prayers more real

Evening, and morning, and at noon, will I pray, and cry aloud;
and He shall hear my voice. ~ Psalm 55: 17 ~

AFTER a sermon on 'Guidance and Prayer', I was asked if I would speak some time on the practical question of how to make prayer more vital: the method of the devotional life, the technique of prayer.

Our first instinct may be to say that that phrase, 'the technique of prayer', involves a contradiction in terms. Has one any right to apply the words 'technique', 'method', to religion? Is it not the very essence of religion to be spontaneous, untrammelled, free? Are you going to imprison the living spirit with the shackles of form and system? Was not that precisely the course of Pharasaism – form and method were there, technique most elaborate; but the living spirit simply smothered? Did not Jesus insist that correctness of religious observance can be a terribly hollow and hypocritical thing? And do you propose to talk about 'the technique of prayer' tonight? Yes I do, and for two reasons.

The first is this. Prayer is such a tremendous act – approaching the presence of an infinitely holy God – that it is simply not good enough to have no method about it – with a kind of hit-or-miss casualness. Think who it is we are coming to:

The Lord doth reign, and clothed is He
  With majesty most bright;
His works do show Him clothed to be,
  And girt about with might!

~ Hymn 140: *CH3* (Psalm 107) ~

It is not good enough to think we can rush into that august presence and out again without due thought and preparation. It is not good enough to kneel down and repeat some familiar sentences, with minds wandering here, there and everywhere, and rather relieved when it is over. Better have some technique than just that!

But there is another reason. Take any subject – engineering, medicine, education, literature, art, music. To each of these there are two sides: there is the theory of the subject, and there is the technique of its practice. Take the Forth Bridge. To make the Forth Bridge there had to be two things: first, a body of mathematical principles, the abstract dynamics of engineering; and second, beyond that, the actual technique of the engineer. So in medicine: on the one hand, you have the theory of physiology; on the other, the technique of the surgeon. So in music: there's the theory of harmony, and there's the technique of the pianist. So in education: there's the theory of education, and there's the technique of the teacher.

Now it is exactly the same in religion. On the one hand, there is a great body of religious principles; on the other, there's the technique of the religious life. There are the reasons for believing in prayer, and there is the method of the devotional life.

And for many people tonight the crux lies in the second, rather than the first. They are convinced of the validity of prayer: they are haphazard about its practice. They are clear about the theory of the thing: they are hazy about the method. They have got the arguments for prayer all right: they have not got the technique. 'I know,' they would say, '*why* I ought to pray: but tell me *how!*'

So we are going to think of the practical question tonight. We are deliberately, on this occasion, *not* touching on the theoretical questions. Mark you, that is not to evade those questions. Questions like: Can prayer be effective in a universe of natural law? Why should an all-wise, all-loving God need our prayers at all? Why are some prayers answered, and others not? – these are real questions, deserving to be met sympathetically and realistically; and we have often faced them together in this church. But tonight our concern is different. Tonight I am addressing myself to the person who says, 'Granted that I believe in prayer, how am I to set about it? How am I to make my prayers more vital?

Now, I take it that we don't come to church for human advice; otherwise a church service would be no different from a public meeting. We come, not for any expression of individual opinion, but for the Word of God. So I ask you to realise that the seven maxims which I am now going to give you are based, every one of them, on Scripture and on the mind of our Lord.

I

The first is obvious, but essential. *Pray regularly*. Have set seasons for it, and stick to them. I know my own heart, and you know yours, well enough to say that the day is not safe without the morning prayer, nor the mind at peace without the prayer of the evening hour.

Paderewski used to say that if he stopped practising on the piano one day he noticed the difference; if he stopped two days his family noticed the difference; if he stopped three days his friends noticed the difference; and if he stopped for a week the public noticed the difference. There's no earthly chance of a vital devotional life unless we put real discipline into it.

But here there are two difficulties. 'All very well,' says someone, 'to talk about regular seasons of prayer; but what if I don't have time? Have you any idea of the rush that my life is?'Yes, friend, I do: I know and sympathise and understand. But the point is this, that the time you borrow for prayer will not be lost to your work: it will be recompensed to you a hundredfold in the poise and steadiness and equanimity it will impart to the rest of the day. I am not going to dwell on this.The busiest man – if he really wants to – will find time for prayer.

The other difficulty is more serious. 'What about the days when I am not in the mood? Isn't prayer bound to be awfully unreal and artificial then? Would it not be better to drop it, until the better mood returns?' This is a point on which both the Word of God and religious psychology are adamant. It is quite fatal to start making moods the arbiter of the soul's duty. In the direct and downright language of our Lord: 'Men ought always to pray, and not to faint!' In fact, it is precisely when the mood is all wrong – it is then, more than ever, that we need to maintain the spiritual discipline.We would not consent to be swayed by moods in any of the important issues of life: why, then, in the relationship of the soul to God, which is the most momentous of all? Would you say – 'I won't go out to work today: I am not in the mood' What would a C.O. say to a soldier who excused his absence from early morning parade with the plea, 'I wasn't in the mood'? Suppose you had made an appointment to meet a friend: would you say, when the time came, 'O bother! I'm not in the mood – I shan't go'? With one voice, all the saints who have ever lived give this instruction: 'Keep your appointments with God.' It is the first basic condition of a healthy spiritual life.

II

Second, *pray continually*. The set seasons, morning and evening, are necessary, as we have seen. But now I go on to add this: don't limit prayer to that, don't rail off two bits of life and leave the rest quite prayerless. Why shouldn't you drop into an open church sometimes for five minutes? It is a move in the right direction that so many churches are kept open for this very purpose now. But there is more than that. You can lift up your heart to God while you are going along the street: that is prayer. You can let God in on the work you are doing: that is prayer. You can touch the hem of the garment of Christ in the press of a throng of duties: that is prayer.

Have you ever asked yourself what Paul meant when he said – 'Pray without ceasing'? He didn't mean literally speaking to God without interruption. He didn't mean shutting yourself up in a monastery for a life of undistracted contemplation. He didn't mean anything so impracticable as consciously meditating on God every moment of every day. The express engine-driver who falls to meditating on God when he ought to be concentrating every atom of his attention on the distant signals down the line is a danger and a fool. What Paul meant was different: it was keeping the Godward channels open by frequent momentary acts of recollection. It is a great thing to know, it is indeed an epoch in a man's life when he discovers that at any moment of the day or night, in any sort of surroundings, his heart can wing its way to God, and touch the power that sways the world: like Nehemiah, when the Persian King asked him about his native land, and he realised in a flash that the whole future of Jerusalem might depend on his answer – so, standing there, with no time to kneel down, no chance even to shut his eyes, 'I prayed,' he said, 'to the God of Heaven'. Like Sir Thomas Browne, who declared there was no street in the city that could not bear witness how he had lifted up his heart to God. Like Robert Murray McCheyne of Dundee, of whom it was said, 'he made the mercy-seat his throne'. It is a proved fact that such frequent, momentary upward thrusts of the spirit to God can change the whole fashion of a man's life. And let us remember what St Augustine said long ago: 'We may pray most when we say least, and we may pray least when we say most.'

III

Pray concretely. One cause of the weakness and failure of many prayers is that they are vague generalities. So now I would say – be explicit! Go into particulars with God. For example, in the morning, take the day that lies ahead – that specially difficult task, that important committee, those hours in the office or classroom or the shop, that bit of national service, that meeting with a friend – hold every item of it up in God's presence, and let Christ in upon it.

In this connection, let me say a word about distractions. You kneel down to pray. You endeavour to 'be still and know that He is God'. And immediately a score of distracting thoughts invade your mind – a letter you should have written, a visit you ought to pay, a plan you'd like to try, a meeting you hope to arrange. What are you to do when into your quiet time whole troops of distracting thoughts come flying on the wing? Your best wisdom is not to try to suppress them forcibly – that is poor strategy: it is deliberately to turn these very distractions into subjects of prayer. Mention them quite concretely: and then they will cease to distract, and for the rest of your prayer-time your mind will be stayed upon God.

IV

Pray methodically. I mention this because a praying man will have so many people, so many causes, he wants to remember in his prayers. This is the value of such a directory of prayer as the little book *The Holy Tryst* – which takes you systematically over a wide range of themes for intercession. For myself (if you will allow a personal word), I have been in the habit for some years now of using the Communion Roll as a manual of prayer – taking three families each day: so that there is not a soul of the 1560 on the Roll who is not prayed about personally by name at regular intervals. But each of us in these matters has to arrive at his own method, remembering that more things are wrought by prayer than this world dreams of.

V

Pray affirmatively. It has never been adequately recognised that one of the most vital forms of prayer imaginable is the prayer of positive affirmation. This is the prayer in which, instead of begging and pleading with the Almighty, a man upon his knees reaffirms the great verities of faith. Instead of concentrating on his own frailties and handicaps and negative perplexities, he concentrates on the great positive convictions of faith. The Bible is full of this kind of prayer. The psalmist didn't say: 'O Lord, be my Shepherd. Don't let me want!' He said: 'The Lord *is* my Shepherd: I *shall not* want.' That is the prayer of positive affirmation; and religiously, no less than psychologically, it is much more efficient than the other. Jesus didn't say, 'O Father, don't leave Me alone! I implore Thee to be with Me'. He said, 'I am *not* alone, because the Father is with Me'.

I am sure we all need to learn this lesson, and to pray far more affirmatively. If we have got troubles, perplexities, temptations, there is a way of praying about these things that, instead of helping, simply drives them deeper into our consciousness, and roots them more fixedly in our minds. There is no liberation in such prayers. Here is a man with some besetting temptation: and he says, 'I've prayed about that thing till I am tired: I have begged and besought God about it for hours on end – and it is still there!' Of course it is still there: and the reason is that that kind of prayer, by concentrating on the man's pathetic problem, instead of on God's strong grace, defeats its own end. If you and I learn from the Word of God, we will pray far more affirmatively: not asking God if He can come to us, not begging and beseeching and persuading Him to be a refuge from our woes – but saying, with the saint of old, 'The Lord of hosts *is* with us, the God of Jacob *is* our refuge'.

VI

Pray meditatively. We narrow prayer unduly when we think of it as supplication, confession and intercession. To meditate quietly on the qualities or attributes of God – His serenity, His pity, His love – to walk in thought with Jesus on the Galilean road: that is prayer at its highest. Just think of the helps that are available for this kind of meditation – your New Testament, the immortal pictures of the Gospels, the lovely Hymns of Bernard and Francis and Charles Wesley, the great and moving prayers of Augustine, and Thomas à Kempis, and Martin Luther. And you have one great instrument for this kind of prayer – your imagination. Don't, I beg you, be suspicious of that. It is God's gift to you, and you are meant to use it. When you read a page of the Gospels, picture yourself present when that was actually happening – yourself the blind man crying for his sight, yourself Peter weeping in the dark for his denial, yourself Mary Magdalene kneeling at Jesus' feet in the fresh wonder of the Easter dawn. All that is prayer: and in that silent meditation, you 'will hear what God the Lord will speak'.

VII

Pray sincerely. It was inevitable to come round to this at last. For ultimately, if prayer is to be worth anything, we have to back it with our life. What is the use of racing the engine of a motor-car if you never let in the clutch? And what is the use of being fervent or assiduous in prayer, and slack or static in life, not harnessing prayer's power to character and action, not letting in the clutch. By all the laws of the spiritual world, such prayers can't be real. 'If I regard iniquity in my heart,' said the psalmist bluntly, 'the Lord will not hear me!' – not because God has gone deaf, but because that kind of prayer never gets through for God to hear it. Do you remember Shakespeare's Macbeth, listening to the sentries at their prayers?

> *Why could not I pronounce 'Amen'?*
> *I had most need of blessings, and Amen*
> *Stuck in my throat.*

Yes, indeed; for there was a sin clutched to his heart.

Mark you, this prayer-sincerity can be a desperately costly affair. It may mean taking the dearest idol you have known, and tearing it from a throne where it has no right to be. It may mean, as General Gordon said it meant for him, 'hewing Agag in pieces before the Lord'. It may mean, as Temple Gairdner said of one of his own temptations, 'taking it into the desert with Christ, and throttling it'. It is a desperate business – this demand for total sincerity. But if I want a real prayer-life, it is worth it! 'So shall my walk be close with God.'

CHAPTER 6

Singing the Lord's Song in a Strange Land

How shall we sing the Lord's song in a strange land?

~ Psalm 137: 4 ~

DOWN by the river that night, when the sun has set and the day's hard slavery is done, a little group of Jews have gathered, too weary to talk, too heartbroken to sing, silent and dejected by the river's bank. But by and by, one of them, greatly daring, takes his harp and touches the strings and begins to croon an old song, 'The Lord is my shepherd: I shall not want'. But he does not get very far. He has only got to 'He maketh me to lie down in green pastures' when the others interrupt and stop him reproachfully. 'Not that song, man! For any sake, don't sing that. Don't you see we can't bear that tonight?'

I think we can understand that. Think of an emigrant ship going out from the Clyde, and someone on shore, well-meaning perhaps, but terribly blundering, beginning to sing 'Home, sweet home'. Or a troop-train steaming out of the station, and a thoughtless, unimaginative bandsman striking up (of all ghastly things for such an occasion) 'Will ye no come back again?' So those exiled Jews felt when their unthinking comrade began that night to play the dearest of all the Psalms of Zion. 'The Lord is my Shepherd' was a dreadful thing at a time and place like that, tearing torn hearts to shreds. 'We might have been spared that!' they say. And I think I can see two of the more fervent spirits taking his harp from him almost by force. 'You won't go on with that! You won't!' And so silence falls again, silence broken only by a sob. 'By the rivers of Babylon, there we sat down; yea, we wept, when we remembered Zion.'

But stay – who are those coming down the river path? A group of roistering, swaggering Babylonian soldiers out for an evening's amusement. And they catch sight of the Jewish exiles. 'Why, here is the very thing! We'll get those wretched slaves to entertain us! A splendid idea!'

And they approach the Jews. 'You there, take your harp and sing us something! Let us hear one of your National Anthems! Sing us one of the songs of Zion!'

But not a man moves or responds.

'Don't you hear this? We are telling you to sing! Give us something with a real Hebrew lilt in it! Let us see if your Jehovah has as good a taste in music as our Gods of Babylon! Sing and amuse us!'

And still there is no answer, nothing but one of those exiles muttering to himself something that sounds like, 'Give not that which is holy unto the dogs!'

But their tormentors keep pestering them, until at last, blurted out and brokenly it comes – 'How shall we sing the Lord's song in a strange land?' And then, a great, bitter cry – 'O Jerusalem, if I forget thee, let my right hand forget her cunning! Let my tongue cleave to the roof of my mouth, if I remember not thee above my chief joy!'

But by this time the Babylonian soldiers are tired of waiting. 'Well, don't sing then! It would only be some poor barbaric song anyway – not worth our listening to!' And with that they move away.

And then – then that awful imprecation that still as it stares at us from this page makes our blood run cold: 'O daughter of Babylon … ' (please remember these men were living away back in the dim years before ever there was a Christ) … 'O daughter of Babylon, who art to be destroyed; happy he that rewardeth thee as thou hast served us! Thy children, thy little ones, thy bairns in arms – happy he who dasheth them against the stones!' And then, maybe, with a sob, 'O God, we don't know what we are saying! Forgive us – Lord, have pity!' And by the rivers of Babylon, silence reigns again.

Well, you see what it was that kept them songless that night? *It was loyalty to the memory of Jerusalem.* The years, the bitter years of exile might come and go, but still the biggest fact of their life was the city out of sight. All around was this sordid, blatant, alluring, God-denying thing called Babylon – but away yonder was the real thing, the land of their dreams. And they would sooner lie down in their graves than let the memory of Zion go.

How does it stand with us? Here are we tonight, exiles of eternity, pilgrims and sojourners before God as all our fathers were, children of the unseen, men with a citizenship in Heaven – here are we, with all that for our home and background; and yet all round about us the hard, workaday, tempting world, the jarring, jangling jostling world, the world of sense and flesh and the temporal – and it is out to absorb our every thought – *are we remembering Zion?* Epictetus, in one great place, speaks of the danger of our settling down content with our work and ambitions and pleasures and achievements, as if these were the end of life.

'That is,' he says, 'just as if a man on his journey home were to find a pleasant inn on the road, and, liking it, to stay on always in it. Man!' cries Epictetus, 'thou hast forgotten thine object! Thy journey was not to this, but through this – home!' And what is home but God?

'If I forget thee, O Jerusalem – if I forget the spiritual side of things, let my right hand forget its cunning!' Ah, but we do forget. And there are three things determined to make us forget.

1   *The creed of materialism is determined to make us forget.* 'What is all this about an unseen reality?' it says. 'The only real things are the things you can touch and handle and measure and see!' What a sad, dingy creed – even science is repudiating it now: and yet it slays its thousands!

2   *The dust and heat of life are determined to make us forget.* 'You've got enough to think about,' they say, 'without indulging dreams and fancies. You've all the worry and care and fret and tangle of the days, all the ceaseless struggle for existence!' And it is true – so true that prayer gets crowded into a corner, and then out of sight altogether, and God's precious intimations of immortality are smothered, and the blessed angels sing for us no longer – all through the dust and heat of things!

3   *Yes, and the Tempter is determined to make us forget.* 'You with your other-worldliness!' he sneers at us. 'Do you know what you are missing?' And with that he holds up his glittering bribes, his sensations and thrills and pleasures, the things to carry a man off his feet, and to sweep him away, God knows where! 'All that,' he says, as he once said it to the Lord Jesus Christ, 'all that, if you'll forget!'

Yes, there are things in this world determined to make us forget Jerusalem. And, friends, we have got to fight for the spiritual view of things, fight for the right to believe in God, fight for our soul's relationship to Christ, fight the stranglehold of Babylon and the suffocating pressure of the world! Do you remember how, by those same rivers of Babylon, one man discovered how to do it? The only way to do it, he found, was to fling his western windows wide, and then to go down on his knees and gaze and gaze and gaze away to the horizons that only the pure in heart could see – until away in that far Jerusalem some breath of God began to stir, came wafted across the intervening spaces, came in at his open window and fanned him on the brow. That was how Daniel kept memory alive and kept his soul! And do we want to remember Zion and God and Calvary and Christ and all the spiritual side of things? Then fling those western windows wide! God can't be real to a man who doesn't pray! The unseen can't grip and hold a man who is never on his knees! Jerusalem can't be vivid to a man who never turns his face that way! It grows dim and distant and recedes and fades away; and to be left in Babylon with only Babylon to think about – that is the death of the soul, the nearest thing on earth to Hell.

> *Lord God of hosts, be with us yet,*
> *Lest we forget, lest we forget.*

Well, it was loyalty to the memory of Jerusalem that kept those exiles silent and songless that night. And yet, on second thoughts, I wonder – was it not maybe a mistake, that silence? Don't you begin to feel that the real victory of faith would have been, not 'How shall we sing the Lord's song in Babylon?', but 'How shall we sing it anywhere if *not* in Babylon?' And so the picture in this psalm fades, and I begin to see another picture in its place, the picture of what might have been.

Again, it is the evening hour by the rivers of Babylon. Again the captives are being commanded by their captors to sing. But tonight they are taking it, not as a half-amused jest, but as a serious challenge. They take up their harps. A few notes, and then – they begin to sing. Quietly and gently the song begins, a plaintive, haunting melody; but gradually it gathers force and power, gradually rises higher and higher, until it breaks into a mighty, marching rhythm, with the beat and tramp of an unseen host in it, and the ring of iron in every note; and the song is this – 'Lift up your hearts, O ye gates! Lift them up ye everlasting doors, and the King of glory shall come in!' And now those Jews are singing it as they have never sung it in their lives before, singing it with a fervour and a passion that even their happiest days in Jerusalem never heard, singing then their very hearts out – 'Lift up your heads, O ye gates!' – until up on the ramparts of Babylon that night the sentries, hearing it, move uneasily at their posts, and in the streets of Babylon people stop to listen with a strange fear at their hearts as though that music were fate knocking at the door, and in the temples of Babylon the very gods begin to tremble. And still louder and louder rises the song, until with one great jubilant shout – 'Who is the King of glory? The Lord of hosts, He is the King of glory' – suddenly it ceases, and along the rivers of Babylon the echoes die away. But those Jews have gained the biggest moral victory of their lives. *They have sung the Lord's song in the strange land.*

Now then, have we ever done it? It may be a great thing, in loyalty to our unseen Jerusalem, to say – 'How can we sing the Lord's song in a strange land?' But it is a far, far greater thing to sing it! 'A strange land' – this earth? Yes, it is a strange land with sorrow in it, and pain, and death, and broken hearts; with clouds that gather and tempests that howl eerily, and winds that blow and beat upon the soul; with things, too, as Babylonian as Babylon, spirits of Avarice and Lust and Pride and War. How shall we sing the Lord's song here?

Nay, how shall we sing it anywhere else? It will be easy singing 'Worthy is the Lamb' when we get to Heaven. The real valour of faith is singing 'Worthy is the Lamb' into the face of your Tempter now. It will be easy breaking into the Hallelujah rhythm yonder, when the warstle of things is over ...

> *Where loyal hearts and true*
> *Stand ever in the light,*
> *All rapture through and through*
> *In God's most holy sight!*

But the real saints are the men who can send up a Hallelujah for God to hear *from this low earth,* the men who, nailed to some little cross, with the nails running like hot agony through their souls, can cry 'Hallelujah', and 'Blessed be God', and 'All praise to Christ' – even *there* and even *then!*

Others have done it – so why not we? I open my New Testament at Paul's Epistles, and I come on this – 'To the saints in Colosse who are in Christ'. In Colosse – in Christ! And Colosse was one gigantic, painted iniquity; and yet, white-robed and spotless and uncorrupted, they walked though it – those men and women of Jesus. There you have it – the Lord's song in the strange land! I think of Savanarola marching to the stake with the *Te Deum* on his lips; of Margaret Wilson singing in the Solway tide; of Milton, out of his blindness, fashioning Paradise; of Dante, out of his desolation, making music for God. Above all, I think of Jesus, the Christ of the Upper Room, ringed round on that last night with enemies and treacheries and plots, with all the sorrow and sin and shame of men gathering itself up to hurl itself down on Him and break Him – I open the story of it, and what do I read?

> 'Jesus took the bread – *and gave thanks.*'
> 'Jesus took the cup – *and gave thanks.*'
> 'Jesus, *when He had sung a hymn,* went out.'

I think I can hear Jesus' voice starting that hymn, one of the old Psalms of David it was, and the disciples trying to join in, and breaking down, and begging Him – 'No, Jesus, no! We just can't sing tonight, our hearts are too sick and sore to sing' – and with that, I hear Jesus' blessed voice finishing the song alone, singing it right through to the end, out on that

Gethsemane journey. Verily – the Lord's song in a strange land! And that is the Christ who is standing beside every burdened heart tonight. 'My brother, my sister,' He is saying, 'why aren't you singing? I've been waiting, listening for your song, and I haven't heard it!' And we look at Him almost reproachfully. 'Singing, Jesus, how *can* you ask it? Don't you see? Don't you know? Don't you understand? How can we sing?'

Ah, but then perhaps, as in the old story of Caedmon and the angel, 'Sing to me,' says Jesus to us: and with that, everything is different, and somehow we can. Others have sung God's song in the strange land, Christ has done it – and why not we?

I am going to close by giving you two reasons why it is our duty to sing the Lord's song in the strange land.

The first one is this – we've got to do it to let Babylon see *our spirit isn't broken!* My friend, when you are feeling downcast and cowed and beaten, try for a tonic the fifth chapter of Revelation! The man who wrote that chapter was far more downcast and cowed and beaten than you will ever be, and yet the whole thing is one red–hot riot of doxology! The man who wrote it was at his last gasp, with nothing left to hold on to – and yet, listen to this: 'Worthy is the Lamb that was slain to receive power, and riches and wisdom and strength and honour and glory and blessing!' – and every word there is another nail hammered into the coffin of the enemy Despair, another arrow of faith shot out of the depths to Christ! Here was a man singing the Lord's song out of the blackened pit of Hell! And why not? For God was there, as much as anywhere! And there is no strange land of the soul tonight, and no desolate captive shore, and no bitter rivers of Babylon of which you can't say – 'Even there shall Thy hand lead me, and Thy right hand shall hold me!' Sing that song of the Lord then, and let Babylon see your soul is your own!

That is the first reason. And here is the second. *We've got to be singing the song in the strange land in order to be practising it for our homecoming.* For we are not going to be in the strange land always. One day we are going home to God. And the question is: Are we going to have the music ready for that day when it arrives?

You know, I can imagine those Jews of the rivers of Babylon saying this: 'Doesn't it stand written in our prophet – "The ransomed of the Lord shall return, and come to Zion with songs, and everlasting joy upon their heads"? And if we are not keeping up our music here, how shall we able to join in it there? We must keep singing and practising every day – practising in Babylon for Zion.'

And if you and I, friends, have the great hope set before us (as in Jesus Christ it is set before us), that one day, away home yonder in Zion, we are going to sing the new song before the very throne of God, don't you think we had better be practising it now? And the words of that new song are faith and hope and love and valour and kindness and truth, and its keynote is likeness to Christ. Don't you think we should be practising it now?

For out of all nations and peoples of the earth, that great final choir is going to be gathered – the festival choir of Jesus. And all over the world tonight there are smaller choirs practising the music of the new song, the music of faith and hope and love that is to be rendered in perfection on that great day. North, South, East and West at this moment they are practising it – each separately in their own corner. But one day all are coming together in one united choir, the 'multitude which no man can number', you and your loved ones you have lost, reunited there and their voices blending again with yours, all the generations of mankind united to sing the one great song of Zion! Isn't it worth doing some practice for that? Practising those notes of faith and hope and love every day we live? 'The Lord's song in a strange land?' Yes, we'll sing it here, that we may be ready to sing it in Heaven.

CHAPTER 7

Thanksgiving:
Theme with Variations

I will praise Thee with my whole heart: before the gods will I sing
praise unto Thee ... forsake not the works of Thine own hands.

~ Psalm 138 ~

IF I were asked to prescribe a tonic for someone depressed and spiritually below par, I'd suggest this short, immensely stimulating psalm. It has spoken to my own soul many and many a time. I hope it may speak to yours today.

If you want a title for this psalm, I'd call it 'Theme with Variations'. The theme is thanksgiving. Here are the variations.

I

First, the *character of thanksgiving*. Look how abruptly it begins, how impetuously the man who wrote it bursts in upon us, without ceremony or introduction, his eyes shining, his face glowing, his voice vibrating with excitement, like a man overwhelmed with some marvellous piece of incredible good fortune. His first words come tumbling out in a torrent of irrepressible gratitude – 'With all my heart I thank Thee. With all my heart I sing Thy praise!'

Whereupon perhaps we look at him askance, in some misgiving and distaste. Knowing life as we do today, the international strains and stresses, rival ideologies menacing world peace, yes, and all the problems on our own doorstep – what Wordsworth called 'the heavy and weary weight of all this unintelligible world' – knowing that, we feel that this sort of unadulterated enthusiasm for life is not quite seemly, indeed positively exasperating.

'This,' we say, 'must have been a man with a singularly sheltered, fortunate existence. He had obviously escaped the jars and jolts of this rough world. Did he really understand what life means in terms of hardship, strain and difficulty for multitudes of people? Did he have any conception of the sheer mass of misery which this world at any given moment contains? Just listen to him! "I bow before Thy sacred shrine, to praise Thee for Thy love so true. With all my heart I thank Thee".'

We feel like flinging back at him, 'Man, if you had any discrimination, you would say rather – "With all my heart I'd thank Thee to make this world quite different, to shatter the whole sorry scheme of things to bits and remould it nearer not only to the heart's desire, but also to the basic principles of justice and equity and fair dealing".'

Is that perhaps our first reaction to these glowing words? Well, it is understandable enough. There are such outrageous inequities in life that it would be quite natural. But I want you to see that if we do react like that we'd be quite mistaken.

We'd be doubly mistaken. For on the one hand, this man in the psalm was not a man who had lived in the sunshine and never suffered. Look, lower down, he tells you he had been in the midst of trouble, in the grip of hostile forces. And on the other hand, surely one of the basic functions of religion is to make us thankful, not in proportion to favourable circumstances – no atom of credit in that – it is precisely to help us to keep thanking the Lord in face of the most testing circumstances.

Anyway, here you have this man singing forth his praise in face of all the facts – not in a demure, apologetic murmur, but with jubilant doxologies and exultant hallelujahs – 'With all my heart I thank Thee.' This is faith's achievement. This is the essential *character of thanksgiving*.

II

So let us read on. We pass to the second variation on the thanksgiving theme: first, the character; second, *the cause of thanksgiving*. You will observe that, among all his other causes of gratitude, the psalmist singles out one thing specifically, one all-important discovery. He had discovered the fact of *a prayer-answering God*.

Listen how he puts it in verse 2: 'Thou hast magnified Thy word above all Thy name' – meaning by that, 'Lord, you have gone beyond everything I had ever imagined of the divine character, in the way You have responded to my petitions!'

And then this magnificent testimony in verse 3: 'In the day when I cried Thou answeredst me, and strengthenedst me with strength in my soul' – or, to translate it otherwise, 'The very day I call, Thine answer comes, with courage to inspire my soul!'

I wonder how many of us here today can say that has been our experience? Honestly? There comes back to me across the gulf of years (more than fifty years now) the voice of Professor Hugh Mackintosh of beloved memory, lecturing to us students at New College on the theology of miracles. 'Be sure,' he would say, 'when you think of miracles, be sure to start from two facts – the forgiveness of sins and *answers to prayer* – both of them *sheer miracle!*' 'The very day I call, *the answer comes*' – has it been our experience?

There was a day when a little company of Scottish Covenanters, hunted across the moors, were in imminent danger of being surrounded and cut off by the pursuing dragoons. But there among the heather, for one fleeting moment, the men of Christ's crown and covenant knelt down, and their leader Alexander Peden lifted up his voice in prayer. 'O Lord,' he prayed, 'we be dead men unless Thou help us. Lord, throw the lap of Thy cloak over this poor company!' Instantly, says the historian, a Highland mist enveloped the fugitives and hid them from their pursuers, just as though the prophetic word was being fulfilled: 'Before they call, I will answer, and while they are yet speaking, I will hear!'

'The very day I call, the answer comes.' On the north-east coast of Scotland, one black and stormy night, a woman came to the house of her minister, and knocked and roused him and said, 'Rise, sir, pray for my husband, for he is on the sea in a storm'. And there, in the little study together, they knelt down and prayed for the safety of the sea captain. Sure enough, at that very hour the ship was being battered by monstrous seas. It plunged in the trough of the waves, descending again and again into that hell of swirling waters. So colossal was the onslaught that all hands on board were beginning to give up hope. And then suddenly the tempest had spent its force. 'Men,' said the captain afterwards to his crew, 'surely there was some God's soul on land praying for us tonight, or we could never have come out of that!' 'The very day I call, the answer comes.'

Whereupon we retort – 'Oh, yes, very dramatic, no doubt. But unconvincing! It certainly hasn't been my experience!' Some here might tell how years ago they called on God, told Him of their heart's desire – and there hasn't been any answer yet. No ... not my experience, they say. Besides, doesn't the Bible itself tell us, 'If the vision tarry, you must wait for it'? Are there not sayings, parables of Jesus, urging perseverance, tenacity, sheer downright importunity? What is all this, then, about instantaneous answers? The man's romancing!

III

Not in the least. For mark well his words: 'Thine answer comes, *with courage to inspire my soul.*' Here we pass to the third variation on the theme. We have seen the character and the cause of thanksgiving. Here is *the courage of thanksgiving.*

Look at it like this. You are carrying, let us say, some heavy load of trouble or anxiety. It is beginning to be just a bit too heavy for your resources. You take it to the Lord in prayer. You commit to Him your situation. There are two ways in which God can answer that petition. The one is *to level down that burden to suit your strength.* The other is *to level up your strength to suit the burden.* It so happened that the answer the psalmist got was of the second kind: 'courage to inspire my soul.'

That spiritual and intellectual giant of a man, St Paul, had what he called a 'thorn in the flesh', a crippling, frustrating physical malady. He tells us in II Corinthians that he prayed to God again and again to take the thing away; yet apparently it stayed with him to his life's end. But that did not mean all those prayers of his were fruitless and unavailing. Definitely not. The answer came. And the answer was – 'My grace is sufficient! Strength made perfect in weakness' – like an army with banners marching into the beleaguered fortress of his soul.

Jesus, too, had His Gethsemane, His cry out of the darkness: 'Father, let this cup pass from Me! If it be possible, let this cup pass!' And yet to the last bitter dregs He drank it. But that did not mean His crying was unheard. 'There appeared unto Him an angel strengthening Him.' 'The very day I call, the answer comes.'

I know that if today I were to ask the men and women in this Church to stand up, all you who have found God to be a prayer-answering God – I am not going to do this, but if I were – the great majority, perhaps nearly all, would stand. Particular petitions may be granted or denied; that is a mystery beyond our power to fathom. But this is certain: prayer itself is always answered. Indeed, you get far more than you asked for. You get God. You get Christ. You get an invasion of supernatural strength from another world. Lightning has no speed, nuclear energy no power, compared with that invasion. 'The very day I call, Thine answer comes, with courage to inspire my soul.'

I wish our services today would lead someone to put this to the test. You know you can. For the whole life and power of the invisible God are standing beside you at this moment, to penetrate and transform any situation. If that is not true, then nothing in the Bible is true. 'Lord, I believe; help Thou mine unbelief.'

IV

Come back to the psalm. The next verses – four, five and six – are an interlude: the psalmist pictures the kings and kingdoms of the world bringing their homage to the Lord.

But look! In the closing verses – seven and eight – the main thanksgiving theme returns. Here comes the fourth variation on the theme: this time, *the confidence of thanksgiving.* For here the psalmist turns from past experience to face the future. *'Though I pass through the thick of trouble, Thou wilt preserve me.'*

It is difficult sometimes, terribly difficult, being confident about the months and years that stretch ahead into the unknown future. So many disquieting contingencies are lurking there. What if, on the international scene, 'the sky grows darker yet and the sea rises higher', till tensions between East and West reach breaking-point? And on the more personal level, what if health gives way? What if plans fail? What if sorrow strikes, hard, inexorable? There is no assurance that these things will not happen. No. But there is an assurance that the man in Christ will come through with head unbowed. As the Lady Julian of Norwich put it, away back in the fourteenth century: 'He said *not* "Thou shalt not be tempted, thou shalt not be travailed, thou shalt not be afflicted!" He did not say that: He said, "Thou shalt not be overcome".'

Oh, you say, if only I could be certain of that! If only I knew in advance that I'd hold out to the end!

But that's just the point! I *can't* be sure of it. There is no guarantee of getting through this world victorious.

Is there not? The psalmist at any rate says there *is*. He says there is one sure rock on which a believing man can build his confidence.

V

This is *the crown of thanksgiving.* For look at his closing words. The psalm finishes as abruptly as it began. It finishes with the psalmist looking up into the face of God and saying not simply, as it usually runs, 'Forsake not the work of Thine own hands' – but saying this tremendous thing: *'Thou wilt not drop the work Thou hast begun!'*

Think of that. It means the question is not: Will I hold out to the end? Will I keep on with God to the end of the road? No … not that. But this: Will God keep on with me? And that is not a question – *it is a certainty.*

The guarantee is not my courage, my confidence, my tenacity: it is God's fidelity, God's constancy, God's dependability. 'Thou wilt not drop the work Thou hast begun.' This is the final variation of the theme. This is the crown of thanksgiving.

What did you expect? Did you think God would undertake a task, and leave that task half finished?

Put yourself into this. Did God once begin a work in you? Look back today along the road you have travelled, and see if you can't mark one experience after another – 'There it was, there again, and there yet again, Providence delivering my eyes from tears, my feet from falling, my soul from death.' Have you not had days when you actually felt the touch of His Spirit on yours? Then, when you are discouraged, ready to give up the struggle, speak to your own heart and say – 'He did begin a work of grace in me. He did lay the foundations of my house of life for me.'

Martin Luther, when the devil of depression was trying to get hold of him, had two words, two Latin words, he held on to like grim death, repeating them over and over again: '*Baptizatus sum*' – 'I have been baptised.' By which he meant 'God did claim me for His own. God did *begin* a work in me'.

You be like that! Tell yourself that, whatever happens, even though the mountains be cast into the sea, and the stars crash and fall, *God cannot and will not go back on His word.* For that is true. I can do nothing else but proclaim that that is true. 'Thou wilt not drop the work Thou hast begun.'

If this old psalmist could be sure of that, how much more we! For the fact has been sealed by the Cross of Jesus and the Resurrection. Do you think God would have allowed the Cross to happen, if He were not going to finish the work? Do you think He would have staked so much, if He were not set on seeing His Kingdom through to victory in the world and in the lives of men?

We talk of the Cross as the symbol of God's love. It is that indeed. But I want you to go further today and see it as the symbol of God's determination. It tells of tender mercy, but it tells also of inflexible resolve. Hymn 258 says:

Inscribed upon the Cross we see
In shining letters, 'God is love'.

I see something more inscribed upon that Cross today. I see inscribed there: '*God will not fail nor be discouraged!* God will not let the world He died for slip through His fingers at the last. God will not let His plan for you remain unfinished and incomplete.'

What's the evidence? That Cross, that Resurrection. After *that* I know God will not drop the work He has begun. This is thanksgiving's crown.

And it spans this world and the next. For it gives me a horizon away beyond death itself, the sure glory of Immanuel's Land beckoning yonder across the Jordan, our eternal inheritance, with the trumpet-call sounding the reveillé of the Resurrection, and the hosts of the redeemed shouting the praises of Jesus – sin conquered, God glorified, Jesus seeing of the travail of His soul and being satisfied. Thanksgiving's crown indeed!

Oh, why are we so dull and thankless often, grudging our gratitude? I am sure the saints in heaven must sometimes be nonplussed at the stinginess of our Hosannas here on earth.

The Gospels tell us of the first Palm Sunday, when loud reverberating Hosannas greeted Jesus riding in to Jerusalem. Some sour-faced Pharisees tried to stifle the thanksgivings that cheered Him on His way. Do you remember our Lord's reply to that? He said – 'If these people should hold their peace, the stones would immediately cry out.' Just that. The dead, inert stones of the street would have to shout Hosanna, if His men and women kept silence.

And He is here today! And He is waiting. Do you remember those lines from Hymn 360?

> Ransomed, healed, restored, forgiven,
> *Who like me His praise should sing?*

I tell you now – no, I don't tell you, *He* tells you – that if you and I, yes, indeed, 'ransomed, healed, restored, forgiven' – for that is not just a familiar hymn with a good-going tune, it is the truth of your life and mine at this moment – if you and I should hold our peace and have no real gratitude to bring, then the stones of this Church, the stones of the city streets, might well cry out and offer the Hosannas we have failed to render.

Therefore, here in God's Word it stands, to challenge and incite us in God's House today:

> 'With all my heart I thank Thee.'
> 'The very day I call, the answer comes.'
> 'Thou wilt not drop the work Thou hast begun.'

And so – thanks, yes, a thousand times, thanks be to God! And may there be rejoicing among the angels in Heaven when our thanksgivings rise to mingle with theirs before the throne.

CHAPTER 8

The God
of Jacob

Happy is he that hath the God of Jacob for his help.

~ Psalm 146: 5 ~

THAT fervid exclamation immediately starts a question in our minds. We want to interrogate this psalmist. 'Yes,' we say to him, 'happy indeed to have God to help us – but why the God of *Jacob* in particular? Why, out of all the figures in the great portrait-gallery of Israel's history, do you choose just *this* one, and say that we are specially happy to have *his* God for ours? Why not the God of Abraham? Why not the God of Moses? Why not the God of Elijah? Why the God of Jacob?'

It is clear from the very frequency with which it occurs that, to these old psalmists and prophets, this way of describing God had a quite peculiar appeal. They prayed with greater confidence when they remembered it was the God of Jacob they were praying to. They sang with more glowing rapture when they reflected that it was the God of Jacob who was listening to their praises. They faced life with firmer courage when they knew that it was the God of Jacob who was with them. Whatever the reason was, they found that to connect God with Jacob, to call Him 'Jacob's God', brought them a strange sense of strength and comfort and consolation. Perhaps, in some dim, vague way, we have felt that too. Perhaps we felt it when we sang the words this morning:

> *O happy is that man and blest,*
> *Whom Jacob's God doth aid.*

But what's the reason? Why should we rejoice that we have not only got God, but the God of Jacob for our help? I am going to suggest three reasons now.

I

If He was the God of Jacob, that means that *He is a God who can make something out of my crude materials.*

The God of Abraham – He certainly was that. But Abraham stands towering infinitely above us, a sublime, original, glorious man, a blazing lighthouse beacon of a man, of a kind of which only one might appear in a century or in an age. God might be the God of Abraham, and yet not be ours. The God of Moses – He certainly was that. But Moses is wrapped for ever in the mystery and darkness and solitude into which he went to commune with the Eternal, that day when, on the mountaintop, with all the world left behind, he saw God face to face.

The God of Elijah – He certainly was that. But Elijah was of the stuff of which thunderbolts are made: no common clay, but a soul which, when its days were done, simply had to go up on a whirlwind into heaven. Tell me that God is the God of Abraham, and Moses, and Elijah, and the knowledge of it may leave me cold. But tell me that He is the God of Jacob and 'Ah!' my heart immediately cries, 'That's different! That's more like what I need. There *is* some hope for me after all. Jacob, with his queer mixed nature, his blundering ways, his sins and his repentances, his drabness and ordinariness, mediocrity and averageness – the God of Jacob? Then there *is* a chance for me. I needn't give up. He is a God who can do something with *my* crude clay, the crude stuff that I am'. 'Happy is he that hath the God of Jacob for his help!'

We do feel sometimes, don't we, that our very ordinariness is shutting us out from God? We are like the man in the story who was given one talent. And as soon as his master's back was turned, he looked at it. 'What am I to do with this?' he wondered. And he held it up to the light, and looked at it again. 'This, then, is all the Master thinks of *me,* is it? All very well for these others with twice or five times this, but obviously I'm nothing. I'm lost in the common herd – in God's sight just don't count! This talent – come, let me bury it!'

But if it is the God of Jacob you've got for your God, then that low mood is *finished!* 'Even out of me,' you now say, 'God may yet fashion something!' Robert Burns was walking along Princes Street in Edinburgh one day with a fashionable acquaintance, when he saw a poorly-dressed peasant, a man he had known away back in Ayrshire; and he ran up and took him with both his hands and greeted him with warm affection. And when he rejoined his companion later, 'Really,' said the man, 'you know you shouldn't! That common creature, that peasant .... ' And Burns' eyes flashed with fire. 'Fool!' he cried, 'it wasn't the dress, the peasant's bonnet and the hodden gray I spoke to, but the man within!' It's not our drabness, our crudity, our commonplaceness God sees – it is the soul within: it is the brother, the sister of Christ, that He can make of us!

The great and good Lord Shaftesbury one night was visiting one of the so-called 'Ragged Schools' he had founded; and there were about a thousand waifs gathered in off the streets. 'Talk about sacraments?' he said to a friend next day. 'Talk about the Real Presence? Our Lord was there last night – the Real Presence of Christ – as much as at any time or place!' And we who so often feel our littleness, who feel huddled, lost among the crowd of God's creation, can lift up our heads and say, 'The Lord is here!'

'Where are the angels?' Francis Thompson found himself asking one day, when the terrible solitude of London engulfed him. 'Where are the guardian angels men spoke of long ago?' And here was how he dared to answer his own question:

> Not where the wheeling systems darken,
> And our benumbed conceiving soars!
> The drift of pinions would we hearken,
> Beats at our own clay-shuttered doors.

> ~ Francis Thompson: 'The Hound of Heaven' ~

As much as to say to himself, 'Soul! The angels are *here!* Hark! Don't you hear the beat and throb of wings – they're here!' And you and I, lost in the crowd more even than Francis Thompson was, can raise our heads and say – 'Where is the Lord God of hosts? Ten thousand miles from our poor lives? An infinity away? No, the Lord is here! And He is mine, and I am His!'

When *Principal Rainy was dying, a friend came in and prayed with him. And when the prayer was over, 'I wonder,' said the dying man, 'at the love of God to me. And I believe that for all my short-comings, I am not shut out, but – shut in!' That's it – in spite of all our short-comings, all our poverties, all our sense of being lost and lone and too poor for God to notice – not shut out, but *shut in* with God and with His love! For if God could work a spiritual miracle out of the crude stuff that Jacob was made of – and He did – then He can do it also with our poor clay. He may be the God of Abraham, the God of Moses and the God of Elijah, and we just tremble before Him: but happy is he that hath the God of Jacob for his help!

---

*Principal Rainy (1826-1906) was Principal of New College, Edinburgh from 1874.

II

Turn to a second thing now. If God was the God of Jacob, that means that *He is a God who plans and guides our life.*

There was that night at Bethel when Jacob had left his home for the first time in his life, and was facing the great world for himself. And he wasn't finding that world an easy place; Providence and fortune seemed to have deserted him, and life was proving harder and lonelier than he had expected; and there was more than a touch of rebellion in his heart. On he went trudging up the mountainside as the gloaming deepened into darkness, with night all round him and black night in his soul; on and on, past the lower levels and green pastures, up amongst the bare rocks and crags; until at last, dead beat and exhausted, he lay down with a stone for his pillow and the biting night-wind in his bones, a poor, lonely pathetic thing. And then – the sudden glory, the open Heavens, the vision of God!

'Surely,' he cried, 'the Lord is in this place, and I knew it not! I thought that there was nothing here but these bare rocks and loneliness and darkness, and lo! I've blundered into Paradise! I thought my pillow was a stone, and lo it was the very bosom of God!'

And so he made his great discovery – that there was a God unseen, guiding and planning – all his way, and that his steps were moving on a path prepared. That is still one of the supreme discoveries of life. It changes the whole aspect of the world. It is a new world when you have discovered that you can hold God's hand each step of the way. Robert Louis Stevenson tells of a humble friend of his, a Welsh blacksmith, 25 years old and unable to read or write: and one day, in a farm kitchen, he heard a chapter of *Robinson Crusoe* read aloud in Welsh.

'Up to that moment,' says Stevenson, 'he had sat content, huddled in his ignorance, but he left that farm another man.'

What happened? Down he sat, taught himself to read Welsh, and then returned to borrow the book. It had been lost. The only other copy he could find was in English. Down he sat again, learned English, and at last, with joy and delight, read *Robinson*.

It was a new world that night in the farm kitchen had opened to him. And it is literally a new world you enter on – a world of glorious meaning and zest and happiness – when you come awake to a God who guides.

And I am convinced that half the strain, half the feverishness in the world today, are due to the fact that we won't believe that, just won't credit it that our lives, and the lives of our dear ones, are in higher hands; won't sink back even for a moment and feel underneath the everlasting arms. We think that if we aren't forever taking thought for ourselves, no one else will; that it is our responsibility, and ours alone, to put this business of life through, and that therefore we've *got* to worry and be anxious about it, and run about feverishly, and fret ourselves to death about things. Which simply means that we are tying on to our own shoulders a burden that needn't be there at all, because it is meant for *God's* shoulders. And as long as that is the way of it, we'll never be really free, never that feeling of release and exhilaration that is the hallmark of true religion.

Will you trust God to guide you? 'My life,' said Thomas Browne of the *Religio Medici*, 'my life has been a miracle of 33 years' – God's hand, all the way through.

Will you trust that guiding hand, that mind, even when things look dark and fearsome? 'The darkness,' said Kagawa, the great Christian leader of Japan, 'the darkness is my holy of holies, where I meet God!'

Bunyan's pilgrim, trudging through the dismal valley, suddenly heard a song in front of him; and his heart leapt up. 'I'm not alone,' he cried 'there are two of us in this darkness.' Yes, there are always two in the valley – you, and God. Caesar's victories, we are told, were due to this: that never did Caesar say to his men 'Go!', but always 'Let us go!' – and went himself at their head. That's God, if you'll only believe it – never 'Go!', always 'Let us go!' – God in it with you, planning the way, every step of it. If I didn't believe that, I'd go home today and never try to speak a word for God again. But I *know* it. This was Jacob's Bethel discovery – a God to guide him. Happy is he that hath the God of Jacob for his help!

III

Turn to the third and last thing now. To have the God of Jacob means to have a God who can make something out of crude materials; it means to have a God who guides and plans; it means, finally, to have *a God of infinite patience*.

You remember how in Jacob's story, after that glorious night at Bethel, comes what you can't help feeling to be a period of anticlimax – the man back at the old levels of life, the old scheming of stratagems, the old earth-bound ways and habits – so that, like Wordsworth, you begin to wonder:

Whither is fled the visionary gleam?
Where is it now, the glory and the dream?

~ 'Intimations of Immortality' ~

But all through those subsequent years of spiritual anticlimax, you can see a dim shadow moving at the man's heels, the shadow of God, God in infinite patience refusing to be shaken off or give the man up, refusing to be finally disappointed or turn away.

And then, at last, at Peniel, came the crisis. To Jacob, walking alone that night in the dark gorge, beside the rushing river, something happened. He felt himself suddenly gripped by hands of steel. He tried to break away, fought desperately to break away, and the question was beating in his brain, 'Who can this be? Who must this be? The spirit of the river? The ghost of my own past perhaps? Or is it my old enemy Esau? Or is it not flesh and blood at all, but a spirit, an angel? Is it …' – and his heart almost stopped beating at the thought – 'is it perhaps God Himself?'

'God?' he thought, and suddenly a wave of anger flooded him. 'The God who has been dogging me all these years? Then I'll finish with Him tonight! I'll end this business once for all!' And he fought wildly like a tiger; but the grip of the unseen wrestler held him, flung him, lamed him, broke him down at last into a little child, shattered the sinner and left a saint. God had won. The love, which never all these barren years had let go, had conquered. Here was a man saved by the sheer patience of God.

Happy is he that hath the God of Jacob for his help – the God of infinite patience! If it weren't for that, if God were even for a single day to treat these exasperating lives of ours, with all their spiritual anticlimaxes, as they deserve, where should we be? But you remember Jeremiah's great picture – the potter toiling with his clay, watching it take shape beneath his hands, growing into a thing of use and beauty, almost finished, just a few last touches, when suddenly – snap! – the thing shivers to pieces in his hands. And he looks at it. What does he say? 'Throw it away! There must have been a flaw in the material – poor, shoddy, trashy stuff – and all my work's been wasted. Away to the rubbish-heap with it!' Is that it? No! But this – 'I must give it another chance. I'll start all over again from the beginning. This time I may succeed.' This, says Jeremiah, is God – the God of all patience.

Or look at Christ with His disciples – giving those twelve men His very best, his very self, every day He lived with them: and yet, after it all, the old rivalries breaking out among them – what a blow in the face to Christ it must have been! The old unspirituality, the old touchiness – why, even on the night when He was going to die, there wasn't one of them who would stoop to wash the others' feet; even then they were babbling about their rights.

'Oh!' Christ might have cried, if He had been anybody but Christ, 'Oh! can't you see, will you *never* see, that if you're mine, that kind of thing is finished, gone? But you,' He might have flamed, 'you'll never see it, you're useless to Me, I'm tired of you, back to your homes with you –

and I'll get others!' That *might* have been it. But no! Not a word – only that love that loved them through it all, and doggedly refused to despair of them, and so made them saints at last by its sheer patience with them. That's Christ – and that's God.

> *Thy foes might hate, despise, revile,*
> *Thy friends unfaithful prove:*
> *Unwearied in forgiveness still*
> *Thy heart could only love!*　　　　　~ Hymn 216: *CH3* ~

There is a man – one of God's best servants in our generation, toiling in the London slums – Lex of Poplar, as he is now familiarly known. He tells how, going into a house one day, he found the father, a great sullen bully of a man, beating his child until she was almost unconscious, blow after blow being rained down on her poor prostrate form. Lex dragged him off, and the man stood scowling against the wall. Slowly the girl regained consciousness, and, looking round, saw her father there, and extended her arms as though asking him to come to her. And when he never moved, she rose and tottered towards him, a smile lighting up her poor battered face; and then she flung her arms around him, and kissed him. 'Oh father dearest,' she said, 'I know you didn't mean it! I know you didn't!'

And so we turn and think of Jesus on His Cross, Christ broken, battered by the sins of men, but smiling still. 'Say you didn't mean it,' He says to you and me, 'you can't have meant it.' And when we fling back, as sometimes we do (though not in words), 'Yes, Jesus, I did mean it, and to show that I meant it I'll do it again – see! there's another nail for your Cross,' still He repeats, 'Nay, you *can't* be meaning it, I know that you can't, and I'll endure till I've won you, and you're Mine!'

That's Christ, and that's God – the God of an amazing patience, the God whose patience followed Jacob, and followed, and still followed, and never wavered once all those weary years – until it had got him in the Kingdom, a Prince with God, a real man at last, a saint. A God whose patience follows you and me, and will go on following to journey's end. Then give Him your love. Give Him your trust. Give Him your heart. For happy is he that hath the God of Jacob for his help!

CHAPTER 9

God's Sentinels

But if the watchman see the sword come, and blow not the trumpet, and the people be not warned; if the sword come, and take any person from among them, he is taken away in his iniquity; but his blood will I require at the watchman's hand.

~ Ezekiel 33: 6 ~

TRANSLATE that into Christian terms, and what do you get? *Every Christian a watchman!* This is the immense responsibility to which Christ our Lord is calling us. Every Christian on sentinel duty, with the well-being of society and the immortal souls of others committed to his care. Every Church member – you, myself, all of us – witnesses on whose fidelity in Christian witness other lives depend. This is where the old prophet's dramatic, disconcerting, rallying message hits *us,* and bids us stop and ponder. Let us do that now.

The watchman is one of the great figures of Scripture. Again and again as you turn these pages, you come upon him, standing sentinel on the outposts of armed camps or on the battlements of slumbering cities. You see him, alert and keen-eyed, scanning the far horizon where the noise of battle rolls, or peering through the darkness where the enemy patrols are lurking. In how many a moving and memorable Scripture scene, the watchman plays a part! David, waiting with terrible anxiety for news of his son Absalom, sends the watchman to the tower above the gate, to scan the plain for the first courier from the battlefield. Nehemiah, rebuilding Jerusalem in face of a threatened invasion, arms his builders, and every fifty yards sets a watchman on the walls.

Isaiah, standing amid the encircling gloom of Israel's agony, when the strife is fierce, the warfare long, and morale strained to breaking-point, hears a cry – 'Watchman, what of the night?'

'We wait for Thee,' cries a psalmist to his God, 'more than the watchman watching for the morning!'

'Blessed are those servants,' declares Jesus, 'whom the Lord, when He cometh – [whether it be in the first watch of the night, or the second, or the third] – shall find watching' like watchmen at the gates.

'The peace of God,' exclaims St Paul, 'which passeth all under-standings, shall keep your hearts and minds' – or, as the Greek word really means, 'shall be the watchman standing sentinel over your minds' – 'through Christ Jesus'.

The watchman is one of the great figures of Scripture.

Nowhere does he come in more dramatically than in this great passage of Ezekiel. There are two pictures that these flashing words conjure up before us.

The first – a great open plain where an army lies bivouacked beneath the stars. All round the camp, before darkness descended, a line of sentries was drawn; and now through the darkness there are steady eyes gazing out into the 'no-man's land' beyond. One slow hour passes, and another, and nothing happens; the camp-fires flicker out where men lie sleeping, dreaming of their homes; far down on the Eastern horizon, the first faint streak of dawn appears.

Then, all at once, the silence is shattered by the sudden blare of a single trumpet! Again it comes, and again, and again; and men, starting from their slumbers, gird on their armour, and stand to their posts, know-ing what it means: it means that out there in the dark a sentry has seen something moving, an enemy raiding party creeping near. But now the defenders are ready for them, the element of surprise is gone, the attack foiled, and the raiders fall back in confusion. All honour to that one gallant watchman! He has been the saviour of his comrades' lives.

That is the one picture Ezekiel's words suggest. Now for the other. Another camp, another night, another watchman. Tonight it is so peace-ful that the enemy might be a thousand miles away. Everything is so quiet that war seems strangely unreal. Deep and sound are the slumbers of the weary men. Then suddenly, without warning – the tramp of feet, the rush of the attack, the bewildered, terrible cry: 'The enemy! The enemy! They are upon us – they're here!' And in a moment, the whole camp is in confusion, men struck down before they can reach their armour, others taken prisoner without a fight. Someone has blundered! There was no alarm, no trumpet. Why? Away at the outposts one sentry had fallen asleep; and through that gap in the lines, the foe has snatched his victory. It is at that man's door the disaster lies; and the God of the slain will require their blood at that watchman's hand.

There, then, are the two pictures which God flashed one day into His servant Ezekiel's mind. And as Ezekiel pondered them, the question he found himself asking was: 'Who is this watchman? What does God intend this figure in His parable to represent?' And that is what we naturally want to know. What is the hidden meaning here? What is the interpretation? Who is this watchman?

Well, if you will look at the words immediately following our text, you will find that Ezekiel got his answer. And the dramatic force of God's answer was terrific. 'So thou, O son of man, I have set thee a watchman unto the house of Israel.' Imagine the effect on Ezekiel! The parable had shaped itself in his mind quite impersonally. He had pondered it in a spirit of detachment. He had wondered what this picture from the front line in the day of invasion could mean. And then, overwhelmingly, in one swift flash, like Nathan's thrust at David, came the word of the Lord – 'Thou art the man!' 'I have set thee, O son of man, a watchman to the house of Israel.'

Is it not clear that this has been the authentic conviction of every great prophet who has ever lived? 'If the watchman see the sword come, and blow not the trumpet, the blood of the slain will God require at the watchman's hand.' *That* was why the prophets pled with men in season and out of season. They were the watchmen on the ramparts of the world. They could detect the invisible perils threatening the souls of men, and far down the future the shining of the footsteps of the Christian. They could tell when the powers of darkness were mustering in battle array, and when the Kingdom of God was at the doors. They had to keep vigil, and safeguard the immortal souls committed to their care: else – God would ask the reason why!

But you can see it even more vividly in the New Testament apostles. Why did Paul declare – 'Necessity is laid upon me: woe is me, if I preach not the Gospel'? Why did he say, near the end of his life, 'I am pure from the blood of all men: I have declared to you the whole counsel of God'? Was that just rhetoric? Just Paul's vehement, declamatory way of talking? I should say not! God had said to him – 'See, Paul, here are all those immortal souls in Jerusalem, Antioch, Ephesus, Rome. Here are all those men and women who have never heard of Christ – "bound who should conquer, slaves who should be kings" – slumbering in sin who should be awake in righteousness. Behold I have made thee their watchman! And thou must face me at the last, and render account of this thy sentinel duty.' Is it any wonder that Paul from that moment lived like a man driven by some resistless and relentless Spirit, flinging himself into the work of Christ with every atom and energy of his being?

> Give me a voice, a cry and a complaining,
>   Oh let my sound be stormy in their ears!

Is it any wonder that this young Church of the Redeemer awakened the whole earth with its message, defying weariness, difficulty, danger and death, to thrust Christ upon the conscience of humanity? 'If the trumpet be not blown,' said God, 'their blood will I require at the watchman's hand!'

'So thou, son of man, I have set thee a watchman unto Israel!' To whom does God say this today? To our national leaders certainly. Was not this the tragedy of France in 1940, as Marshal Petain himself confessed, that the leaders saw the menace of the darkening skies, saw the increasing love of pleasure, the factions and the loss of discipline – and said nothing? And are there not in *our* national life today things that are incompatible with the will of God and the sovereignty of Christ? Think of the hundreds of millions squandered on drink and gambling. I think of the sub-Christian culture, the false, boring sophistication of sex, keeping up this daily perpetual bombardment of impressionable minds in television programmes and the cheaper press. I think of the emphasis on rights rather than duties, the altars reared to the blatant vulgar deities of success, the re-erection of walls of partition in social and racial groupings which Jesus came to level to the dust. We are celebrating the Reformation: but do we not need a new *moral* reformation in this land today, the Spirit of God to go through this land like cleansing flame? Tremendous is this God-given responsibility of national leadership. It stands as sentinel to a people's life.

But God says this even more emphatically to the Church. If the trumpet give an uncertain sound, the blood of the perishing will God require at the Church's hand! 'Thou art the watchman!' And if the Church should grow lethargic, and Christendom complacent and composed, prophesying smooth things and leaving the crying injustices of life untouched; if the sense of a terrible urgency should die out of the Christian message, and men hear no longer the pleading and passion of Christ; if we who claim to be Christians are not really *witnessing* Christians, not realising that every Christian today is in the front line, that is, that he must be a witness, or he is not a Christian; if we are refusing to see that in some sense even Communism is God's judgment upon Christendom for all the things it has left undone, and God's challenge to Christendom to rise and do them now, to champion the exploited and defend the helpless, to enfranchise the racially disinherited and give food to the hungry and rest to the weary – if we are not doing all this, it is a denial of Christ as flagrant as Peter's 'I know not the man'. And 'judgment must begin at the House of God. What a travesty it is when Christ's Church becomes content to cultivate inoffensiveness, a sentimental irrelevant quietism – the Church of One who for love of men came right down into the fearful pit of history and into the miry clay of the multiple miseries of all the world.

O Church, O watchman on the walls of Israel, what wilt thou say, when God enquires after the slain?

But if God says this to national leaders and to the Church, He says it in some degree to every individual soul. He says it, for example, to parents. He says it to every father and mother in every home. 'I have set thee a watchman!' What, then, of the homes where none of the safeguards of religion are in action? What of the homes where children, growing up, are launched forth at last into the world unarmed with the defences of prayer, unhelped by the shield of faith or the sword of the Spirit or the helmet of salvation? Then, these innocent lives are being sent forth in jeopardy, to face a risk God never meant them to meet; and if anything happens, God knows at whose door the account will lie. 'For their sakes I sanctify Myself,' said Jesus, 'for them I keep vigil' – and should not every parent say it too?

But indeed we are all involved in this. When one man, away back in the dim dawn of time, exclaimed high-handedly, 'Am I my brother's keeper?', he had perpetrated the first heresy. He was the forerunner of all those who have tried to shuffle off corporate responsibility, to take refuge in the craven security of an individualist attitude to life – as some have done even in religion, clutching greedily at the bliss of a little private salvation, and devoid of a conscience for humanity. There is an entry in John Wesley's *Journal,* under the date April 1740, which tells how one day Wesley visited Newgate Gaol, and was informed that there were some poor wretches under sentence of death who were very anxious that he should speak to them. However, this could not be allowed, as one of the authorities – Alderman Beecher by name – had given express orders against it. Wesley's entry in the *Journal* closes with the words: 'I cite Alderman Beecher to answer for these souls at the judgment-seat of Christ!'

'Am I my brother's keeper?' demands the religious individualist.

God answers him out of his own mouth. 'Your brother's keeper? That is exactly what you are! Ye are members one of another.'

> *Heaven's gate is shut to him who comes alone;*
> *Save then a soul, and it shall save thine own.*

'Inasmuch as ye did it to one of the least of these, ye did it to Christ.'

For One there was who fulfilled the watchman's task as no one else before or since. 'Of them Thou gavest me,' He said at the end, looking up to the face of God the Father, 'I have lost not one.' For Jesus stood as sentinel upon the ramparts of faith. He saw sin's dark attack massing against the city of Mansoul. He saw the Kingdom of Heaven locked in deadly grapple with the powers of Hell. And never has the trumpet blown so clear a blast and challenge as the trumpet of the Cross. So the watchman saved others, but could not save Himself: and with a great price have we received this freedom.

I remember reading a story of a hero of the Chinese rice-fields during an earthquake. One day when the sky was like thunder, he saw from his hill-top farm the ocean suddenly receding, like an animal crouching to leap, and he knew the leap would be a tidal wave. And he saw that his neighbours working in the low fields would then be swept away. Without a second thought he set fire to his own rice-fields and furiously rang the temple bell. His neighbours saw his farm on fire, and rushed up to help him. Then, from that safe height, they saw the swirl of waters over the fields they had just forsaken and they knew their salvation and its cost. So Christ, our watchman, has given us salvation by His sacrifice, and life by His death.

And now today under God, you and I are watchmen too. And if the call of God sends some young soul here out to the ends of the earth, to be God's sentinel in Africa, India, China – God bless you and keep you and equip you with His grace. But let all of us, wherever we are placed, be sure of this – there is some other soul whose eternal destiny is bound up with *your* keeping the faith and letting your light shine clear!

The real problem of Christianity today is not the hardened sinner, nor the charming pagan, nor the blazing red-hot atheist: it is the nonwitnessing Christian, the secret unidentifiable disciple trying to smuggle his soul into heaven. Look at Christ today! Why is He weeping still? Has He not got over the death of Lazarus yet? He is weeping for the professing followers who will not stand up with Him in the light.

There is a great passage in Virgil's *Aeneid* where lovely, queenly Dido, her head held high, sweeps away at last from poor stammering, tongue-tied Aeneas, 'leaving him,' says Virgil, 'leaving him hesitating and preparing to say many things'. Isn't that terribly like ourselves, where witness for Christ is concerned – hesitating, and *preparing* to say many things – yet never getting past that, and actually saying them?

'Ah,' said the great artist Doré, looking at a picture of Jesus he had just finished, 'I would have painted Him better if I had loved Him more.' That is what it comes to. I'd have served Him better, shone for Him better, witnessed for Him better, preached for Him better, been a better business man in my office, a better parent in the home, a better worshipper in the pew – if I had loved Him more.

So dare we reverently imagine two scenes at journey's end? Here is one – a soul standing solitary before the throne of God, and a voice from the throne inquiring, 'Where is that other soul I gave thee, to light for him the way to heaven?' And that startled soul looks round, and there is no one there: that other must have missed the way. And with that it remembers the day when its own light was dimmed; remembers the word it might have spoken and failed to speak, the example it might have given and failed to give. And now it can only answer, 'Lord, have mercy! I cannot tell Thee where that other is. Him whom Thou gavest me, I have lost. The sword came, and I blew not the trumpet – Lord, have mercy!' And the words trail off into the silence ....

Would *you* like to stand before God like that?

But here is the other scene – another soul coming up that last slope into the light, and coming not alone, but bringing another with him; then standing before God the Judge, and saying, 'Lord, you set this other in my home, my Church, my place of business; and I tried to let my light shine, and to go straight myself for this other's sake; and I have not always succeeded, I've bungled and blundered often; but the light has never quite gone out, the road has never quite been lost; and see – the soul you gave me is here! Lord, I render back the gift you gave'. Wouldn't you like to stand before God like that? In Matthew Arnold's noble lines in 'Rugby Chapel' about his father:

> *Therefore to thee it was given*
> *Many to save with thyself;*
> *And, at the end of thy day,*
> *O faithful shepherd! to come,*
> *Bringing thy sheep in thy hand.*

There is a certain Hebridean island, where once there was a little township full of fisherfolk. It is said that in the olden days, the fishermen used to steer on dark nights into the bay by the light of a certain cottage window, which marked the fairway between the rocks. One wild night of storm, all the boats had come home but one. An anxious wife stood down on the shore, peering out to a sea now lashed to fury – and still the boat did not return. Hour after hour she waited; and then suddenly another woman caught her arm, and pointed back to where the cottages stood above the cliff.

'Cairstine, where's your light?' she cried. 'Where's your light?'

And Cairstine looked. The lamp, the guiding light, had gone out. Or ... had she forgotten that night to light it? With a sick dread clutching at her heart, she turned and stumbled home. Next day her man was washed up dead on the sea wrack. And terrible beyond words was her remorse for the light that had failed. From that hour till the day she died, she set her light in the window, and always the panes were polished, always the wick was trimmed, always the bowl of oil was full; that she might make atonement for the mistake that had cost so dear.

'So thou, O son of man, I have set *thee* a watchman unto Israel!' Is your candle in the window? Is *your* Christian witness pointing out the way to others? Are *your* Christian life and character the guide to some poor wandering pilgrim of the night? Or is Christ saying to us what that Hebridean woman said to Cairstine – 'Where's your light? Where's your light?'

CHAPTER 10

The Challenge
of Life

Can these bones live? ~ Ezekiel 37: 3 ~

HERE you have one of the most vivid and most dramatic flights of imagination to be found anywhere in Scripture. To understand it, it is necessary to appreciate the historic situation that produced it.

Israel was in exile and her heart, by this time, was broken. The iron of Babylon had gone right into her soul. The national spirit was crushed, the national patriotism extinct, the national existence ruined for ever.

This good man, Ezekiel, had tried to raise the flag of faith, and they had only mocked him. He had tried to fire them with the flame of God; and they had only looked at him in a dull, unresponsive, insensible way, and had muttered, 'What is this madman talking about?' and then settled down to their abject apathy again. The very air was thick and heavy with that spirit of defeatism and despair and futility that you get in Swinburne's words:

> *From too much love of living,*
> *   From hope and fear set free,*
> *We thank with brief thanksgiving*
> *   Whatever gods may be,*
> *That no life lives for ever;*
> *That dead men rise up never;*
> *That even the weariest river*
> *   Winds somewhere safe to sea.*   ~ 'The Garden of Proserpine' ~

Now it was to rebuke that defeatist spirit that this parable was spoken. Will you look at it again? The prophet seemed to see himself standing in a great, deep valley, through which some ancient tide of war and battle had rolled. The Latin historian Tacitus tells us, in his *Annals,* how once the Roman general Varus, marching through the German forests with his troops, had been ambushed by barbarians and his whole army cut to pieces; and how, years afterwards, another Roman legion, marching that same way, had come upon great gruesome heaps of bones – all that was left where their fellow-countrymen had died. So Ezekiel dreamed that he was standing in this grim valley, over which there hung the brooding silence and the utter desolation of an ancient battlefield; and all round about him, turn where he might, were great piles of human bones, bleaching and rotting beneath the sky. 'That is my nation,' he said, 'and that is what the spirit of Israel has come to – broken, smothered, dead.'

And then, suddenly, his sad reverie was interrupted. God Himself broke in. 'Son of man,' said God, *'can these bones live?'*

We'd better be frank about this and say that, over and over again, men looking at Israel, the Church of God, have answered that question with a ringing and emphatic *'No!'* Many a time they have seen Christianity, to all intents and purposes dead, the whole soul gone out of it, the living spirit of the thing crushed and stifled and exterminated, the Church, which once had the fire of Jesus in her eyes, a mere encumbrance and incubus upon the earth, nothing left but some poor, pathetic skeleton; and they have said – as Celsus said, and Julian, and Voltaire, and Hume, and many another – 'This, then, is the end! Here is the finish of Christianity! Here lies Christ!'

Thomas Hardy, in the year 1919, was writing a letter to someone who had been congratulating him on having passed another birthday. 'I should care more for my birthdays,' he wrote, 'if at each succeeding one I could see any sign of real improvement in the world.' And then, in a sudden burst of bitterness, he added this: 'Why does not Christianity throw up the sponge and say, "I am beaten", and let another religion take its place?' So many, I say, have answered the question 'Can these bones live?' with a confident and dogmatic *'No!'*

You'll observe, however, that Ezekiel hesitated. He didn't quite know *what* to say. He was too much of a believing man to answer 'No'. And yet, he was too vividly aware of the desperate situation to answer 'Yes'. And so he answered neither the one nor the other. He left the question for higher hands to settle. 'O Lord God,' he said, *'Thou* knowest.'

And then, straightaway, he got his commission. 'Prophesy unto these bones, and say, "O ye dry bones, hear the word of the Lord".'

Isn't your first reaction to that to say, Poor Ezekiel! Prophesy to the *bones!* What a task to have to face! What a deadly soul-destroying duty – preaching to the dead bones! Paul, at a later date, was to speak of 'the foolishness of preaching' with a vengeance!

Yes, but then, you see – the foolishness of preaching is the wisdom of God! Read on. 'Son of man, prophesy, and say, "O ye dry bones, hear the word of the Lord".' But this is worse than ever! The word! What can a mere word do, do you say? Words, words, words, the endless, incessant deluge of words! But this was to be different! The word was the Lord's. One word – if it is *God's* word – can get right through a man's defences, can shatter the ignoble peace of a lifetime, and bring down the iron walls with a crash, and burst the stoutest strongholds of sin, and tear through the soul like lightning – so that this man will never be the same again. One word!

There was Luther, the monk, poring over his *Romans* – he had read it a hundred times; and then at the hundred and first time, it got him – 'the just shall live by faith' – and the lightning flash of that moment changed not only Luther's face, it changed the face of Europe and of the world. One word of God!

And you remember Wesley, going into the little meeting-house in a back-street in London, his soul frozen with the ice of years; and there was a man speaking, a poor, halting, stammering speech it was, but it was a personal witness to Jesus, and Wesley came out of the room that night, with the frost all broken up, and his soul set free, and shouting Hallelujahs to the skies – 'Praise God from whom all blessings flow!' One word!

There is a legend about St John, the great apostle, that when the end drew near for him and the last days of his long life were closing, there was a moment when all who were watching round him were sure his spirit had fled; for they had tried this, that and the next thing to revive him, and nothing happened – no sign of life at all. 'He's gone,' they said, 'it's over now!' – until at last someone standing there happened to repeat the words of Jesus, 'I am the Resurrection and the Life'; and at that, the dead man stirred – says the legend – and sat up, and began to speak to them again. One word! No doubt it is a mere legend, but it is a legend big with truth, this truth – that one word, if it is from the mouth of God, can smite the dead awake!

'The foolishness of preaching'? Yes, indeed, the human element is all folly, poor, bungling and pathetic folly; but what if, in spite of the human element, the God of heaven speaks? What if there are words in this Bible that are nothing less than Resurrection trumpets blown by the lips of the Almighty? And I've seen this happening – for one soul and another – words of God that stand written here, and they have leapt out, and changed the world for somebody! What can a word do, do you ask? A poor, weak fugitive word? It can do anything – if it is not man who speaks it, but God!

And yet – there's no denying it – it was a tremendous act of faith that Ezekiel was called to; and I have the feeling that many a man, confronted with that valley of bones, would have cried out at the callousness of God.

'Don't send me here, Lord! Don't break my heart with a task so desperate and futile! If there were even one spark of life in this valley, one faintest atom of hope, I'd go gladly and at once; but as it is – the thing is mad, insane, absurd! You can't mean it, God! Don't ask me to do it. Don't bring down my grey hairs in sorrow to the grave!'

Many a man would have turned round on God like that. Not so Ezekiel! Listen to the gallant soul's reply. 'Go, prophesy,' said God. 'So I prophesied as I was commanded.' What an act of faith and of obedience!

Do you remember Simon Peter on the Galilean lake, returning after his all night's unsuccessful fishing? And there was Jesus standing on the shore, and Jesus asked to be taken on board.

'Now then,' said Jesus, when they had pushed out a little way, 'let down your nets for a draught!'

And Peter looked at Him. 'Master,' he said, 'we have toiled all night, and taken nothing' – as though to say, 'What's the use? We have done our best, and failed! We've given it every chance. It's wasting time and effort to try again. It's no good, it's senseless, it's defying reason' – and then he suddenly pulled himself up – 'toiled all night and taken nothing; *nevertheless – at Thy word I will let down the net.'*

Everything against it – but, 'at Thy word, O Christ of God'. And there's the task of the Christian Church – in the face of a thousand discouragements, to go back undiscourageably, and once again let down the Gospel net!

So with Ezekiel in Babylon: 'I've done my best,' he said. 'I've pled with them, and they won't listen. I've cried to them, and it has fallen on deaf ears. I've sought for souls, and not a soul have I found. I've toiled all night, and taken nothing. Nevertheless ... ' (and at that, I think, the man threw up his head and defied his whole mob of doubts), 'nevertheless, at Thy word, great God, I will let down the net!'

'So I prophesied as I was commanded.'

Isn't it a mirror of the ministry of Christ? The thought that strikes me is – how wonderfully like Jesus! What a valley of dry bones it was that Jesus had to wake! And how easily Jesus might have flung up the commission in sheer despair. Is there anything more amazing in the world than just Christ's dogged, stubborn hope for men, as you see it in the Gospels, His refusal to acquiesce in their deadness and worldliness and lostness, His almost reckless confidence – standing there on the ancient battlefield of sin, where souls that might have walked in light were just heaps of ghastly corpses and rotting bones – his reckless and defiant confidence, 'Something can be made of these if God wills – even yet'?

So natural it would have been, so understandable, if Christ had cried, 'I'm finished with the hopeless task! For I've loved them, and they've hated Me; I've wept for them, and they've laughed at Me; I've prayed for them, and they've spat into My face; and I've comforted their sorrows and they've crashed this crown of thorns about My brow. God and Father, I'm finished!' So understandable, so justified, it would have been!

But not once did Christ's hope for men break or waver. He looked at a nasty, blotched, shifty little figure of a Zacchaeus, and cried, 'Here is a conquering son of God to be!' At a blundering, undependable, disloyal Peter, and declared, 'Here is sheer Rock! And on this rock I build My Church'. At Mary Magdalene, crying her heart out at the foot of the Cross; and though in that hour all the world had forsaken Him, and though destruction and death were shouting in His ears, 'You've failed Jesus! You've failed!' – He swept that mocking cry away, for there at least was Mary 'out of whom seven devils had gone', one soul at least whom He had saved, and He looked at her kneeling at His Cross, and His heart was exulting, 'this, this, is the firstfruits of a world redeemed!'

Thank God that this is the Christ whom we've to deal with; and when we're so ashamed of ourselves, that all our hope should be gone forever, this undiscourageable Jesus will hope on still; and when our souls feel dry and dead as the bones in the valley, Christ is still sure that He can thrill them back to life! Thank God for the hopefulness of Jesus.

'So,' says Ezekiel, 'I prophesied as I was commanded.' And then, with a few strokes of vivid imagination, almost eerie and uncanny in their vividness, he pictures the result. Do you remember Samuel Taylor Coleridge's Ancient Mariner, standing on his ghostly ship, with all the crew lying dead around him on the deck? And then a blessed wind stirred in the calm ...

> *They groaned, they stirred, they all uprose,*
> *Nor spake, nor moved their eyes;*
> *It had been strange, even in a dream,*
> *To have seen those dead men rise.*

> ~ 'The Rime of the Ancient Mariner' ~

So, Ezekiel, in his parable, heard suddenly a rattling and rushing, and saw bone leaping to bone, and flesh and sinews covering them. 'But,' he adds, 'there was still no breath in them.' A wonderful thing had been achieved, but the one thing needful was still lacking.

Do you see what Ezekiel was driving at? You can organise religion, as those bones were now fully organised; a skeleton is a marvel of organisation, but what is the good of it when it is done, if the breath of the Spirit is not there? You can say of a man's religion, or a generation's religion, or a Church's religion, that it is hardworking and painstaking and devoted and godly and conscientious and believing; but we are being driven to see this – all the energy and all the elaborate machinery in the world can't cover the lack if there is not a vital experience of God!

And so much present-day religion is of that kind. So much of it is trying to do by committees and schemes and bustling activities what can never in this world be done by anyone except the living God! Committees and schemes and activities are all needed – God bless them all – but they can't create life; and that is what is needed more than anything; and that is what only the Holy Ghost can do.

O for the living flame
From His own altar brought,
To touch our lips, our minds inspire,
And wing to heaven our thought!   ~ Hymn 39: *CH3* ~

Let us get this clear – no Church is ever going to conquer the earth for Christ, that is not living on the right side of Pentecost. And no man will ever know the real rapture and joy and power and abandon of the Christian life, till he has felt the winds of God blowing full in his face.

And that is what the story makes clear. Read on and see how Ezekiel, having prophesied to the bones, was now called to a higher ministry:

Prophesy unto the wind, prophesy, son of man, and say to the wind, 'Thus saith the Lord God; Come from the four winds, O breath, and breathe upon these slain, that they may live'.

And always it comes to that. Always when we have done everything that mortal wit can do to regenerate the earth and stir our own souls into life, we are thrust back and driven back upon God.

Why is the world in such a mess today? It is because the world, with no reference to God or spiritual things at all, has been trying to control forces and powers which only God-filled, Christ-inspired men will ever be able to control. Why do our own lives so often get at sixes and sevens, restless and fevered and furtive and hectic and strung up and tragically ineffective and unhappy? It is because we've been forgetting, as the psalmist put it, to 'be still and know that He is God'. The God-contact that comes by prayer and fellowship with the Father is the supreme issue for everyone of us. 'Wait on the Lord, and He shall strengthen thy heart: wait, I say, on the Lord!'

So it was here in Ezekiel's vision. 'The breath came into them, and they lived, and stood up upon their feet, an exceeding great army.' And I want to close by asking you to ponder that final touch – not a rabble, but 'a great army'. Do you see it? After the miracle of Pentecost, the march of the sons of God! Here surely is what it means. After regeneration – service. After the breath of God has come into the bones – a disciplined host waiting for the command. After Christ has put His Spirit into our own poor helpless souls, we're not units any longer, we're a fellowship – a Kingdom, a Church, 'fair as the moon, clear as the sun, and terrible as an army with banners'!

It is a wonderful thought that, over the wide world today, there is in that fellowship, out of every tongue and nation and tribe (Africans, Europeans, Chinese, Japanese, Indians), a great host of men and women who have signed on beneath the blood-red banner of the Cross. It is blood-red for so many. Just think of the multitude of young men and women there are who have been wakened by the challenge of the Christ, welded into a fellowship of the Spirit, and who have seen that the coming of Christ's Kingdom is the one thing now worth looking for and living for, and are *in* this thing with mind and strength and heart. The dream of the seer of the Book of Revelation is coming true, when he saw a great concourse of ransomed spirits streaming out after Christ the King. Do you realise that the Church of Scotland is just a tiny fraction of the great universal Church of today? Do you realise that our own congregation is only an infinitesimal unit in the great host? And our loyalty as Christians is not ultimately to our own congregation, not ultimately to the Church of Scotland, but to the vast world Church which is the Body of Christ? And I lay it upon every soul here now – Are *you* in that fellowship? Have *you* got out of the valley of death into the light of the morning? Have *you* felt the down-wind of God blowing in your face? Have you risen up and given your life to Christ's campaign? For remember, in the poet's lines …

An empty tomb is waiting, and the East is silver grey,
As the angels of the morning trumpet in another day,
See the risen God go walking down the world's eternal way,
For His task is never done.

There's an army thronging round Him as He takes the road tonight,
Can't you see your sons and brothers lined before Him left and right?
Can't you hear their voices calling you to join the host and fight
For the God who marches on?

CHAPTER 11

The Tenderness, Tenacity and Triumph of the Love of God

Ephraim, how can I give you up? Israel how can I let you go?

~ Hosea 11: 8, Moffatt ~

MARTIN Luther, the great Reformer, was a man of rugged, downright speech, never mincing words, sometimes disconcertingly plainspoken and daring in his language; and one day, brooding on the apostasy of the world, 'If I were God,' he flamed, 'and the world had treated me as it has treated Him, I would kick the wretched thing to pieces!' Now that was not just the old Adam in Luther breaking through. Nor was it merely a fantastic extravagance of diction. It was the bewilderment of an ardent, impetuous nature at the incredible patience of God.

And we may well share with Luther in that bewilderment. For when we think how persistently man has desecrated and made havoc of this earth which is God's creation; how stubbornly the human heart has crucified Christ afresh in every age, and put Him to an open shame; how defiantly it has refused the light of life, preferring the darkness and chaos of its own wrecking passions and sinful egotism and ruthless self-assertion; when we think of these things, do we not (like Luther) stand amazed at the self-control of heaven? Why has not the Creator despaired utterly of His creatures long ago? Why isn't the whole tragic performance swept away into oblivion? The sin of man – how *can* God bear it?

It is this bewildering patience of God that is Hosea's theme. He was the first religious genius in Israel to grasp and proclaim the miracle of divine long-suffering. That is why he stands for ever as the great evangelical prophet. That is why again and again you can see, looking out at you through his pages, the very face of Jesus.

Contrast Amos – you could not conceive two men more radically different than Amos and Hosea. It is no part of the intention of God that His servants should all be cut to one identical pattern. God does not stereotype His grace, or standardise His saints. What a deadly monotonous thing mass-produced sanctity would be! Men as wildly dissimilar as John of Bethsaida and Saul of Tarsus, as Kingsley and Newman, as Browning and Spurgeon, can serve Christ in His Kingdom.

Look at this contrast of Amos and Hosea. Amos is a veritable whirlwind of a man; Hosea is sensitive and tender-hearted. Amos is a herald of doom; Hosea an ambassador of mercy. The background of Amos' book is the desert — you can actually feel the scorching breath of the desert in his words as you read; the background of Hosea's book is the home, and the family, and the dearest intimacies of life. Amos is an austere and fiery moralist; Hosea is a passionate evangelical. In Amos, God speaks like the thunder and the tempest and the trumpet; in Hosea, God's speech is like the wooing of love, and the cry of the heart, and music when soft voices die.

The question is — Where did Hosea find his Gospel? What was the origin of his incomparable insight which lifted the whole history of religion to new and higher levels? How did he arrive at a message so inward and so spiritual? The first three chapters of his book supply the answer. He reached it through the events of his own life. He arrived at his new thought of God through the influence of a crushing personal sorrow. And if in these pages, written seven hundred years before the Incarnation of our Lord, you can nevertheless discern something of Jesus and His Cross, it is because the prophet himself was a crucified man.

Is it not true that trouble teaches, that sorrow sharpens insight? 'Tears,' cried Joseph Parker once, preaching to a vast multitude on the tragic element in life, 'tears are telescopes!' Through them you look to God. The Covenanters used to say that they never felt Christ's presence so vividly as when Claverhouse's dragoons were after them. And often it is in the shadows of some dark valley that the soul discovers how near God is, and how marvellous His all-sufficient grace.

What was the nature of this sore experience which revealed to Hosea the heart of the eternal? It was a domestic tragedy. It was an agony of wounded affection. It was a broken home. For the prophet had loved and lost. Gomer, the bride of his youth, the light of his eyes, had left him. Faithless and disloyal, she had wandered to that far country of which Jesus in His greatest parable was to speak so vividly; and shame and degradation had claimed her for their own.

So Hosea sat amid the ruin of his dreams, a man of sorrows and acquainted with grief. But though Gomer had broken his home, had broken his happiness and had broken his heart, as the slow days and nights and months dragged by, he made this discovery — that there was one thing she could not break, and that was the love with which he loved her. That refused to be destroyed. There were too many memories in it of happier days, too much that was holy and sacramental for him ever to be able to put it from his heart, or for the pain of that parting to cease to pierce his spirit like a sword.

> *I will not let thee go.*
> *Have not the young flowers been content,*
> *Plucked ere their buds could blow,*
> *To seal our sacrament?*
> *I cannot let thee go.*

Having loved his own, he loved her unto the end.

Now, see what happened – his love was not merely passive and resigned. It went into action to redeem. The day came when Hosea rose and followed Gomer to the far country. There eventually he found her, forlorn and destitute and a slave. He bought her back from slavery. He paid down the ransom price. With infinite tenderness and pity he cared for her. He brought her home rejoicing. So love conquered at the last.

Such is the story of Hosea, which from broken snatches you can piece together in his book. But come now to the wider issue. I want you to watch how this man, out of his own most moving experience, brought for Israelite religion and for the world a new philosophy of history, and an amazing discovery of the mind and heart of God.

It happened like this. One day, when Hosea was brooding in secret on the sorrow that had wrecked his home and darkened his life, it suddenly occurred to him that there was something strangely similar in national history. Israel, the chosen people, had broken the covenant, had sinned away her soul, had rejected the God who was her home. What would God do? Must He not disown her and cast her off? Was it not inevitable, as the prophets of doom were declaring, that the national fate was sealed, and judgment at the door? But stay! thought Hosea, 'Here am I, crucified in the region of my affections: and yet knowing that, if Gomer came back to me tomorrow, I would sing for joy and take her to my arms and forgive everything – I love her still so utterly. *Shall God love less?* If I would do that for my dearest possession, will God do less for *His?*' This was the swift insight which made this man a prophet, this daring logic of faith rising from the human to the divine. 'If human love can know such agony, how much more love divine! If I can suffer so much for Gomer, how much more God for Israel!'

That was Hosea's argument. Is it valid? He argued, you see, from what was deepest in his own nature to what he believed must be in the heart of God. Is that kind of reasoning valid? Are we entitled to start from what is noblest in human nature, and say, 'That must be what God is like'? Is this 'how much more' legitimate? The answer is that it is Christ's own argument. 'If ye, being evil, know how to give good gifts to your children, how much more will your heavenly Father give good things to them that ask Him?' And when Jesus thus argued from the human to the divine, He gave us a warrant for doing the same. It is no fallacy: it is the soundest logic. If parents will sacrifice themselves for their children, how much more God! If a man will lay down his life for his friends, how much more God! If you will suffer for one whom you love, how much more God! Never forget that the human heart at its highest and best is a true sign-post to the heart of the eternal. 'If you would know,' cried Lacordaire, preaching to a vast throng in Notre Dame Cathedral in Paris, 'if you would know how the Almighty feels toward us, listen to the beating of your own heart, *and add to it infinity!*'

So, Hosea, seven hundred years before Christ, arrived at three of the greatest truths of religion.

I

First, *the Sorrow of God*. The tragedy which had happened in his own home was a kind of miniature of the vast tragedy which had happened in God's world. God's relation to the nation, as he now pictured it, had been one of marriage and romance. Jehovah was the husband of Israel. Listen to the lovely words of 2:19f:

> I will betroth thee to Me for ever; yea, I will betroth thee unto Me in righteousness and in justice, in leal love, and in tender mercies: I will betroth thee unto Me in faithfulness, and thou shalt know Jehovah.

It is a forecast of that lovely New Testament picture – the Church as the Bride of Christ, the New Jerusalem coming down from God out of heaven, adorned as a bride for her husband.

But, as Hosea pondered his country's history, he saw with piercing clearness what had happened: Israel had broken the marriage bond – all the prevalent irreligion and apostasy and worship of false gods that was Israel, like Gomer, being unfaithful to her marriage vow. What was God's reaction to this unfaithfulness? Amos would have said that God reacted in blazing anger and indignation. But Hosea (looking into his own heart, and knowing how he felt about Gomer) dared to picture God overwhelmed and desolated with grief.

Who can doubt which is the truer picture? The misery of all our tragic human wrongness and rebellion is not that it breaks a law, but that it smites love in the face. An impersonal law can't suffer; and if God is merely an impersonal law, a kind of philosophic Absolute, then of course God can't suffer; and the people who think that the notion of suffering is incompatible with divinity and a degradation of the idea of God are perfectly right. But it is quite certain that love can suffer horribly; and if God is love, then immeasurable must be the agony, overwhelming the burden, that weighs on God today. That was Hosea's startling new insight. That is why the central symbol of the Christian religion is a cross. 'I will betroth thee unto Me' – it is the word of God to the human race, inscribed in shining letters upon the Cross – 'betroth thee unto Me in leal love and tender mercies.' And that means for everyone of us, in the words of Faber's hymn: 'Thou hast stooped to ask of me/The love of my poor heart.' And therefore, when I am faithless and indifferent; when men, breaking troth with God, follow the devices and desires of their own hearts; when the world prefers darkness to light, because its deeds are evil, and chaos comes again – don't you see what is happening? It is love that is being wounded, it is God who is being persecuted.

'Saul, Saul, why persecutest thou Me?'
'O Sacred Head, sore wounded!'
'O Lamb of God, slain from the foundation of the world!'

If that realisation does not make us hate sin, nothing will. If the sight of the sorrow of God at a thousand Calvaries does not stab the world's conscience into activity, nothing can.

Last night, when I was waking,
   I saw the bitter Rood,
And One upon it breaking
   His heart in solitude.

Dear God, my heart was shaken,
   And in the utter black
I heard Him cry 'Forsaken' –
   For Christ's sake take me back.

II

So Hosea preached to his people the sorrow of God. But beyond that first great truth, he discerned another. This was *the undiscourageable Patience of God*. His own love for Gomer, he found, survived the wrecking of his home: he loved her still, and could not let her go. How much more then would God refuse to let Israel go! 'How am I to give thee up, O Ephraim? How am I to let thee go, O Israel?'

Don't these words remind you of something? As I listen to them, seven centuries fall away, and I see a greater than Hosea standing on the brow of Olivet, gazing at the city of God: 'O Jerusalem, Jerusalem, how often would I have gathered thy children together, and ye would not!' The tears of Jesus! Or, coming back to Hosea, listen to this: 'When Israel was a child, then I loved him, and called My son out of Egypt. I taught Ephraim to walk, holding them in My arms. With bands of love I drew them' – that picture of a parent teaching a little child to walk with God, remembering the happy days of Israel's innocence. And always comes the refrain – 'How can I let thee go? How can I give thee up?' Or once again, take this, at the close of Hosea's book: 'I will heal their backsliding, I will love them freely. I will be as the dew unto Israel, and he shall grow as the lily.' Seven hundred years before Christ, Hosea had learnt to sing – 'O Love that wilt not let me go!' We break faith with God, and He loves us still. We multiply our sin, and He multiplies His love. We put Him to an open shame, and He refuses to despair. Verily, as the apostle said, 'the long suffering of our Lord is salvation.'

III

So Hosea preached the sorrow of God and the patience of God. But beyond these two great truths, he proclaimed another – *the final victory of God*. The midnight of Hosea's own domestic tragedy led on to a brighter day; for he found Gomer in the far country, and brought her back to the home of her youth. How much more would God win the love of Israel yet! 'Behold, I will allure her, and bring her into the wilderness, and speak home to the heart of her; and she shall sing there, as in the days of her youth, as in the day when she came up out of the land of Egypt.' That is the final picture – God, not now sorrowing passively, or merely watching patiently, but going further in action to redeem.

What is that but the Christian evangel? In Jesus Christ, crucified, risen and exalted, God has acted in history. In that life and death and resurrection, God has intervened decisively against the hosts of evil. If you have seen Christ, you have seen the living God going forth to war, with power and great glory, against every wrecking force that desolates the earth, and every sin that rots the souls of men. This Cross that we proclaim is not a poignant memory of a moving human heroism. It is not the language of pity or pathos that I need to express what meets me there: it is the lan-

guage of victory, songs of a conqueror's march, such language as John
Henry Newman's:

> *O loving wisdom of our God!*
> *When all was sin and shame,*
> *A second Adam to the fight*
> *And to the rescue came.*

It is God in action. It is a lever strong enough to move the world.

Can there be any doubt of the issue when God thus takes the field?
Even Hosea, seven hundred years before Christ, had no doubts whatever:

> *I will ransom them from the power of the grave; I will redeem them from death:*
> *O death, I will be thy plagues; O grave, I will be thy destruction.*
>
> ~ 13: 14 ~

Did you know that Paul's greatest triumph shout was but an echo of
Hosea? 'O death, where is thy sting? O grave, where is thy victory?' All
the deadly forces of history, the tyrant principalities and powers, the
ruthless blight of wickedness in high places, shall yet yield, aye, and the
sins from whose stubborn grip you and I could never ransom ourselves
or be our own redeemers, shall yet bow to the Name that is above every
name. 'I have gotten me Christ,' shouted Donald Cargill, the Covenanter,
when they led him out to the scaffold, and his soul marched on to God,
'and Christ hath gotten me the victory!' It is not that God will take action
some day to redeem. It is that God once and for all in Christ has acted.
Let us walk through the world as souls that have a faith. Let us march
through the furnace as men that have a God.

Do you remember how Christopher Smart, two hundred years ago, in
his great 'Song to David', mounts up, through all the mighty acts of God,
to the Cross of Jesus, the mightiest of them all?

> *Glorious the sun in mid career;*
> *Glorious the assembled fires appear;*
> *Glorious the comet's train:*
> *Glorious the trumpet and alarm;*
> *Glorious the Almighty's stretched-out arm;*
> *Glorious the enraptured main:*
>
> *Glorious the northern lights astream;*
> *Glorious the song when God's the theme;*
> *Glorious the thunder's roar:*

Glorious Hosanna from the den;
Glorious the Catholic Amen;
      Glorious the martyr's gore:

Glorious — more glorious — is the crown
Of Him that brought salvation down,
      By meekness called Thy Son:
Thou that stupendous truth believed; —
And now the matchless deed's achieved,
      Determined, dared and done.

CHAPTER 12

Builders of the City of God

I lifted my eyes and there I saw a man carrying a measuring-line. I asked him where he was going, and he said, 'To measure Jerusalem and see what should be its breadth and length'. Then, as the angel who talked with me was going away, another angel came out to meet him and said to him, 'Run to the young man there and tell him that Jerusalem shall be a city without walls, so numerous shall be the men and cattle within it. I will be a wall of fire round her, says the Lord, and a glory in the midst of her'.

~ Zechariah 2: 1-5, New English Bible ~

SOME people have a God-given vocation to be encouragers of others. That is what they have been raised up for. Such a one was this man Zechariah.

There were his people, emancipated at long last from the Babylonian exile, back home on Judah's sacred soil. Now they were contemplating the desolate ruins of their city, and facing the colossal task of creating a new Jerusalem for the new age. A daunting prospect indeed; so much so that a kind of hopeless lethargy was settling down upon them – till it looked as if nothing would ever galvanise their sluggishness or sting them into real activity.

But then quite suddenly, among the poor squalid huts and shacks on the scene of Zion's departed glory, there occurred one of those un-predictable events which no one can ever forecast, mysterious like the wind – a religious revival. Immediately the whole situation was changed; the evil demon of sloth and slackness was cast out; every man of them was now a fellow-worker with God; and the new Jerusalem began to rise.

Now Zechariah (if I may put it so) was the Martin Luther, the John Wesley, of that revival. God's message came to him in a series of visions. This text gives one of them.

What happened was this. One night, when the labours of the day were over and the builders had gone to rest, Zechariah went out alone to meditate and pray. Suddenly he seemed to see a young man moving quickly through the shadows, carrying in his hand what looked like a surveyor's measuring-chain; and he accosted him, asking where he was going and what he was proposing to do. Whereupon the stranger answered, 'I am going to measure Jerusalem, to find its length and breadth, to make sure it tallies with the city that was here before'.

Then in his vision Zechariah saw two dim angels in the background, and heard one say to the other, 'Run to that self-confident young man, and tell him to throw his measuring-line away. Tell him to think twice before attempting to measure the bounds of the City of God!'

Now that was a two-fold challenge; and it is important to observe what the two factors in it were.

On the one hand, it was *a warning against allowing the past to dictate and determine the future.*

That was what Zechariah's people had been doing. Their one idea in rebuilding Jerusalem was to construct the new city strictly on the lines of the old – an identical facsimile of the city their forefathers had known: just as today there are plenty of people hoping the world will be able to revert to the old settled order of things when international Communism has passed its zenith and decayed; yes, and just as in the life of the Church there are those who cling to tradition and fear all novelty, and who demand that the Church of today and tomorrow should be constructed – in its methods, worship, institutions – on the lines which proved adequate for a bygone age.

'It was good enough for our fathers,' said the builders on the site of Jerusalem, 'it was good enough for the prophets of the past. Here were the walls that David and Hezekiah and Isaiah knew. Should that not be good enough for us?' To which, with devastating directness, Zechariah replied, 'Your fathers, where are they? And the prophets, do they live for ever? .... Throw away your measuring-line,' he tells them, 'it is not the will of God that the old should dictate the limits of the new, or the past cramp and smother the future!'

And today, surely, God's Providence has some other and better intention in sending us through the strains and stresses of this revolutionary age than that we should just sit back eventually into a kind of nineteenth century comfort and security. Wherever God means to lead us, it can't be back to that; and if that is all our hope and dream, we may find an angel with a flaming sword barring the way.

James Russell Lowell, the poet-Professor of Harvard, proved himself a prophet of the same breed as Zechariah when he cried ...

Time makes ancient good uncouth:
They must upward still, and onward, who would keep abreast of Truth;
Lo, before us gleam her camp-fires! we ourselves must Pilgrims be,
Launch our Mayflower, and steer boldly through the desperate winter sea,
Nor attempt the Future's portal with the Past's blood-rusted key.

'Throw away that rusted key,' cries the American poet, 'it's finished!'

'Throw away that rigid measuring-line,' cried the Hebrew prophet, 'it's finished!'

And today it is Christ Himself who tells us to throw away the backward-gazing spirit. 'No man,' said Jesus, 'having put his hand to the plough, and looking back, is fit for the Kingdom of Heaven.'

Oh yes, certainly there have been great days back yonder in the past, when revival was in the air, and the spiritual tide was at the flood. But now, says Zechariah, listen to the word of the Lord. 'Jerusalem shall be inhabited as towns without walls for the multitude of citizens therein'; and he could have added, catching sight from afar of the vision of an apostle Paul, 'Greeks and Jews, barbarian, Scythian, bond and free'; he might even have gone on, 'Protestant and Catholic, Russian and African, Zion a city without walls, her only ramparts that wall of fire which is the Lord, her only bounds and battlements the boundless grace of heaven: men, women and children crowding her gates with thankful songs, filling her courts with sounding praise'.

Oh, don't say that is wishful thinking, whistling to keep our courage up. Emphatically not. This is – this *really* is – the Church that is to be. And if you will receive it, it can be the word of the Lord for this congregation.

So Zechariah warned his people against allowing the past to dictate and cramp the future. That was the one side of the challenge of his vision of the young man so intent on measuring Jerusalem.

Now here is the other. *Don't think the material can measure the spiritual. Don't allow your human reckoning to delimit the sovereignty of God.*

It is not without significance that the man in Zechariah's vision was a *young* man. We are less inclined, all of us as we grow older, to imagine we can bring the mysteries of life and death, earth and heaven, within the span and compass of our dialectic and our logic.

This young man's error was not only in failing to see that the Jerusalem of the future was far to outstrip the Jerusalem of the past. It was in *thinking you can apply material standards to spiritual realities.* 'Run and tell him,' was the message, 'tell him that Jerusalem being the House of God and the Home of God, the sooner he loses that absurd yardstick the better! And that notebook with its columns of calculations and statistics, tell him to burn the thing or bury it. Tell him the measuring-line has never yet been invented that can take the measure of anything in which the living and eternal God is dwelling.

> For the love of God is broader
> Than the measures of man's mind.

So Zechariah, speaking to his own people, speaks still to you and me.

It is characteristic of human nature that it loves to measure and analyse and calculate and define. Of course, in a sense, we *have* to do that. We can't help ourselves. Science has to do it. Psychology has to do it. But so often, when the analysis is complete and the definition has been given, whether, let us say, it is the botanist defining the construction of a lovely flower he has pulled to pieces and stuck into his collection; or the physicist defining the universe of space; whether it is psychology seeking to define the experience of conversion; or the newest of new theologies trying to define the image of God in ways quite alien to the Fatherhood revealed by Jesus — so often, when the definition has been given, one finds oneself retorting (and I think one *ought* to retort): 'Canst thou measure Jerusalem?'

I want to ask you — have you ever heard a sceptic explaining religion away? I have — many a time. 'Religion?' he says in effect, 'I have taken its measure, can tell you all about it: twenty per cent sentiment, twenty per cent credulity, twenty per cent utilitarian social contract, and all the rest just psychological projection. The Word of God? I have taken its measure: a venerable volume now antiquated by the surging advance of enlightened secularism. The Church? I have taken its measure: a redundant anachronism, totally irrelevant. The Kingdom of Christ? I have taken its measure: such stuff as dreams are made of, dreams now scattered by the dawn of technology.' And so, measuring-line in hand, he goes on his way, proudly brandishing the wretched little footrule of his peddling logic, thinking himself learned because he knows that there are twelve inches to a foot and three feet to a yard.

'Run and tell him,' said the angel in Zechariah's vision, 'tell him not to make himself ridiculous! Tell him to throw that absurd inadequate measuring-stick away! Canst thou by statistics apprehend the mystery of God, its breadth and length and depth and height?' As the Book of Job puts it with trenchant sarcasm, 'Canst thou catch Leviathan with a bent pin?'; or, as we might add, 'Can you tack down the secrets of the universe with drawing-pins?' *Stop measuring Jerusalem!*

We have our Church statistics, and I am not saying these are not important. Indeed they are. Most important. Just as the national tables of birth-rate and death-rate and the like give a real indication of the health of a nation, so the records of Church membership, Christian liberality and so on do form a reasonably reliable criterion of the health of a Church. And yet sometimes, when that complicated schedule comes down to a congregation from headquarters at the end of the year, asking how many meetings of this kind or that we have had, how much money we have raised, what sort of activities we have organised, how many names have been added to the roll, and how many removed, I fancy that many a minister, when he appends his signature at the foot, must feel like scrawling across the page, 'Canst thou measure Jerusalem?'

Where is the column in this document for the secret prayers that have gone up to God, the widow's mite given sacrificially for love of Christ, the fellowship of the cloud of witnesses and the communion of the saints? Where is the column for tabulating the multitudes of men and women who have come alive to the reality of another order of existence, a spiritual order, penetrating and transcending the world of sense and time, men and women who by their immersion in the Spirit know for certain the love of God, and actually themselves radiate a measure of Eternal Life – where is the column for all that in any document of statistics? It isn't there! But that – not the thing you can measure – is the real Jerusalem of God.

Don't you know, says Zechariah, that one stammering soul's grateful confession of spiritual discovery may mean more to God than a dozen meetings with record attendance? Don't you know that Zion is spirit, not mechanics? Don't you know that all your triumphs are worth nothing if God is not in them; yes, and all your difficulties and failures and oppositions are less than the dust of the balance if, to one soul here and another there, the living God has been drawing near? Don't you realise – you *must* realise – that the Holy Spirit will persist in embarrassing your confident ironclad preconceptions with fresh invasions of Divine truth and love? The man-made institution, the human city, you can assess and measure; but O City of God, how broad and far outspread thy walls sublime!

Do you remember Elijah, for once in his life visited by a really uninspired complaining mood? 'Alas,' he moaned, 'I only am left faithful, of all God's people in Israel.' He measured the Church and found that its membership had dwindled down to one. But God tore up that dismal schedule. God looked down from heaven and said – 'I see seven thousand who have not bowed the knee to Baal.' It is good to know that our reckoning and God's reckoning don't necessarily tally.

Elijah said one; God said seven thousand.

There was once a poor monk called Martin Luther. The principalities and powers of his day weren't worrying much about *him*. They had his measure all right – one restive, troublesome, insignificant monk. But the day came when Luther stood up and cried – 'Here stand I! I can do no other. So help me God!' You can't measure that. That set all Europe ablaze. Canst thou measure Jerusalem?

There was a day when Robert Morrison was a passenger on a ship to China. The captain of the ship had *that* passenger measured all right.

'What do you imagine you're going to do?' he scoffed, 'Convert China?'

'No,' came the quiet reply, 'I don't think I'll ever convert China. I think God will!'

You can't measure that. All the dreams of Christ were there. Canst thou measure Jerusalem?

And so I finish with this. What did *Jesus* say about our measuring of Jerusalem? He said – 'Where two or three are gathered in My name, there am I in the midst of them.' And then of course the statistician comes along. 'Only two or three,' he says, 'how disappointing! What a dismal failure!' But listen: 'There am I,' says Jesus. Tell me, can you measure Christ? Have you a calculus for the Cross? Have you an equation for the power of the Resurrection? Have you a standard gauge for the Holy Spirit; a ready reckoner for Pentecost? Man, throw your measuring-line away! Jerusalem the spiritual city is greater than you know. Ten thousand, without the Spirit of Christ, are a helpless rabble: two or three, with Jesus in the midst, are an irresistible host. For the real Christian is a man or woman belonging to a new race, with a new name and a new song.

And don't you begin to see what this means for you personally? I trust you will never reach a point where you say – 'There's not much for me to hope for now. My character is fixed, set, circumscribed long ago. I know the narrow confines of my powers. I know the dull impoverished measure of my days.' Won't you listen to Christ when He tells you He can stretch those horizons illimitably? It is an enormous claim, but it it true. So throw that measuring-line away!

At this very moment God may be seeing in you the potential to be something you hadn't realised you had it in you to be. Don't say that is romantic pious nonsense. If you believe Christ, you must never say that. For He knows you far better than you know yourself. He sees the living soul of you behind all circumscribing circumstances.

More than that! The miracle is that He can inject into you something to make that potential become real and actual. 'I live,' said St Paul, 'yet not I, but Christ liveth in me.' Measure that? Thank God you can't! And that is the real miracle, the daily miracle to crown all miracles, the miracle *you* can experience.

'Not I, but Christ!' 'It is not I who live, but Christ who lives in me.' That is *the* miracle of divine loving-kindness. And it gives you in this present world joy, peace, victory, here and now – yes, and in the world to come, life superabundant, everlasting.

CHAPTER 13

The Touch
of Jesus

He touched her hand, and the fever left her.

~ St Matthew 8: 15 ~

HAVE you ever thought of the significance of a touch, how much a touch can convey, how sometimes a touch can change the world? Alfred Lord Tennyson comes to one's mind at once:

> O well for the fisherman's boy,
>   That he shouts with his sister at play!
> O well for the sailor lad,
>   That he sings in his boat on the bay!
> And the stately ships go on
>   To their haven under the hill!
> But O for the touch of a vanished hand,
>   And the sound of a voice that is still!

~ Break, Break, Break ~

That missing touch – all the difference between being inside the gates of Paradise, and being out in the cold and dark, alone.

Or take this. The poet Campbell, in his ode to the memory of Robert Burns, says: 'And rustic life and poverty/Grew beautiful beneath his touch.' Others, he means, might have seen only the squalor in it, felt only the smell of the earth in it, there where folk were huddled together on their poor crofts, and in their tangled, muddy village lanes, with their own minds often grown coarse and muddy, their faces blurred and dimmed with the toil from which there was no release, their very vocabulary showing the smallness of their interests (for it has been reckoned that in some of those districts people used no more than 500 or 600 words altogether, while Shakespeare used no less than 15,000), the whole thing indeed to outward appearance unutterably mean and sordid and unlovely, irredeemably commonplace; and then Burns came, and he just touched it with the magic of his art, and behold! it became a perfect pageantry of loveliness, a whole world of beauty and charm and nobleness. And it was only a touch!

Or take this, from one of the familiar poems of our youth: 'Her feet have touched the meadows,/And left the daisies rosy.' Mere fancy, you say? Perhaps it is. Yet sometimes a touch can change the world.

Look at it like this. The soul of man has got three ways of communicating with other souls, three bridges to throw across the gulf that separates it from the rest of the world. These three bridges are: the language of Speech; the language of Art; and the language of Action. Now sometimes the first breaks down. Words fail, we say; there are thoughts that lie too deep for words. Well, when that happens, there is the second bridge – the language of Art – the haunting beauty of a Mozart or a Raphael that takes you near the heart of things. But if that bridge too should fail, there's still the third – the language of Action, the language of gesture and symbol and touch. A mother caressing her baby, for example, a doctor laying his hand on a patient's fevered brow, the handclasp of two Scotsmen meeting away out on the rim of the world, the laying on of hands at an Ordination service, the father running out to meet his poor, shamed, ragged boy coming home, and not speaking, but just falling on his neck and kissing him – ah, yes, what things beyond words a touch can convey! 'Give me,' said a young officer to the Duke of Wellington, who was sending him out to a dangerous, almost impossible task, 'give me one grip of your all-conquering hand, and I'll see the thing through!' The magnetism of a touch!

Now think of the touch of Jesus. Wasn't there something there that meant more than words? I think of all the fine things Jesus said about childhood, for example, all the revolution in the world's attitude to childhood He brought about by His teaching: but I know this – that far, far mightier than anything He ever *said* about it, is just the sight of Jesus Himself laying His hands upon the bairns of Galilee, as they clamber to His arms, their tousled heads on His own shoulder, their little grubby hands clutching at His seamless robe, their laughing merry eyes looking up into His own. Jesus (as Isaiah put it long before) carrying the lambs in His bosom – and doing it not because He wanted to teach His disciples a lesson (just fancy! there are some pedantic, witless commentators on the Gospels who tell us solemnly that Jesus took the children to His arms in order to impress the disciples, to make a theological point! I think not!) – He took them to His arms because He loved them, and for no other reason. And that touch of His has unconsciously taught us more than all the treatises on childhood ever written.

Or think of all the great things Jesus said about the virtue of compassion, all the mighty sermons He preached with the duty of sympathy for His theme, those deathless words of His about 'Blessed are the merciful', 'Whoso shall give a cup of cold water', 'Greater love hath no man than this', 'Inasmuch as ye have done it to one of the least of these' – whole pages of the Gospel sparkling with the pure gold of this message of sympathy. And yet I know this, that gripping and powerful as those passages are, dazzling with an unearthly radiance some of them, yet for me far more gripping and powerful is just seeing Jesus with His own hands on a wretched leper, Jesus not saying anything, but *touching* that poor, pitiful, cringing, untouchable wreck of God's creation! Yes, the touch of Jesus means more than any words. 'Give me,' we too may say to Christ, like that soldier lad to the Duke of Wellington, 'give me one grip of your all-conquering hand, and I'll see life through!'

Now tonight I am going to suggest that the touch of Jesus meant, for those to whom it came, three things.

I

First, it meant *the kindling of a great expectancy*. Take this patient here. Why did Jesus touch her? – Why the touch?

I believe that, in every instance when Jesus used this method, it was with a definite end in view. *It was to strengthen his patient's faith*. It was to quicken hope. It was to elicit the feeling, *'Now* something is going to happen!' That is what the touch was for – to give Christ's healing power a chance to work by kindling a great expectancy.

Now see what this means for us. Here we are tonight, many of us I am sure disappointed at the poverty of our own spiritual achievement, and the years passing over our head – and we have only one life to live, and before we know where we are, we'll be past the summit of things and be going down the long slope on the other side – the years flying past, and so little real gain in character to show; and if we had been told five to twenty years ago that (here tonight) we should still be confronting the same humiliating temptations that were plaguing us then, we wouldn't have believed it. But there it is – and why? It is because we have not really been expecting anything else! 'Ye have not,' says St James bluntly, 'because ye ask not!' Others – yes, others may occasionally see mighty things happening in their life, but we – what can we do but dodge along in the old well-worn groove? 'Blessed,' said Alexander Pope dryly, 'blessed are those who expect nothing, for they will never be disappointed!'

But that is what baulks Christ all along the line. 'Blessed are they,'

Christ would say, 'blessed are they who expect everything, expect the impossible – for they shall yet see miracles happen!' But as it is – why, the old story is true again: Christ can't do any mighty works because of our unbelief, because we're not *expecting* mighty works to happen.

But then perhaps one day Christ touches us – 'strikes His finger on the place,' as Matthew Arnold said, the sore place in our life, the place where there are wounds that very shame would hide – touches us perhaps by some word in hymn or prayer or conversation, touches us by some old far-off memory or by the look in someone's eyes, touches us perhaps by a little child's birth or by a loved one's death, touches us by something in the evening sky or by the vision of a lonely cross on a green hill far away. Jesus touches us, and then, only then, what happened here in Galilee happens to *us* – faith is born, and hope kindled, and expectation crystallised; and then, our hardness is broken up, and we are ready to receive at the deeps of our nature the seal and imprint of God. Give Christ an expectant spirit, and I tell you – miracles will happen still!

II

The first thing the touch of Jesus meant, then, was *the kindling of a great expectancy.* Notice now that the second thing it meant was *the announcing of a great truth.* And that truth was this: *it's never God's way to deal with life's ills from a safe distance.* God is not fastidious. God comes right down to the desperate morass of human need.

Indeed, when you come to think of it, wasn't the whole life of Christ symbolic of that? Bethlehem, for instance: what was Bethlehem but just God touching man, the Lord of glory coming as near to us – our poverty, our weakness, our humiliation – as near to all that as He could possibly get? And Calvary: what was Calvary but just God touching us again, the everlasting arms going round our fallen manhood and gripping it and lifting it up, Love making contact with us even though it had to stoop to Hell to do it? Yes, the heart of the Incarnation, and the heart of the Atonement are here – *God in Christ touched us.* God didn't stand at a safe distance. God came.

Now that, mark you, was a new thing in the world. Take your Old Testament sometime, and glance through the rules and regulations about lepers. Pages and pages of diagnosis and instruction you'll find, everything devised to cope with the disease that the wit of man could devise, enormous precautions about isolation and segregation, and so on – but the one thing you'll look for in vain is any story of anyone *touching* a leper. No, the burden of it all is: 'Outside the camp with him! Outside the gates! Let him keep well back from the road! And you who are clean, if you come upon him standing there, draw your robes about you, and hurry past, and get away!'

And you know, it wasn't only the lepers who were treated like that: it was all the world's unfortunates. The Pharisees were great at *lecturing* sinners, revelled in that indeed, talked down to them from the height of their own holiness; great at throwing coppers at a blind beggar or two on the Temple steps ('Poor soul!' they would say. 'How grateful he will be to us!' – and went in to worship God with conscious virtue glowing in their breasts); great too at discussing schemes and projects for reclaiming the outcasts. ('Isn't it scandalous,' they would say, 'another young life gone wrong, another foolish soul thrown itself over the precipice of temptation? We must do something about it!') Ah, yes, great at all that kind of thing they were, for, you see, they could do all that *at a distance;* but personal contact with the lost and the fallen, why, they would have been shocked, staggered, indignant at the very idea! But Jesus touched the sinner. Yes, it was a new thing on the earth.

Tonight, I put it to you, friends: which is *our* way – the way of those good religious folk of Jesus' day, who threw their help and advice from a distance; or the way of Christ, who touched? The way of the philanthropist, doing what he feels to be a duty; or the way of the lover, doing it because he can't help it?

Thank God, Christ's lesson has not gone quite unlearnt. I think of Father Damien on his Isle of Lepers, living in that polluted, deadly atmosphere, dressing these poor sufferers' sores, telling them of Jesus on their deathbeds, digging their graves and burying them with his own hands when they died, until at last the dread disease seized himself. But even then he continued his work happily, felt indeed it gave him a new power, for now when he stood up to preach he could begin, not 'My brethren', but 'We lepers'.

I think of that Cambridge student whom Canon Raven tells us about in his book *A Wanderer's Way*. The student was a man of brilliant prospects who might have risen to distinction in almost any walk of life, a passionate lover of nature and the open country, and all beautiful things – but for Christ's sake he gave it all up for a slum charge in a sordid Midland town, living in some sort of a garret in a dingy back street, his health breaking under the strain, but still holding on; and Raven tells how, when he went to see him, this friend of his, when he sought out the mean street, and climbed the rickety stairs, and opened the door of the poor room, he came face to face with Christ – Christ living and present and there in that so utterly self-surrendered life. Ah yes, the lesson has not gone for nothing; and many a slum-worker, many a missionary on the field, many a friend of the poor, many a hospital nurse, is following in His steps who did not stand afar off from human need, did not keep a safe distance from us, but came all the way, came and *touched* us.

III

The first thing the touch of Jesus meant was *the kindling of a great expectancy.* The second was *the announcing of a great truth.* But third and last, that touch of Jesus meant this: *the achieving of a great victory.*

'Jesus touched her hand,' says the Evangelist, 'and the fever left her.' Now there must be thousands of people tonight for whom this, if they could only hear it, would be *the* good news above everything else, the most blessed news imaginable – this fever (I don't mean bodily fever: I mean the fever of a fretted mind and an unhappy soul) is a thing that can quite definitely be cured, and cured in a moment. For aren't there thousands for whom this fever of the mind is (a thing that is) simply ruining life and happiness?

What causes it – this fever? Partly just the steady strain of life, the burden of work that takes it out of us, the rub of other people on us. Partly it is our inability to relax, to let ourselves go – so that even when we try to rest, the muscles are taut and the mind is racing. Partly it is a general worry and depression, the sense of something wrong somewhere that we are powerless to put right, the feeling that life is not as kind as it might have been. Sometimes it is the result of hope defeated or deferred. Sometimes (I think it is necessary to add this), sometimes it is the result of trying to satisfy the restless, hungry, eternal bit of us with the poor little pleasures of this world, drugging our souls with sensations when all the time they're crying out for God. So the fever comes. And life grows hot and flurried and unquiet.

But 'Jesus touched her hand, and the fever left her'. And there are souls tonight who know that this story in Matthew must be true, because it has happened to them. Christ touched them – perhaps it was just a chance word somebody spoke, perhaps something in the sky at sunset, or a few notes of an old melody, or an illness that took them awhile out of the bustle of life, or a little child's voice, or the quiet of a Communion Sunday – Christ touched them and the fever left them. Yes, friends, here is the good news I bring you from this text tonight, that at any moment, whatever may be worrying you, whatever may be straining and fretting and depressing you, you *can* relax your spirit, can let yourself go upon Jesus, and know the healing of His peace. There's far more in Christ to steady you than there is anywhere else in life to trouble you.

And may I add this? Sometimes the fever is not the fever of worry and trouble, but the fever of sin. What then? Can a touch cure that? If things have been said, things done, that shame a man, keep him down in the dust, make him feel he can never lift his head again, that whoever Christ may be for, He is not for him and it's no good struggling away any longer, for the scars will always be there now, the fever poisoning his blood – can a touch cure that? Yes, it can – *for it is the touch of a pierced hand.* It is the touch of a hand with wounds in it that speak of a love that would not be turned aside even from the worst of men.

And now it doesn't merely touch, that hand – it grips. There is a story told of a party of men with a guide who were climbing in the Alps, when suddenly a crevasse opened in the ice and snow, and one was cut off. And as he stood there trembling and irresolute, 'Jump, man, jump!' cried the guide, reaching out his hand, 'I'll get you! That hand has never yet lost a man!' And the other jumped, and was pulled to safety. Yes, you can trust Him – this Guide of ours. For that Hand of Christ, that pierced Hand, has never yet lost a man.

Thy touch has still its ancient power;
No word from Thee can fruitless fall:
Hear in this solemn evening hour,
And in Thy mercy heal us all.   ~ Hymn 52: *CH3* ~

CHAPTER 14

What is the Sin against the Holy Ghost?

Whosoever speaketh a word against the Son of Man, it shall be forgiven him; but whosoever speaketh against the Holy Ghost, it shall not be forgiven him, neither in this world, neither in the world to come.

~ St Matthew 12: 32 ~

WITHOUT any shadow of doubt, this is our Lord's hardest saying; and vast has been the distress it has occasioned. It is a simple fact that by these words thousands of sincere souls have been brought to the very verge of the pit of despair. Now with all my heart I believe and am sure that these feelings of distress and despair have almost invariably been due to a fundamental misunderstanding of Jesus' meaning; and that if it had always been clearly seen what Jesus really did mean when He said this, and what He did *not* mean, all that mass of misery could have been saved. So I want to take the opportunity of tonight – this night of Pentecost when the Holy Spirit is the focus of our thoughts – to explore with you this deep, mysterious saying; and, please God, we'll find it not charged with menace and dismay, but big with strength and hope and reassurance.

Certainly the problem is an acute one. That Jesus, who was the pity of God incarnate, should have said a thing so stabbing; that the Voice which a thousand times over declared that any wretched soul that cared might come – ragged, shamed, lost, perishing though he were – might come, and God would most certainly welcome him and kiss him and gather him to His heart; that that same Voice should nevertheless have declared that there was one exclusion, final and irrevocable, and disastrous; that the Lamb of God who took away the sins of the world should have laid His finger on one brand of sin, and stigmatised it with a dreadful notoriety, and said that it was so abysmal, so God-forsaken, so *rank,* that no fragrance of love, and no water of cleansing, and no washing of absolution, and no blood of the Cross of Calvary even, could possibly achieve that sin's forgiveness – that Christ should have said that, is the most startling thing in the world.

'What *is* this sin?' troubled souls have asked. 'Has anyone ever committed it? And if so, who?' And it has been only a step for sensitive souls to the next question: 'Am *I* perhaps guilty of it? May not I – quite inadvertently even – have fallen into it? And am I, then, whatever I may do, shut out from grace forever?' That's the question. That's the black spectre.

The historic instances of it will occur to you. You remember John Bunyan's *Grace Abounding* – how for days and nights and years on end, before he won through to the peace and assurance that produced the *Pilgrim's Progress*, one thought kept haunting him, one sentence ringing in his ears – 'You've sold Christ! You've sold Christ! You've sold Christ! You're ruined!'

'Oh,' he exclaims, looking back on it, 'no one knows the terrors of those days but myself!'

The other instance is in George Borrow's *Lavengro*, where you meet Peter Williams. And you remember how one day, while still a lad, he heard this text quoted in the farm kitchen by his father, who added the words, 'Thank God I never committed that'. And that night the boy lay awake in bed wondering about this strange sin, and what it would feel like to commit it – until the thought became an obsession; and at last one night, getting up when all the household was asleep, he went out to the verandah and looked up for a moment at the stars that were like the watching eyes of God; then, laying himself down on the ground, he muttered the words of horror, awful, dreadful words which he thought constituted the sin; and then went and lay down again. And from that boyhood day, for the rest of his life, he was a haunted man. Sometimes, mingling with the crowd on the street, he wondered how they would look at him if they knew; and sometimes he felt a wild impulse to cry to them, 'Stop! Do you know who I am? I am the man who has committed the sin against the Holy Ghost!' How they would shrink in loathing, he thought! He couldn't pray. What was the use of prayer? He was never to be forgiven. What was the use of work, love, life, anything? He was never to be forgiven. He was a man branded like Cain.

In greater or lesser degree, many a sensitive soul has been troubled by these words of Jesus. What *is* this sin? Is it, as the man in *Lavengro* thought it, some word or set of words? Is it, as Bunyan once conceived it, some deed that can be committed almost inadvertently? To find the truth, let us re-examine the text itself.

Notice what comes first. 'Whosoever speaketh a word against the Son of Man, it shall be forgiven him.' Now there is a point that is often overlooked. It is this. Christ by these words is obviously implying that anyone who speaks against Himself will *need* to be forgiven for it: in other words, He is making the tremendous assumption that anyone who speaks against Him *will always be wrong*. Do you see the point? If Jesus could say that, how sure of Himself He must have been! Verily never man spake – never man would dare to speak – like this Man. But who of us can doubt for a moment that Christ had a right to say it? It is not that the Church's critics are always wrong – they may be wrong, or they may be right – that is a different matter. But Christ's critics – this is what it says – will always be wrong. So declared Christ Himself, and so He had a right to declare: for it is true. They will need to be forgiven for it; but, He added, forgiveness they can have. A man speaking against Jesus, a man taking his stand against Christ – whether the Pharisees, or Saul of Tarsus, or the Emperor Julian, or Nietzsche, or a twentieth century sceptic – can be forgiven.

Then comes the difficult thing. 'Whosoever speaketh against the Holy Ghost; it shall not be forgiven him, neither in this world, nor in the world to come.' Now the only way to find what was in the Master's mind is to take these words strictly in relation to the context in which they stand. More harm has been done by the practice of isolating Scripture sayings from their original context than by all the heresies. If you take single verses from Scripture, with no thought of their context, you can prove almost anything under the sun you want to prove. Let us take this saying strictly in its context now.

The situation was this. Jesus had just wrought a miracle. There was a man in the crowd, blind and dumb, possessed of a devil; and Christ had cast the devil out. It was a manifest work of the Spirit of God.

But notice the Pharisees' reaction to it. They didn't like Jesus. They had never liked Him. And now, when His popular influence was growing every day, they liked Him less than ever. It was partly because Christ was a challenge to their own secret conscience, and made them feel uncomfortable; and partly because they were jealous of His success. And so they went about insinuating discreditable things about Jesus. They hinted that He was no better than He should be. They ascribed His deeds of love and kindness to low and selfish motives.

Now that is what happened here. As soon as this noble miracle of compassion had been wrought and the evil spirit cast out, what did the Pharisees say to the crowd? 'Don't let yourselves be impressed by it,' they said. 'Compassion? Goodness? Nothing of the kind! *We* know how it happened! He's in league with the evil spirits – it's Satan's power He wields!' They kept saying – 'He hath an evil spirit.' They repeated it so often that they at last began to believe it.

Now watch how Christ answered them. He said two things about that attitude. He said it was irrational; and He said it was sinful.

Irrational – why? Because here He had cast out an evil spirit, and yet they said that it was by an evil spirit that He had done it. 'How should Satan cast out Satan?' It wasn't sense.

Sinful – why? Because face to face with a patent work of God, they had called it of the devil. They had refused to recognise goodness when they saw it. They weren't only rejecting Christ as Messiah (that *could* be forgiven): they were rejecting the voice of God in their own souls. This, said Christ, was the first step towards a blind and hardened state of soul, impervious to spiritual realities, incapable of spiritual repentance, and therefore unable to be forgiven. It was a signpost on the road to the sin against the Holy Ghost.

Now mark you, Christ didn't say that these Pharisees had committed it. They hadn't. But He warned them of the direction in which their attitude might lead. And the warning still stands. If a man, says Christ, indulges in a cynical depreciation of goodness; if he suggests bad motives for other people's good actions; if he is forever detecting selfishness behind generosity, and vice behind virtue, and the work of the Evil One behind what is manifestly the work of the Spirit of God – let him beware, says Christ: that minimising of other people's goodness, that imputing of low motives to others, is the very essence of sin; and, if he persists, he may damage his own soul irreparably.

Here, then, is what we have now found: the sin against the Holy Ghost is not any word, or set of words; it is not any single act, or number of acts – it is *a state of soul*. It is *an attitude whose distinguishing mark is an entire spiritual numbness and unconcern.* When a soul reaches that condition, it is incapable of seeing anything in goodness at all that is worth having. Evil and good are then all alike. 'Evil, be thou my good' has become its motto. And if there's no forgiveness possible, it is not because the good God can't or won't forgive; it is because, in that condition, there is no *repentance* possible. Obviously, if a soul is spiritually numb and unconcerned, it can't repent. God may offer forgiveness, and that soul will take it and look at it. 'Forgiveness?' it says. 'What is this? I don't want it! I've no use for it!' – and it takes the gift, and with a contemptuous laugh flings it back in the Giver's face. 'Take it, God, keep it!' This, said Jesus, this atrophied, unrepenting state of soul can never be forgiven, because it won't accept forgiveness. This is the sin against the Holy Ghost.

Whether any soul has actually come to that, Christ didn't say; and it is not for us to enquire. But for those to whom mistaken interpretations of the Master's words have caused distress, let these facts be underlined.

First, it is not possible that a soul may have fallen into this sin *inadvertently.* And therefore any soul that has known that particular fear can set it aside once and for all.

Second, it is not a matter of saying certain sinful words, or doing some sinful deed. However bad or wicked such word or deed may be, it is *not* the unpardonable sin.

Third (and this is quite crucial), the very fact that a soul can be concerned about this sin, can be worried and troubled about it, is an absolutely infallible proof that that soul has *not* committed it. Now this is not any personal opinion — it is on Christ's authority. For the mark of this sin, as we have seen, is an utter spiritual numbness and unconcern; and therefore the very concern a soul feels is proof positive that, of this sin at least, it is guiltless. If that had always been realised, what a mass of desperate and quite needless fear would have been banished!

Fourth and finally we come to this (and this I would fain underline again and again, for this is the blessed implication of everything we've said tonight), that nothing on the face of the earth, no blackest, shamefulest shape of sin need stand unpardoned: for the soul that repents, there are no limits to the grace of God, and no end to the love of Jesus Christ.

And if anyone has taken these solemn words of Jesus to mean that there are some sins that God refuses to remit, some cries for mercy which God spurns, some souls from whose appeal God turns away, I beg you to put that thought away once and for all, for Christ never said it, and it is not true.

There is an old legend from the days when Jerusalem for her sins was going down before her enemies, which tells how one night the priests in the Temple, praying for God's mercy and help, heard suddenly a mysterious voice behind the veil of the Holy Place, crying, 'Let us depart! Let us depart!' — and then there was a sound of wings through the darkness, a sound that faded into the dim distance like wings vanishing up the sky; and they knew then that God, for their sins, had thrown them off and left them; and next day Jerusalem fell, and the Temple was a ruin. Thank Heaven that, in the temple of the soul at any rate, this can't happen: a man will never cry to God for pardon, only to find that God has gone. It is not true.

Let Omar Khayyam say what he will:

The moving Finger writes; and having writ,
Moves on; nor all thy Piety or Wit
  Shall lure it back to cancel half a line,
Nor all thy Tears wash out a word of it.

     ~ Edward Fitzgerald: 'Omar Khayyam' ~

Let him say it. We have seen Christ: we say to him that it is not true! Do you remember how, at the end of *King Lear*, Shakespeare has one line that consists of a single word five times repeated, and the dramatic force of it, coming where and when it does, is simply terrific and over-whelming? Lear, with his poor broken heart, is dreaming of his dead Cordelia: 'Thou'll come no more,' he cries, 'never, never, never, never, never!' And sometimes a man in his sins has felt like that, has felt that, for him at any rate, it was too late. 'Thou'll come no more, O God – never, never, never!' Christ looks that dread in the face and declares it's not true. Call, says Christ, and God will answer: for even when your bed is in hell, He's *there!*

There is a picture an artist once painted, a picture of the Lord Jesus Christ, with averted head and face, moving slowly away: and in the fore-ground of the picture there is a soul caught in a pit, with flames round the edge, and the man's arms are stretched out to that retreating figure in agonised entreaty, and it is just as if he were crying – 'God, God, have mercy! Christ, Christ, have pity!' But still that retreating figure moves away, and His whole attitude seems to say, 'Too late now, too late!' I don't know who painted it, but this I do know – that the whole thing was a lie! It was Satan's lie upon God's Christ.

Did ever Jesus look into the eyes of any poor penitent who came to Him and say – 'No, my friend! Some sins I can deal with, but not yours, not yours! You've gone too far in sin for Me'? Did ever Jesus, who bade Peter forgive unto seventy times seven, do less Himself? Did ever Jesus, meeting one faintest, dimmest spark of penitence, fail to rejoice, and give glory to God, and cry – 'Father, My Father, here's another soul, another child of Thine own for Thee'? And think you that Jesus tonight, for all our sins, and all our shabbiness, and all our stabbing memories that smite us to the dust, is going to take the one door of hope we have, which is His love, and slam it in our face, and we be left standing desolate there hearing the bolts run home, and then battering with both desperate, maddened hands on that closed door in vain – 'Jesus! Let me in! Let me in! For pity's sake, let me in!'? Is that the way of it? A thousand times *no!*

But this – the door flung wide, the lamps all burning bright, the table set and laden – bread of Christ's broken body, wine of the blood of God – and at the door the Host Himself, crying, 'Welcome, friend! In God's name, welcome!' And now He has got both your hands in His, drawing you to His heart. A moment so, and then – they pass in together – your soul and Jesus – into the glory of that perfect love.

CHAPTER 15

The Extravagance of God

To what purpose is this waste? ~ St Matthew 26: 8 ~

JESUS said that, wherever the Gospel was preached throughout the wide earth, this deed of Mary's would have to be retold. I think every preacher and evangelist must sometimes feel that to be a personal injunction laid upon him by our Lord Himself; and though it seems almost sacrilege to touch a tale so exquisitely lovely, so moving and profound, I believe we are meant – specially on such a day as this, this Sunday of the week of Calvary – to dwell on it together; and to hear, through this story of a woman's devotion, what God the Lord will speak.

'To what purpose is this waste?' Waste was a thing Jesus abhorred. Again and again He denounced extravagance. 'Gather up the fragments,' He had said, 'that nothing be lost.' I wonder what Jesus would have said about one country dumping its surplus wheat into the sea to keep up prices, while another starved – which has actually happened? Waste of any kind – waste of God's mercies, waste of opportunity, waste of the means of grace, the young man wasting his substance in riotous living, Jerusalem wasting the precious day of visitation – all that to Jesus was sheer tragedy. Extravagance was anathema.

It is therefore worth inquiring why one of the most extravagant actions in the Gospels should have won His unstinted praise. 'To what purpose is this waste?' asked the critics. 'Let her alone,' said Jesus, 'she hath wrought a good work'; or (for this is what the Greek really means) 'it is a lovely thing that she has done'. Now why? What was in the Master's mind?

Well I think, to begin with, that Jesus praised her deed because *He saw something divine in it, something akin to God's own way of working.* Did it ever occur to you to think how extravagant God is? There would be a fine subject for a meditation some day – the extravagance of God. I must not linger on this now, but may I just point out, ere we pass from it, how one could illustrate this prodigality of the divine from the spheres of nature and of grace?

What seeming wastefulness there is in nature! Across the vast deeps of space, God's hand has scattered countless millions of stars. Every tiny flower of the heather on all the moors and glens is fashioned with patient, consummate artistry and perfection of detail, though no eye may ever look upon it. 'To what purpose is this waste?'

Full many a gem of purest ray serene
The dark unfathomed caves of ocean bear:
Full many a flower is born to blush unseen,
And waste its sweetness on the desert air.

~ Edward Gray: 'Elegy written in a Country Churchyard' ~

That is the divine prodigality in nature – the breaking of God's alabaster box; and you must call it either colossal waste, or else the token of a love 'broader than the measures of man's mind' and lavish beyond our wildest dreams.

Or turn from the sphere of nature to the sphere of grace, and behold God's extravagance there. Isn't the very meaning of grace just this – that God is for ever squandering upon His children things that none of them deserve or would ever dare to ask for? We ask that the way to the mercy-seat may not be totally barred against us: and God flings wide all the gates and says, 'Whosoever will, let him come!' We ask, knowing that we have sinned against heaven and in God's sight and that we are no more worthy to be called His sons, we ask to be taken on as His hired servants: and the Father says, 'My son! Here is the best robe in the house, here is a ring for your hand, and shoes for your feet. My son, My son!' We ask, like Whittier, at journey's end, for 'Some humble door among Thy many mansions/Some sheltering shade ... ' and God says – 'Come in, ye blessed, come in – inherit the Kingdom!' We are all immeasurably debtors to the royal extravagance of the divine unstinting hand.

It is God's way, alike in nature and in grace, to break the alabaster box, and fill the world with the fragrance of His love. I wonder if that is why Jesus praised this woman? He saw her deed was so akin to God's.

There is a *second* factor that makes this one of the loveliest acts in the Gospel. It leads us, in the second place, to notice this – that *Mary gave Jesus her very best*. It did not *need* to be alabaster, her vase – earthenware would have served quite well. It didn't *need* to cost three hundred pence, that ointment – quite a good perfume could have been obtained for fifty. In any case, she did not need to break the narrow neck of the vase, and let all its contents escape – she could have poured it out slowly, drop by drop, and a few drops would have sufficed. 'To what purpose is this waste?' Why this lack of economy?

Ah, surely the thought in Mary's mind was this − 'How can I give Him less than the best, after what He has done for me?' Think what Christ had done for this woman. Have you ever had a loved one given back to you from the very gates of death? And if you have, was any thank-offering too great for that? Well, this woman had had her brother given back to her, not only from the gates of death, but actually from beyond the gates. Lazarus had been restored, the broken circle mended, the desolate place made into a home again. She owed Christ that. Yes, and even before that had happened, there was something else. For in a very deep sense, she owed Christ herself. 'He has made the whole world new for me: He has lifted me out of my restlessness and dissatisfaction and the misery of divided loyalties into a life of marvellous horizons and joy and confidence and steadfast, settled peace. I'd be ashamed to pause and calculate how little need I bring! Must I not later ask how much can I bring, to the Christ who has done all this for me?'

So Mary gave her best. Shall we do less? Has Christ really been getting the best of everything from us − our best affections, our strongest mental powers, the freshest of our morning moments in prayer? If you are a parent, you know that *your* best possession is the child whom God has given you: have you brought that gift to Jesus yet? If you are a young man or woman, you know that those years of youth, when all the faculties are at their keenest and most wide-awake, are your best offering. Has Jesus got that yet − from you?

> I would not give the world my heart,
>   And then profess Thy love;
> I would not feel my strength depart,
>   And then Thy service prove ...
> O choose me in my golden time!   ~ Hymn 435: *CH3* ~

Don't bring Christ the left-overs of life, the earthen vessel and the fading fire: bring Him the alabaster box! The best is not too good, for the Christ who died for you.

There is yet a *third* factor that makes this deed so lovely − the noble impulsiveness of the act. It had all the vivid loveliness of a truly spontaneous emotion. Had Mary noticed, I wonder, a look of strain on Jesus' face that told of the awful burden He was secretly carrying? Did she sense that something dreadful was going to happen soon? Did some swift insight of love reveal to her that the end was very near? It may have been that: Jesus' strange word, 'She did it for my burial', appears to hint at that.

And one great word of God to us out of this story is this – Never despise the promptings of the heart to do something impulsive for your religion, even if it looks quixotic and unconventional. The shrewd, hard-headed man who prides himself on being guided solely by reason and common sense is not to be congratulated. He is to be pitied. Mere brain, without heart, is such a poverty-stricken thing, and the world it inhabits so arid and limited and narrow! We tend to be far too prosaic, and matter-of-fact, too wooden and utilitarian, too frightened of anything unusual, too enslaved by rules and reason and convention to remember that, as Pascal says, 'the heart has reasons which the reason knows not of'.

We need a dash of Mary's spirit. This deed of hers was sheer poetry. That was why those hard-headed, prudential onlookers, those wor-shippers of commonsense said, 'Put her out! The woman is irrational! It is a disgraceful exhibition of herself she is making!' And that was why Jesus said that the fragrance of Mary's ointment, which was already beginning to fill the house, would eventually fill the whole House of God which is His Church, and would one day fill the world.

Notice *how gratefully Jesus accepted it*. Here, He felt, was one glimmer of understanding in a dark and callous world. Did you observe when the story was being read to us, that this bright picture stands in a very sombre frame: it stands in the Gospel, hemmed in between two other incidents – here the plotting of Caiaphas, there the treachery of Judas, and this Bethany incident in the midst, like a shaft of sudden sunshine through the blackness of a storm, like a blessed momentary relaxation of the tension and the strain? And it meant so much to Christ – to have found even one soul who understood ...

> My table Thou hast furnished,
> In presence of My foes.
> My head Thou dost with oil anoint,
> And my cup overflows.   ~ Hymn 387, *CH3* (Psalm 23) ~

He was no grim, self-contained Stoic: it made a difference to Him. Do we realise the difference loyalty and help can make to Christ today? He is still being furiously misunderstood and hated and opposed: and your love could mean so much!

And He accepted it from her so graciously. He might have said to Mary – 'It is kind of you to be so lavish; you mean it well, I know. But really I can't accept this.' He might have denied the gift. Can you guess how that would have hurt her? A child brings you a bunch of flowers one day, some daisies from the garden clutched tight in its hot little hand. Would you spurn a gift like that? It is doubtless more blessed to give than to receive. But remember, there is a gracious way of accepting a gift, no less than of giving it. So grateful Jesus was to Mary; and when, later in that same week, He wore the crown of thorns and hung dying on the cross, and at last was laid within the tomb – the fragrance of her ointment was still upon his hair.

But it is *the criticism from the bystanders* we must come back to, for the crux of the story lies there. I do not think we can condemn those disciples out of hand for complaining about waste. After all, they were poor men themselves, and the gaunt spectre of poverty was all around them. Three hundred pence – why, that was a labourer's wages for a whole year! It could have kept them in food and raiment for many a long day. So their grumble about what seemed so glaringly extravagant may have been sincere enough.

But John's Gospel tells us significantly that it was Judas from whom the criticism first emanated. The others certainly joined in, as Matthew tells us, but *he* began it. The immediate impulse of this man, confronted by this deed of Mary's, was to translate it into terms of money! There are some people who will always do that. They know the pence value of everything. In other words, they know the real value of nothing. As if a deed like this could be measured in terms of pounds, shillings and pence! Can you put a price on a spring morning? Can you assess the market value of a sunset, or a Symphony, or a heroic deed, or a woman's love?

'It might have been sold for three hundred pence and given to the poor': did *they* care for the poor? I should have thought that Mary of Bethany was a better friend of the poor than her critics. One of them got thirty pieces of silver for selling Christ (less than half, by the way, of what Mary's ointment cost): did he intend giving *that* to the poor? It was an insult to the poor that this man should have come forward as their champion. No, the objection to Mary – not that it shouldn't have been wasted, but that it should have been given to the poor – was just, in psychological terms, a 'rationalisation', a defence mechanism, that is to say it was the argument created in self-defence by stingy minds when confronted with an exasperatingly generous deed. Such generosity, so alien to their own spirit, made them actually uncomfortable; and so it had to be denounced. 'To what purpose is this waste?' They never saw that, in thus passing judgment on her act, they were really judging themselves.

So it is still today. Wherever Mary's spirit reappears, this criticism is sure to be renewed. And they are not bad people who make it. Not fundamentally selfish people. They are just people who want a modicum of religion, and can't really see why our Lord and Saviour should claim everything. Florence Nightingale leaves a home of culture and luxury for a life of hardness and sacrifice and scenes of ugly squalor, and a hundred voices cry – 'What waste! Waste of beauty, waste of homelife, waste of friendship, waste of love!' Albert Schweitzer, born musician, world-renowned theologian, with a brilliant literary career opening out before him, throws it all up to go and bury himself in the heart of Africa, and again the voices cry – 'What squandering of splendid talents! Only one life to live … and the man does *that* with it! What insane, colossal waste!' The Church, under the guidance of the Spirit of God, makes a new determined drive for foreign missions, goes forth into all the earth to carry the Gospel to every creature, and again the voices exclaim – 'Are there no poor at home, that we should have to go spending money on other races overseas?' Ah, but you don't find that it is the people who say that who are the poor's best friends. Actually, it is the very opposite that is true. It is those who are keenest on sharing Christ with all mankind who are also doing the real work here at home. Of that there is no doubt whatever.

Waste? Let those who pass that judgment take care lest they be simply judging themselves. In any case, I wonder what Schweitzer would think if someone said, 'Sir, you are throwing away a brilliant career, wasting your life!' I wonder what Christ would say if someone spoke about 'wasting' time and thought and money on people overseas? 'Let her alone,' Christ said to Mary's critics. 'It is a lovely thing she has done.' And He would say it again. Waste? Yes, the spirit of sacrifice will always seem sheer extravagant, senseless waste in the eyes of a blind world; but in the eyes of God – another alabaster box of fragrance for the head of Jesus!

But there is one thing more that must be added; for I know there are thousands today asking the question 'To what purpose is this waste?' in a deeper and sincerer and more poignant tone. Life has hurt them; disappointment has visited them; the dark, mysterious, tragic side of things has come home to them; and it all seems so meaningless and irrational – so poor the actuality of life compared with what might have been. 'To what purpose is this waste?'

An Arthur Jackson spends long years preparing himself for a lifetime of medical work in the East, and then is cut off by plague before his first brief year is over. Why this waste? A man goes out into the world, born to make his mark; but circumstances are against him, and he never gets a chance. Why this waste? A woman has a great dream of the joy and affection and interest of a home, has a heart just made for that; but life seems to forget her, and the dream of love passes by. Why this waste? To all mankind, sooner or later, sorrow comes, and thwarting, and frustration, and trouble knocking at the door; and the sore heart cries – 'To what purpose is all this? Why this waste?'

Will you believe God when He tells you in His word that those experiences need not ultimately be waste at all, but the raw materials of the highest and most enduring blessing. Not wasted, that heartache of yours; not wasted, the tears and loneliness and loss and sacrifice. Everything depends on what we do with the trouble when it comes. Treat it negatively, brood over it bitterly, and it *is* dead loss and waste; but use it positively and creatively, see in it *your* share of the pain by which humanity's redemption is coming, offer it up as *your* sacrifice, provided you offer it up on the altar alongside the sacrifice of Jesus, then it becomes not waste, but power and character and peace – an alabaster box for God Himself, and the fragrance of the ointment fills the house.

You will notice that I said 'alongside the sacrifice of Jesus'; and I say now in closing that if ever the question might have been asked with apparent reason, it might have been asked of the life and death of Jesus. He came to save the world, and for nearly all His life He was set to drudge at a carpenter's bench. He came to inaugurate a Kingdom, and His lot was cast in a remote, provincial village, and Rome and Athens never saw Him. He came to face a task for which the longest lifetime would scarcely have been sufficient, and He died at thirty-three. He was born for a throne, and they hanged Him on a Cross. 'To what purpose is this waste' – this shocking, mad, incredible waste, this most glaring unpardonable waste in all the records of history? So cries the heart, staggered by the mystery of the ways of God.

But today we know the answer. Was it waste, that life, when it has been the inspiration of ten thousand Christ-like lives in every age? Was it a waste, that death, when it is drawing the whole world to His feet? Was it a waste, that breaking of the alabaster box of Jesus, when there has gone forth a fragrance that shall one day sweeten and redeem the earth? Waste? Let the Cross and Resurrection tell us that the most apparent waste, the most heavy, shattering sacrifice, can be the road to life, and to the coming of the glory of the Lord!

My friend, if you have some sorrow in your heart, some secret tale of sacrifice, will you go home today believing that your life, not in spite of that, but because of that, can be used by God to bless the world with fragrance? Or if there is some treasured thing you have never yet surrendered, some side of human nature never yet committed to the divine control, don't you think that that would be a fine alabaster box to break now at Jesus' feet?

CHAPTER 16

Coping with Life's Storms

Carest Thou not that we perish? ~ St Mark 4: 38 ~

THIS is the question – tonight – in our confused, bewildered world, battered by incessant storms of international upheaval. What is the world to do when God who created it seems to leave it to its own devices? Or, in the more personal arena where we have to live, what is any man or woman to do in face of the hurting insoluble problems of life? What are you to say in the day of trouble when heaven seems indifferent to your cry? 'Carest Thou not that we perish?'

Here were the disciples in the storm; and the first thing I observe is immensely significant: the storm came upon them *while they were obeying their Master's commands*. It was Jesus who was first on board that night. It was Jesus who had suggested, 'Let us go over to the other side'. And it was then that the storm befell them.

Isn't that strange? If they had been out on the sea against their Master's wishes; if they had wanted to sail and He had said, 'No! It is madness to go out tonight – let us wait till morning'; and if, in spite of that, they had insisted on risking it, then we could have understood the storm better. We could have said that the disciples got only what they richly deserved.

Suppose a nation defies the will of God. Has it any right to complain if it runs into frightful trouble? 'Be not deceived, God is not mocked; for what a man, a nation, soweth, that shall he also reap.' That, I say, we can understand.

But this was different. Here it was Jesus who was responsible. It was He who had suggested going across that night. And it was while they were obeying Him that the storm burst upon them.

Do you see the truth behind this? There are storms you are liable to encounter *even on the path of duty and discipleship*. There are troubles from which goodness and integrity offer no immunity. Being Christian – a Christian nation, a Christian disciple – is no insurance against calamity.

There are some good people who think religion *ought* to give a guarantee, who are quite at a loss when they find that in fact it does nothing of the kind, and that trouble falls indiscriminately on good and evil.

But now consider. If religion *were* a means of avoiding trouble in life, if God hid us from the storms, then being religious could be practically equivalent to taking out an insurance policy; and it is certain you would have people paying the premium and being 'religious' simply for the sake of the insurance. And that, of course, would be ruinous to Christ's whole conception of discipleship.

So the question is – What do we want? Do we think religion ought to give exemption? Do we think a Christian nation ought to find everything running its way in this troubled world? Do we call it unfair when someone who is a real saint is struck down by illness and misfortune, while another who is a rotter gets off scot-free? But if we do, don't you see the consequences of that position? We are making religion a sort of favouritism. We are asking God, in return for being worshipped and obeyed, to deal out preferential treatment. Is that a Christian idea? Would it be good for a boy at school to receive exemption from discipline just because his parent happened to know the headmaster?

The fact is – a world where religion is exempted from trouble would not be a better world: it would be definitely worse. Christ came into the world not to keep us safe: He came to keep us loyal. All the saints have witnessed to that fact – from Paul and Peter done to death by Nero, to Dietrich Bonhoeffer executed by Hitler. Jesus never said – 'Sail with Me, and I'll guarantee you smooth seas all your way.' He said – 'Sail with Me, and through the stormiest sea I'll get you to your desired haven.' I urge you therefore, for your comfort and your challenge, to ponder this feature of the story – that it was while the disciples were loyally obedient that they encountered the worst gale of their lives.

And then – look at this – the sleeping Christ! Did you ever stop to think of that? How utterly spent and weary Jesus must have been to sleep on through a night like that! Surely this picture of Christ asleep is a most moving commentary on that great word of the evangelist describing the strain of Jesus' crowded days – 'virtue was going out of Him'; 'Himself took our infirmities and bare our sicknesses.' So here the sleep of utter exhaustion. 'The Son of Man hath not where to lay down His head.' But on this wild hurricane night, a couple of rough boards at the bottom of a boat were pillow enough for Christ's repose.

Of course it wasn't merely weariness. It was trust. It was the serenity of filial confidence. It was the knowledge that the tumultuous waters were the hollow of His Father's hand, and that underneath were the everlasting arms. And if we knew that too, in these violent, frightening days, knew it and confided in it, our fretful hearts could share the strong ineffable serenity of Jesus. 'So He giveth His beloved sleep.'

But looking at that sleeping figure I wonder – what did the disciples think about it? They were expert sailors. They had beaten the elements scores of times. But this storm was no ordinary affair. Tonight the terror of the deep had got them in its grip. Tonight they knew that death was on the sea. And there was Jesus sleeping through it all! There was the One who had brought them here, who had told them to launch out and cross over, who had got them all caught like rats in a trap – there He was, sleeping, heedless and indifferent. It wasn't good enough. It wasn't right of Him to sleep. He had got them into this – let Him now get them out! Just then a bigger wave than ever struck the ship, and sent her staggering; and Peter, hauling like mad at the ropes, looked at John. 'For God's sake, man, don't stand shivering there! Wake Jesus! Get Him aroused. Our one and only hope – wake Jesus!'

Have we ever come to that, amid the tumult of the world today – we who believe in prayer? There was a day four hundred and fifty years ago when Savonarola, of the noble army of martyrs, was preaching in the great Cathedral of Florence. 'Sirs,' he cried, 'the light of faith is being extinguished, the soul of the Church is perishing. The ark of the Lord is going under. The billows of unbelief are going over her. The waves of trouble are swamping her .... Sirs,' he cried, 'what are we to do? What can we do?' And then – with a great shout that startled the Cathedral and heralded the Reformation – 'Wake Christ! Wake Christ!'

I ask again – Have we come to that? With power politics bedevilling the world, and international gangsterdom rife, with a fierce, unpredictable storm of cynicism and hatred battering the frail ship of our hopes and dreams and mocking our visions of the Kingdom of God – have we come to that? To see that Christ is indeed our only hope? That the one chance any of us has to get through this frighteningly complicated life is to bring Him into action at our side? Then act on it, call on Him now. Wake Christ! You will discover He has been awake and watchful all the time.

> *Thy foot He'll not let slide, nor will*
> *He slumber that thee keeps.*
> *Behold, He that keeps Israel,*
> *He slumbers not, nor sleeps.* ~ Hymn 139: *CH3* (Psalm 121) ~

Here in the ship Jesus looked up into His terrified disciples' faces. 'Master, carest Thou not that we perish? Are we to drown, for all You care?' What a question! Shame on the lips that asked it.

But we do ask it still. It is not only those disciples' voices you hear; but right down the ages, a great host of people, baffled by life, battered by its storm winds, overwhelmed by the mystery of evil and suffering, with one desperate challenge on their lips: 'Don't you care? God in heaven, is it nothing to You that we perish?'

'There is only one thing,' said a shattered soldier in hospital to the padre who was visiting him – and there was no mistaking the bitterness in his voice – 'there is only one thing I want to hear about now I'm not interested in anything else – *does God care?*'

There is such a host of people asking that tonight. Here is one of them. He has been a Christian and a Church member all his life. He has had a simple working theology of his own. But he is beginning to wonder if it is all myth and self-delusion. For isn't contemporary history a denial of his creed? All this successful devilry, this trumpeting atheism – how can God allow it? 'Does God care?'

Here is another man, his problems more personal. His life was once full of promise, and the future radiant; when suddenly, down came calamity, and the dream was destroyed, and the cup of heart's desire smashed to atoms at his feet. And he stands there among the ruins. 'Does God care?'

Or here is a woman with a psychological problem, nerves and depression. She can't see any reason for it, but it is there, spoiling everything for her – that intractable neurosis and maladjustment – making her life a misery, so that she wonders, 'How is it going to end?' 'If thou gaze long into an abyss,' said Nietzsche, 'the abyss will also gaze into thee'; and that is how she is feeling – out of the depths a cry, 'Does God care?'

Or here is someone else, whose problem is not the world of failure or depression, but sin – the grip and sting and tyranny of it, wrecking his resolves, vanquishing his vows, making chaos of his hopes. 'O wretched man that I am, who shall deliver me?' 'Does God care?'

Or here is someone for whom the real faith-destroyer is the biological fact of death. 'The grass withereth, the flower fadeth: surely the people is grass.' 'Our outward man perisheth,' declares St Paul. That is the inexorable truth – 'perisheth.' And 'carest Thou not that we perish?'

What a host of them there are, asking that!

Indeed which of us has not asked it at one time or another? In a world where the mystery of evil and the problem of suffering – after all that the saints and philosophers and theologians of two thousand years have done to elucidate them – are still wrapped in obscurity; in a world that is so desperately indiscriminate towards good and evil that it can hang up together on the same Calvary its Christ, its very best, and its thieves, its very worst, in appalling disregard of any difference; in a world where Herod and Nero triumph and the innocent die, and there are so many things blind and meaningless, cruel and unjust – who has not at some time asked the question – 'Does God care?'

Bishop Nevile Talbot has told of a high officer of the fleet, an agnostic, who was talking one day with a naval chaplain. 'Yes, padre,' said the admiral, 'it is all very well for you to talk about religion and the goodness of God – but look at the world! If one of my captains kept his ship in the condition in which the Almighty seems to keep the world, I'd sack that captain in a week!' That's the problem.

It is made almost startlingly acute by a picture in the Book of Job. To say that humanity must one day stand before the judgment-bar of God is indeed no more than we all know already; but Job, with a daring that takes our breath away, has reversed the picture, and actually dared to conceive God standing before the judgment-bar of humanity – man the judge, God the accused – and God summoned to answer at the bar of man's outraged soul!

So also Omar Khayyam in his great poem, brooding on the same mystery, has hazarded the opinion that if there are many things for which we poor mortals need to be forgiven by God, there are some things at least for which God needs to be forgiven by us:

> For all the Sin wherewith the Face of Man
> Is blacken'd, Man's Forgiveness give – and take!

'Master,' cried the disciples, laying rough hands on Jesus, 'Master, Thou hast brought us into this: and carest Thou not that we perish?'

But it is time we came to the Lord's answer. To that fierce demand Christ answered two things, two things as relevant tonight as they were then.

The first was this: 'Where is your *faith?*' Or – for this is what it meant – 'Is it not enough for you to know that *I am here beside you in the storm?*'

It is told that once a Roman ship, a man-of-war, with Caesar aboard, encountered a terrible storm at sea. But not a man was afraid. 'Sail on,' cried the captain, 'the ship can't sink that carries Caesar!' That may have been bluff – but this was not. The Christian doctrine of the Incarnation means that the ship of humanity carries Christ.

It is one thing to say – as some are saying tonight with bitterness and self-pity – 'We are all in the same ghastly mess and predicament, all in the same boat, we poor human creatures in the world.' But it is quite another thing to say – 'We are in the same boat with Jesus!' And that is true. He has been through it, is going through it now. He knows all about the predicament – from the inside. If the ship sinks tonight, Christ sinks with it.

In fact, the doctrine of the Incarnation means something even more profound. It means that we are in the same boat with God. 'In all their affliction, He was afflicted.'

There was a man who was imprisoned politically on an unjust, trumped-up charge, a man absolutely innocent. He was kept in prison for years; and when eventually he was released, his friends sympathised with him. But he said, 'I don't want your sympathy – it's no use: the only man who can help me is someone who has been in the hell that I have been in.'

What the Gospel proclaims is precisely that there *is* such a one, and His name is God the Father – God revealed in Christ the Son.

One of the most famous of the Greek legends tells of Prometheus chained to a rock in the Caucasus Mountains. When he cried out bitterly, the answer came: 'Expect no answer to thine anguish, unless one of the gods themselves be willing to go down for thee into unlighted Hades and through the gloomy depths of Tartarus!' The Gospel declares that this is exactly what has happened. 'He descended into hell.' God has been in it. That is the Cross.

This is a great part of the Christian light on the problem of suffering. It does not tell why it comes. It does not offer exemption from it. It does not meet our questioning with some neat theory that will solve the mystery. That is not Christ's contribution. No. His way is ever so much more wonderful than that. He says – 'When trouble comes, I will be there. I promise it.'

One of the most moving scenes in English Literature comes at the close of Dickens' *A Tale of Two Cities*. The carts were rumbling through the thronged streets of Paris to the guillotine. In one of them there were two prisoners: a brave man who had once lost his soul but had found it again, and was now giving his life for a friend; and beside him a girl in the first flower of youth. She had seen him in the prison, and had observed the gentleness and courage on his face. 'If I may ride with you,' she had asked, thinking of that last dread journey, 'will you let me hold your hand? I am not afraid, but I am little and weak, and it will give me more courage.' So when they rode together now her hand was in his; and even when they reached the place of execution there was no fear at all in her eyes. She looked at the quiet, composed face of the man beside her, and said – 'I think you were sent to me by heaven.'

What is the Christian answer to the mystery of suffering? Not an explanation, but a reinforcing presence: Christ to stand beside you through the darkness, Christ's companionship to make the dark experience sacramental – 'Yea, though I walk in death's dark vale, Yet will I fear none ill: For Thou art with me … ' (Psalm 23) – and I think, Jesus, yes, I know You must have been sent to me by heaven.

Do you remember that marvellous scene in the Book of Daniel?

'Look,' cried King Nebuchadnezzar, pointing to the furnace, 'look! We cast in three men there, and now – there are four! Who is that fourth? Where has He come from? A spirit? An angel? No – his form is like the Son of God!'

It was the truth: God in the furnace, God in the storm, God in the confusion of this bewildered world tonight. 'Carest Thou not that we perish?' There is Christ's first answer: Remember – you are in the same boat with God!

And then His other answer, His final answer? It was that ringing, reverberating cry above the storm: *'Peace, be still!'*

That was addressed primarily, I believe, to the turmoil of the waves: for I have no doubt that this was a mighty miracle of supernatural power. But it was addressed also to the inner turmoil of the disciples' hearts.

You may believe that in all the world's affliction God is afflicted: but you want more than that. You may know that 'In every pang that rends the heart/The Man of Sorrows had a part …' – but you need more than that. You need a ringing voice above the storm: 'Peace, be still!' You can have it – in Jesus.

Those disciples should have known! They had seen Him cast out devils and heal the sick and resurrect the dead. They should have known.

And the nations – the Christian nations at any rate – should know it today. There *is* a personal force in the world – His name is the Holy Spirit – who can conquer where all our fumbling, man-made policies fail.

And certainly you and I as Christians should know it. I can think of one place after another where I have experienced it – and so can you: the energetic rescuing action of the eternal Christ.

I am speaking tonight to someone who is depressed. I am speaking to someone else who feels at war with his or her surroundings in a world that doesn't care. I am speaking to someone else who is encountering some frightful doubt or temptation, straddling like a mad Apollyon right across the path to heaven. But tonight you are going to trust Jesus when He says – 'All power is given unto Me in heaven and on earth', power to bridle the winds and shackle the seas and smash the grim spectre fear – and to make your life actually richer for having faced the storm-wind and the flood. It is to your turmoil He is speaking now: 'Peace, be still!'

'What manner of man is this, that even the wind and the sea obey Him?' Jesus, I adore Thee, my Lord and my God!

CHAPTER 17

Christ and Human Need

And whithersoever He entered, into villages, or cities, or country, they laid the sick in the streets, and besought Him that they might touch if it were but the border of His garment: and as many as touched Him were made whole.

~ St Mark 6: 56 ~

IF the world is ever to be persuaded of the truth of the Christian religion, it won't be so much by argument as by the logic of facts.

'What is your religion *doing* for you? What *difference* is it making?' That's the question the world flings at Christian folk today. 'What practical effects is this faith of yours producing?'

And mark you, when the world asks that, it is not going to be put off with mystical talk or pious rhetoric: it wants hard facts, and will take nothing else.

'These Christians,' growled Nietzsche once, 'these Christians must show me that they are redeemed, before I will believe in their Redeemer.'

'We know what you *say* about faith in God,' the world tells us, 'we know what you *maintain* about the Saviourhood of Jesus, and the presence of the Spirit, and the power of prayer, and the reality of the supernatural: we know all that. But tell us, what exactly has it *done – for you?* Bring out the concrete evidence! Then we'll believe there is something in it – not before.'

That's the demand – and we *have* to face it.

In Christ's own day, indeed, the evidence was plain to see. Wherever Jesus went, the most astonishing things kept happening – sick folk healed instantly; ailing sufferers with years of grey, bleak misery behind them given a sudden new glad lease of life; people at the end of their tether and near breaking, sent out to face the world triumphantly! That, says the New Testament, heaping page after shining page of incontrovertible evidence, that is what happens wherever Jesus comes. Wherever God in

Christ breaks in, miracles are wrought, and world-renewing forces are released.

Therefore – and this, for us, is the immensely important deduction – therefore if, as we believe, Jesus still comes where people gather in His name, these things ought to be happening *for us*. They ought to be happening, for instance, every time we meet in Church. Here the heaviest burdens should be yielding to His touch; here the most desperate worry and anxiety should be sure of calming; here the most crushing impotence of habitual defeat should find supernatural strength for victory; here faith should have its Olivet, and love its Galilee, and the creative God come right through into our souls to meet our every need.

And indeed, to some extent, these things do happen when Christian folk meet for worship and communion with the unseen. A famous evangelist once said in a newspaper controversy that he was prepared any day, at an hour's notice, to summon five hundred witnesses, ready to declare under oath, if needs be, the truth of the Gospel of salvation from fear and misery and sin. And wherever Jesus comes today, there are some who find the conquering life.

Yes, but why not all? If Christ can mean such glorious things to some, why not to this one, and the next, and to every one within His reach? 'Though Christ,' sang the poet …

> *Though Christ a thousand times in Bethlehem be born,*
> *If He's not born in thee, thy soul's forlorn.*   ~ Traditional ~

On this crowded day in Galilee, says the evangelist, 'Whithersoever He entered, into villages, cities, country, the sick touched Him; and all who touched Him were made whole'. And why not some of us today? Why shouldn't this great thing happen to us all?

Well, we had best have a look at the Gospels, and note the conditions under which God's power in Jesus went so marvellously into action, for they are likely to be the same today. You will observe, for one thing, that in nearly every case, before Jesus actually arrived in any town or village, rumour and report had prepared the way by kindling expectation. The strangest tales were being told – of how, up yonder in the north, not so many miles away, in other villages they knew quite well, blind men were seeing, and deaf folk hearing, the crippled walking, the maimed and wounded healed. To how many a poor sufferer that was thrilling news!

And we too, whether we have had experience of it or not, we have at least heard tell of great things Christ has done in our own land; rumours have been blown to us on the winds of the years of mighty works and miracles of grace. We've *heard* of these things happening.

So it was here in the Gospel. The most amazing rumours were flying everywhere. 'They say He can cure anything! They say that never in human memory has such power been seen!'

Some, it is likely enough, were sceptical. 'They say, they say! No doubt they do. But you know what *that* amounts to! These things always get exaggerated in the telling, and grow as they get passed from mouth to mouth. Most probably the whole thing is quite commonplace after all – nothing to get really excited about!' Yes, there were sceptics then as now. But most were strangely stirred and eager, trusting it might be true.

And so it came about that always, long before He reached the next village on His way, the roads were lined with people, where Jesus was to pass; and queer, incredible hopes were starting into life.

The blind man said – 'I've always asked my fellowmen for alms and charity: I'm going to ask *Him* for sight!'

The leper said – 'They tell me there is no end to this misery of mine but death, that there is no single case on record of leprosy being healed: but He'll speak the word that is going to make me whole!'

The mother of the son who had wrecked his home and broken the hearts that loved him, was thinking – 'He'll show me, this Jesus, how to bring my laddie back! He'll do what all my prayers and tears have failed to do.'

Again and again in the Gospels you come on scenes like that – a whole countryside alert for Jesus' coming, all the need and trouble and wretchedness of a whole neighbourhood lining the road where He was due to pass, and crowding round Him when He came.

Is it not, in miniature, a picture of the whole vast world's need today? Who but God Himself can know and measure all the troubles of this wounded earth – the heartache and the blinding sorrow, the battering anxieties and crushing griefs, the fear of life, the fear of death, the fierce temptations that assault the souls of men? And where all that untold mass of human need is surging around Christ today, our own hearts too are found – each knowing its own deep secret need, each waiting for the word, the touch, the healing of the Saviour of the world.

Here in the Gospel it all worked out so gloriously! There was no disappointing of those eager hopes. 'Whithersoever He entered, as many as touched Him were made whole.' And in those village homes that night, the joy! – can you imagine it? – since Christ had passed that way. The lights burned late in many a cottage window; and psalms of David – often sung before – went rising up to God that night with a new note of lyrical gratitude and elation:

When Zion's bondage God turned back,
  As men that dreamed were we;
Then filled with laughter was our mouth,
  Our tongue with melody.   ~ Psalm 126 ~

Yet the Gospels, which are the frankest records in the world, are careful to point out that even in Galilee there were exceptions. 'We wouldn't be honest if we concealed it,' the writers seem to say. There were places where Jesus came, and little or nothing happened. Why? The lesson was apparent. The prevailing mood in these localities was wrong.

There wasn't any sense of expectation. The scoffer and the sceptic had succeeded all too well. 'You can't take the tales told of this Man of Nazareth at their face value,' they were saying. 'All those suspicious stories of unheard-of happenings – just throwing dust in people's eyes!' And so the solemn word stands written: 'Jesus could do no mighty works there, because of their unbelief.'

Don't blame Christ when mighty works don't happen in the name of His religion! Blame the Church if you like; blame the temper of society and the moral climate of the age; blame your own spiritual dullness and mine – the one thing we mustn't do is to lay the blame on God. His power hasn't failed us: it is we who have failed His power. And Christ's ability to deal decisively with every aspect of the human situation is as real *at this moment* as when they thronged the roads of Galilee.

Thou hast arisen, but Thou descendest never;
  Today shines as the past;
All that Thou wast Thou ART, and shall be EVER,
  Brightness from first to last.   ~ Hymn 131: *CH3* ~

The power is there; and there for anyone to take – cleansing, new life, and the baptism of eternity!

There was a day when a distracted father went clamouring to Jesus: 'If Thou canst do anything, have compassion and help me.' And Jesus caught immediately at the implied question in the man's words, repeating them – '"If Thou canst?" Is *that* your uncertainty? Whether I can really *do* this thing?' – and then, thrusting it back upon the suppliant, 'Nay, if *thou* canst *believe*, all things are possible.' It is never the power that Christ can offer that is in question: it *is* the faith that we can offer Him. There may be doubts about the faith: there is no shadow of doubt about the power.

When that fine writer Clutton Brock lay dying some years ago on Christmas Day, he dictated two verses to a friend:

Now my body masters me;
Little, past its pains, I see;
Yet I remember Christmas Day,
Faint and still and far away.

I am a man by sickness worn,
On this day when Christ was born,
Turn for help to that strange story,
All humility mixed with glory.

After a while he asked that 'turn for help' should be changed to 'turn again'. 'I am not certain that I expect help from it, but I am always thinking about it.' But that's sad, unutterably sad, for Christ knows He *can* help – help just where the need is greatest. 'I can do it for you,' He says today.

Yet admittedly, as things stand, such faith may not be easy. I imagine it was anything but easy for some of those needy folk in Galilee.

For one thing, some of them had been ailing so long, so many weary, helpless years. Was it likely that anything could make any difference now?

Perhaps that is the trouble with some of us. We have travelled so far through life, and nothing spiritually dramatic has ever happened to us, and we begin to doubt if it ever will. 'Our character,' we say, 'by this time is fixed and settled. The day of opportunity is past. There will be no re-fashioning of personality now.'

Others again there were in Galilee who had made a score of bids for healing and for freedom. They had tried every medicine they knew. They had followed faithfully every course of treatment that could be suggested. Sometimes the pain was lessened for a day or two, but always it came back – and now they were tired of hoping.

Perhaps we are like *that*. We *have* dreamed greatly, and made strenuous resolves. We have told ourselves repeatedly, 'I can, I must, I will get away from this dull, tedious groove of spiritual mediocrity, this dismal monotony of defeat'. And sometimes for a day or two, a year or two, the thing has seemed to work, and the hot, eager vows have been kept – and then we have fallen back to the old level again, and quite lost heart. 'Vanity of vanities,' we're tired of hoping.

Yes, and there were still others in Galilee who found faith difficult, not because they didn't know Jesus, but just because they knew Him so well. Their very familiarity with Him was the trouble. 'Is not this the Carpenter? Can these great things really be true of Him? Didn't He live and work in that back street, just round the corner yonder? And don't we know His people, His home, His family and all about Him?' It did make faith hard for some.

And perhaps that's our trouble still. We have known Christ so long. We have heard the story of His religion, we have sung the hymns, we have said the prayers, we have learned the doctrine: our very familiarity with it all makes a sudden act of sheer daring faith unlikely. Even the Cross we have grown so accustomed to that it doesn't move us as much.

But 'whithersoever He came,' says the evangelist, and that means *here* – it includes this Church today – 'as many as had faith to touch Him were made whole'. What *is* your difficulty, after all? Is it that you have been ailing so long? But there was that man at the Pool of Bethesda, you remember, he had lain there 38 years – and then Christ came and healed him.

Or is it that you have resolved and vowed, and now you are tired of trying? But – don't you see? – that disillusioning discovery of personal insufficiency is just about the best of all possible preparations for the coming of a really vital spiritual experience. For, as the old mystics used to say, 'Till thou art emptied of thyself, God cannot fill thee'.

Or is it that the whole thing is so familiar? Is it that you have known Christ so long? But wait – are you sure you know Him? It's one thing to know about religion; it's quite another thing to know the Lord. To know about religion, that's dull and academic and mere theory; to know Christ, as St Brendan put it, that's 'wonder upon wonder, and every wonder true!'

In any case, I have the best of authority – Christ's own authority – for telling you that He can meet you now, just where the burden is heaviest and the need is sorest, can meet you there as the God of your salvation. If there is trouble to be mended, if there's sorrow to be healed, if there are sin's binding shackles to be loosed, if there are shame and misery to be forgiven – well, He has done these mighty things for tens of thousands; and there is not one faintest shade of doubt within His eyes as He turns and looks at you. 'I *can do* this thing for you,' He says quietly. 'Given faith, I can make you all you ought to be!'

There was a distinguished American sculptor who once made a noble statue, a speaking likeness of Abraham Lincoln. The sculptor had a negro servant. She had seen the great rough shapeless block of marble lying in the studio before her master touched it. And now she was permitted to see the finished work. And she looked at it, and rubbed her eyes, and just couldn't understand. At last she blurted out – 'How ever did the master know that Abraham Lincoln was in that stone?'

Our character may be a rough and shapeless and unlovely thing. But Christ the great sculptor – who could see a shining saint in a Zacchaeus, and in an unstable fisherman a glorious champion of the Lord – Christ sees an angel in the lump of stone! 'I can make you,' He declares, 'a son, a daughter of God! I can fashion you into *My* likeness, with My character

and spirit and ways. Will you give Me the chance to do it? Will you trust
Me that I can?'

Well — *will you?*

Here faith is ours — and heavenly hope,
*   And grace to lead us higher;*
But there are perfectness and peace
*   Beyond our best desire.*

O by Thy love and anguish, Lord,
*   And by Thy life laid down,*
Grant that we fall not from Thy grace,
*   Nor cast away our crown!*

CHAPTER 18

The Rending
of the Veil

The veil of the Temple was rent in twain from the top to the bottom.

~ St Mark 15: 38 ~

IT had been hanging there for years. It looked as if it might hang there for ever. Gorgeously embroidered in blue and purple and scarlet, the massive curtain hung before the inmost shrine, where God was supposed to dwell; and for centuries it had guarded its secret well. It was there to fulfil a double function. On the one hand, it was there *to keep men out:* a warning to sinful men that where the last mysteries of religion were concerned they must keep a respectful distance. On the other hand, it was there *to shut God in:* for behind that hanging veil there was silence deep as death and darkness black as night, even while the Syrian sun was blazing down outside. It had been hanging there for years; it looked as if it might hang there for ever.

But one day, suddenly, without warning, it was cut from top to bottom, as by a pair of unseen giant hands; the formidable frustration was finished.

Now whatever we may make of this strange mysterious event, certainly for the Gospel writers it was alive with symbolism. For tradition declared that the rending of the Temple veil had happened at the precise moment when Jesus on the hill of Calvary had breathed His last and gone back to God. Surely, they said, the two events were connected. It was no mere coincidence. The death of Christ outside the city gates and the rending of the veil before the mercy-seat had somehow been related. They went further. They said the two things had been *directly* related as cause and effect. It was the death of Christ that had torn the veil. So they dared to believe; and the verdict of Christendom today is that, in the deepest sense of all, they were right.

For that rent veil in front of God's mercy-seat – what does it stand for? It stands in Scripture, and it stands today, for three things: and in each of them the death of Christ is fundamental.

I

First, the rending of the veil means *the disclosure of a secret:* the revealing of the inmost heart of the Eternal.

When Jews worshipped in the Temple in the old days, they were always sure that there was *something* there behind the curtain. But what? That none could tell. Something awesome, they suspected, formidable, mysterious.

Deliberately and jealously the Temple kept its shrouded secret. It was characteristic of Jewish religion that as you passed in from the outer courts of the Temple through the inner courts towards the centre, the lights were progressively dimmed and lowered – until at the very centre, the Holy of Holies itself lay in perpetual darkness. That had been the tradition for centuries. Then one day Jesus died, the veil was rent, and light went streaming in. It was an end of secrecy in religion, and the heart of God lay bare.

There are multitudes of people today back where those Jews were before this thing happened. Like them, they believe there must be some ultimate Reality behind the veil of sense, some transcendent Power behind the world we see. But what? That is what is so difficult to determine. A living Mind, says one. An austere righteousness, says another. 'The ground of our being,' said Paul Tillich. But we don't know. Perception is clouded, and the lights get dimmer as you near the centre. What if, when you get to the very centre, there should be only a heartless indifference, what Thomas Hardy called, 'The dreaming, dark, dumb Thing/That turns the handle of this idle show'? What if there is something irrational in the very constitution of the universe, something which will always defeat man's dreams, make havoc of his hopes, and bring his pathetic optimism crashing in disaster?

What is God like? Multitudes are really wanting to know. Is He a God to whom it is worth my while to pray? Is He a God who knows anything about it when things in my little corner of the universe get tangled and go wrong, and my heart is hurt and sore? Is He a God who can lay any hand of healing peace upon my soul when I am rushed and tired and hectic? Is He a God who knows the miseries of men and all the heartache of the world? Above all, is He a God who can bring this world of men and nations to a new hope and a new beginning? Has He anything to offer – of strength and refuge and renewal – to a world that is baffled and distracted and defeated? These are the questions to which multitudes are vaguely groping for an answer, and finding only an impenetrable veil. And there *is* no answer – *except in the death of our Lord on Calvary.*

But that does rend the veil. That does answer the question. For the death of Christ goes right beyond all words and arguments. It says what words could never say. For this is a *deed*, ploughed into history, an accomplished fact towering over the wrecks of time.

Words can never prove love. Even God could not do it by words. Once and again He had said, 'Come, let us reason together' – all through the Old Testament He was saying that; but even the divinest reasoning could not prove love. Once and again He had made His prophets a herald voice to men; but even the Word of the Lord burning and flaming on their lips could not do it. He had sent Jesus of Nazareth preaching the Sermon on the Mount, heightening the ethical ideal all along the line; challenging men, in tones they had never heard before, to trust God's love for everything. But even that could not do it. The shadow of doubt still lingered.

Then, when it seemed that God could do no more, Jesus died; and from the top to the bottom – mark that, *not* from the bottom upwards, which might have connoted mere human curiosity and inquisitiveness, but from the top downwards – the veil was rent in twain. It is the death on the Cross that reveals for me the very heart of the Eternal. For this is not words. It is a *deed,* God's deed, against which I can batter all my doubts to pieces.

Principal James Denney, strict Protestant as he was, once declared that if there was one thing for which he almost envied the Roman Catholic priest it was this – that the priest could take a crucifix in his hand, and hold it before the eyes of a soul in trouble, and say – 'Look! *God loves you like that!*' Yes, indeed. Like that – for you, for me, for all the troubled world. It is that Cross that takes us past all the secrecy and the trouble and the complaining, past all the clouds and darkness, and lets in a light brighter than the Syrian sunshine upon the mercy-seat and the heart of the Eternal. And behold, that heart is Love!

II

But the rent veil stands for something more than the disclosing of a secret and the letting in of a light. It stands also for *the opening of a road,* the offer of a right-of-way for all who care to travel it.

You see, it was not only the progressive lowering of the lights as you neared the centre that was characteristic of that Temple on the hill. There was also the progressive heightening of the barriers. The whole thing, in fact, was a carefully graded system of exclusion, dominated by contempt for the common herd. There was the outer court, where all might come; beyond that, the inner sanctuary, where only true-born Jews might go, and it was death for any foreigner to enter; further in, the Holy Place reserved for the ministering priests; and beyond that, behind the veil, the Holiest of all, where one man – namely Israel's High Priest – might penetrate, once a year.

Strange irony of fate, was it not, that in Jesus' time that one privileged individual should have been a Caiaphas? That man and God alone together! And all the rest, the sincere and seeking souls, with heart and flesh crying out for the living God, blocked and thrust back by one barrier after another, and finally by that unrelenting veil that it was sacrilege and death to touch!

One consequence was inevitable. Religion became a second-hand thing altogether. You can picture those Jews standing outside, while their High Priest alone went in; and then, when he came out again, looking at him with awe and reverence – yes, even if he were a Caiaphas. They had not seen God, and never would – but there was a man who had; and they gazed at him, and bowed before him, as though he were half a God himself. And that was all. No access to the mercy-seat for them. No grasp of the great hand of the Eternal. What that veil seemed to say was – 'You stand back! God is not for you.'

But one day, between two thieves on Golgotha, a Friend of sinners gave His life; and from that moment the veil was finished, and the road of access opened up for all.

I wonder what the priests thought when it happened. I wonder what Caiaphas thought. I reckon they turned and gazed at one another with dismay on their faces. They saw that this, unless they did something about it at once, would change the face of religion for ever. And no doubt that very night they got the torn veil patched up again.

Men have done that all down the centuries, trying to restrict to a privileged few what God said was to be a right-of-way for all. They are pretending the veil is still there, when actually it is a historic anachronism. It has been gone for two thousand years.

Jesus once said – 'What God hath joined together, let not man put asunder.' May we not perhaps add this – 'And what God hath put asunder, let not man join together'? 'Whosoever will, let him come.' For the track blazed by Christ stands open.

You may have heard of Bishop Hannington, who died for Christ in Uganda. 'Tell them,' cried Hannington, to emissaries who had been sent to murder him, 'tell them I open the road to Uganda with my life!' And with that shout upon his lips, he fell and gave up the ghost. We are in this Church today because a greater road has been opened at a greater price, and we have heard the voice of Jesus crying – 'Tell the world that I open the road to God with My life!' 'Whosoever will, let him come.'

This is why we take our holy faith into all the world. This is why a Church that was not missionary would be a caricature of Christ's intention. This is why we declare that racial privilege and the colour bar, the pride that separates man from man, are a blasphemy upon the universal Fatherhood of God. From the moment Christ died, the road to God has been open equally to all. No Church, no nation, no racial theory dare reinterpose a barrier there. To close up a right-of-way is a crime.

Very specially let me add this – it is an open road for sinners. You won't rebuke me for stressing this. Who is there among us here so good that he does not need forgiveness? No. When we think of all the ways we have blundered; when we hear across the clamour of our God-forgetting days the still small voice of Jesus; when we walk the roads of Galilee where first we saw what love and truth could mean; when we gather for Communion in some upper room with Jesus, and feel His eyes upon our soul – does that not dissipate all proud illusions and turn our self-approval into shame?

But listen! The greatest thing about that road through the rent veil that the death of Jesus has opened up is precisely that it is the sinner's right-of-way.

There is a lovely story about Dr John Duncan – 'Rabbi' Duncan, as his students and most of Edinburgh called him. He was sitting one day at a Highland Communion; and so unworthy did he feel that, when the bread and wine were handed round, he let them pass untasted. But as he sat there feeling miserable, he chanced, looking up, to observe a girl who, when the elements reached her, also let them pass, and broke down in tears. Whereupon the old saint suddenly rediscovered the truth he had been forgetting; and in a hoarse whisper that carried across the church, he was heard to say, 'Take it lassie, take it – it's meant for sinners!' And he himself partook. I beg you to get hold of that. *It's meant for sinners.* And when next time you take the bread and wine of Communion into your lips, I'll tell you what to say. Say, 'This means that I'm forgiven.' You don't need to say it; it is Christ who says it to you in the Communion. It is His voice saying as you receive the elements – 'My son, My daughter, your sins are forgiven.' For Christ's death has rent the veil. Don't fear to travel that open road.

III

Two things that the rending of the veil stands for we have now seen: the disclosure of a secret, the opening of a road. One third and last thing let me mention. It stands for the *confirming of a hope:* guarantee of life eternal.

Listen to these magnificent words about the veil by a New Testament Apostle: 'Lay hold upon the hope set before us – which hope we have as an anchor of the soul, sure and steadfast, *entering in within the veil,* whither the Forerunner is entered for us, even Jesus, our High Priest for ever.' For what the death on Calvary did, with the Resurrection following it, was more than disclosing a secret and opening a road. It was the veil of our mortality rent asunder, and the eternal glory streaming through where Christ has gone before.

And even if that veil of time and transience swings back again and hides the future from our eyes, we *know* that everything is different. It is a rent veil now, and for one clear moment we have seen right past it into heaven.

'Who shall separate us from the love of Christ?' cries Paul, and immediately goes on – 'Shall death?' As though to say – 'Did you not know that that fear was killed, when Christ went through the veil?'

Death's flood has lost its chill
Since Jesus crossed the river:
Lover of souls, from ill
My passing soul deliver! ~ Hymn 271: *CH3* ~

To have any real contact with Jesus is to touch the very heart of heaven. And to have the life of Christ in you, actually interpenetrating you, is to be joined to the immortality of God: and anyone who is joined to *that* immortality cannot die. In fact, the resurrection which we believe awaits us beyond physical death will be just the glorious consummation of the risen life we already have, here in this world which is a mingling of the eternal and the temporal.

There was a December day in Edinburgh in 1666, when Hugh Mackail, youngest and bravest of the Covenanters, was brought before his judges and condemned to the scaffold. They gave him four days to live: then back to the Tolbooth they marched him. Many in the watching crowd were weeping as he went – so young he seemed, so terrible his fate. Four days to live! Four days to see the sun! But there were no tears in his eyes, no self-pity in this young Galahad's face. 'Trust in God,' he cried, and his eyes were shining. 'Trust in God!' Then suddenly, catching sight of a friend among the crowd, 'Good news!' he cried. 'Wonderful news! I am within four days' journey of enjoying the sight of Jesus Christ!'

So they have passed over – those valiant hearts – through that rent veil into the full sunburst of eternity. So loved ones of our own have passed, and all the trumpets have sounded for them on the other side. So, at the end, for us –

When death these mortal eyes shall seal,
  And still this throbbing heart,
The rending veil shall Thee reveal,
  All glorious as Thou art.   ~ Hymn 674: *CH3* ~

It is the miracle of Cana in Galilee all over again – the best wine kept to the last. For the same Jesus who at the first came to us at Calvary, who has been coming to us again and again, who is with us in this holy place now – that same dear Christ will be there when the veil parts, living an unclouded perception of God, 'where in His presence there is fulness of joy, and at His right hand pleasures for evermore'.

Fear death? Why should I fear – as though coming to Jordan at the last I should perish on the shore? No. For what I have been given in Christ is no sham comfort, no soothing drug nor frivolous metaphysical speculation. *It is God's everlasting 'Yes' to life's ultimate question.* It is the fulfilment which here on earth we never reach. Therefore – *I fear no more!* And with one of our greatest hymn-writers we too can say:

Jesus, my Lord! I know His Name,
  His Name is all my boast;
Nor will He put my soul to shame,
  Nor let my hope be lost.

I know that safe with Him remains,
  Protected by His power,
What I've committed to His trust
  Till the decisive hour.   ~ Hymn 591: *CH3* ~

And to His dear Name – now, yes, now, and in that final hour – be all the glory for ever.

CHAPTER 19

When God recalls the Angels

The angels were gone away from them into heaven.

~ St Luke 2: 15 ~

IT is not the easiest thing in the world getting back to normal when Christmas for another year has come and gone. The Christmas festival is full of gladness, friendliness, fraternity. There are even sudden hopes of peace on earth, real peace at last for this distracted world, to banish the demonic fact of man's inhumanity to man and to eliminate the spectre of thermo-nuclear self-annihilation. But like all experiences that lift us for a moment out of the groove of common days, Christmastide can be unsettling. The days that come after Christmas seem by comparison dull and flat and tediously ordinary, and there is sometimes even a reaction into depression. Was it wise to indulge the dream of world fraternity? Were these high moments of hope and vision really salutary? 'Unto us,' cries a great prophet, 'a Child is born, unto us a Son is given; and the government shall upon His shoulder.' And on Christmas Day perhaps it is easy to believe that; but Christmas passes – and we begin to wonder. Was that prophetic insight realistic? Would Isaiah have talked like that if he had lived today? Or was it high-flown rhetoric with no substance in fact? Is the Christmas hope illusory? A poet says:

> We ring the bells, and we raise the strain,
>   We hang the garlands everywhere,
>   And bid the tapers twinkle fair ...
>   and then
> Back to the same old lives again.

It is probable that even Christian people, to whom Christmas is the celebration of a sublime and holy mystery, experience something of that reaction. For through the whole Advent season, the Church has the forward look. Sunday by Sunday, Christendom climbs, as it were, the Advent slope towards Bethlehem. On Christmas Day itself we celebrate the most terrific fact of history, the incarnation of God. And now? Well, it is behind us. Now we are down in the common thoroughfare again. The angels are gone away from us into heaven.

So it could have been with those shepherds in the nativity narrative. The evangelist pictures them in their great hour hearing the angels and seeing the Christ. But next day? Next day, I suppose, they were back at their old task – the fields the same, the monotony the same, the night skies as dark as if no angels had ever pierced them with their Hallelujahs. Who could blame them if they had felt unsettled, or if the aftermath of the glory had been a strange depression? 'The angels were gone away from them into heaven.'

And yet – was that the whole truth? Look at these shepherds again. *Could* everything be the same for them, back at their common tasks? Not if they had seen the Christ! What matter though the angels were gone, if the gift of God remained? Nothing could dispossess them of that vision.

Now what about ourselves? There *are* those difficult times in life when God, as it were, recalls His angels from us. What are you to do then? Two or three such times let me mention.

I

The first I have already referred to. It is *this season following Christmas*. It is this very time we are in now – with another year coming on its way. And to many of us the New Year is mainly a reminder that we are growing older, that some opportunities will now never come again, that one more chapter of life's brief volume is closed for ever. And there are sombre prospects of a different kind. What has this New Year in store for the nations of the world? Advances in mutual understanding? Or perhaps – somewhere across the world – the explosion of fierce pent-up passions in crisis and catastrophe? The New Year stretch of the road is apt to bring thoughts of an altogether different character from the days of Christmas gladness. Some at least of the singing angels have departed.

What should we do? One thing at least we *can* do – and that is to remember that we are still in the precincts of Bethlehem. If we are facing routine tasks again, at least let us face them with the angels' message and God's revelation echoing in our hearts. The poet says:

We ring the bells, and we raise the strain,
                ... and then
Back to the same old lives again.

I challenge that! It is not true – not if we have met Christ. Not if in these recent days we have seen something of the King in His beauty and our hearts cried 'Immanuel – God with us!' No man ever meets Christ and goes away the same. It is not 'the same old life' after that. It is life on a higher level, with a new dimension. The angels may be gone – Jesus Christ remains!

And remember this, with Advent and Christmas behind us for another year and some of the glory seemingly departed; remember that as soon as this season of the Christian Year is over, we start climbing another wonderful slope, the road that leads on through the story of Christ to Good Friday and Calvary, and past that to Easter and the Resurrection, and past that again to Whitsuntide and the rushing mighty winds of Pentecost! All that is before us now in the forward march of the months ahead, a glory greater even than Bethlehem, the mighty acts of God to which the Christmas music was but the prelude and the overture. The overture may be ended, the angels gone – but the great cosmic drama, God in the forefront of the battle for the redeeming of the universe, has begun. To wish it were always Christmas Eve would be weakly sentimental: thank God that the pilgrim road of our redemption leads past the stable and the manger – to Galilee, to Jerusalem, to Golgotha, to the empty tomb of death's defeat and the incomparable victory of love. The Christmas angels may be gone – but thank God, Jesus Christ remains!

II

But there is another time when the angels seem to go away from us into heaven. I am thinking of the way in which *the generous enthusiasms of earlier life are apt to get damaged and corroded by the disillusionments of experience and the attrition of the years.* Wordsworth, in his poem 'Intimations of Immortality', declared we all come at the first 'trailing clouds of glory from God who is our home'; but he went on to lament that, so soon and so inexorably, the shadows of the prison-house come closing in.

Whither is fled the visionary gleam?
Where is it now, the glory and the dream?

The angels were gone away into heaven.

But suppose it is God Himself who recalls the angels? Suppose this is 'the foolishness of God which is wiser than men'? Suppose it is the divine intention that the reality of our heavenly citizenship should be tested in the rough and tumble of the here and now? Suppose that strange disquieting Scripture which says 'Whom the Lord loveth He chasteneth, and scourgeth every son whom He receiveth' is not the expression of an outworn austere philosophy, but a true transcript of life and the secret of a strong secure serenity? Listen to what Dietrich Bonhoeffer wrote in prison before his execution:

> *Of course, not everything that happens is the will of God, yet in the last resort nothing happens without His will: that is, through every event, however untoward, there is always a way through to God.*
>
> ~ *Letters and Papers from Prison* ~

Here surely is one of the simple, basic, elemental facts of life – that hardship, stress and difficulty, 'winter and rough weather', what the mystics call 'the dark night of the soul', yes, even the cruel discipline of suffering, are not the negative, useless, spoiling things they often seem to be, but can through providence be incomparably valuable, positive and creative in the making of character and the fashioning of sons of God. Do you realise that, if the angels leave you, as they left the shepherds, it can be God's doing, God striving to make sure that His supreme gift in Christ shall be all in all?

III

But now, in the third place, is there not something like the shepherds' experience *in the life of the Church?*

The Church has had its great hours, its Pentecosts, its reformations and revivals; it has had its Columbas, its Augustines, its Knoxes, Wesleys, Livingstones. It has had its ages when it seemed poised to take the world by storm, when belief was easy, and the future seemed assured, and the kingdoms of the world looked set to become the Kingdom of the Lord and of His Christ.

And then the glow departed, and the vision was lost, and the rhythm of the march disrupted. The sea of faith which once was at the flood began to ebb. How good it must have been, we think regretfully, to live in those great days of the Church's history when God was visibly, palpably at work; when whole provinces of the world's life were coming under the sway of the Redeemer; when the claims of faith were recognisably no hallucination but a magnificent triumphant reality; when men knew that their chief end was to glorify God and enjoy Him for ever; and when the Church went forth 'fair as the moon, clear as the sun, terrible as an army with banners'.

'No doubt about it,' we say, thinking of the days of Ninian and Columba, of Francis, Luther, Knox and Wesley, 'there was the arm of the Lord made bare, there was the energetic invading action of the eternal Christ, there was the Spirit of life creatively at work.'

But alas! we say, our days are different. This is no age of faith – this is an age of bewilderment, of doubt, of towering question-marks, of confused morals and hesitant theologies, of rough anarchic winds of scepticism blowing out the ancient lamps of faith. At such a time, it is not only the voice of the individual, it is the voice of the whole Church that cries 'Where is the blessedness I knew/When first I saw the Lord?'

We have been losing the vision. The music has been stilled. The angels have gone away into heaven.

But once again, suppose – as at Bethlehem – it is God Himself who recalls the angels? Suppose the destiny of the Church was written in advance that day on the Transfiguration Mountain when Jesus refused His disciples' request to be allowed to stay there in tranquillity, refused to countenance the idea of faith as a perpetual beatific vision, and led them back to earth and its grim struggles and all its crowding clamourous perplexities?

This is surely the challenge and the glory of the Church's destiny today. Why should we waste time looking back regretfully across the centuries? Why wish to recapture past experiences and vanished visions, great historic hours of the open heavens and singing angels we can hear no longer? We may wait a thousand years for another Columba, another Wesley. God is waiting for us. And with God all things are possible – yes, even greater things than Columba or Wesley ever saw. This is the miracle of the Holy Spirit. Let the Church believe its own faith – Christ is alive – now, at this moment – and all power in heaven and earth is His. I am not ashamed of the Gospel of Christ – it is the power of God unto salvation – as much as it ever was! Glory to God in the highest!

IV

Now finally, there is one other time I must mention when the angels go away into heaven – *the time of bereavement*. For sometimes the angels are human angels. Sometimes it is *they* whose music is the gladness of the world.

It may be that someone listening to me now is thinking of one such angel. The angel left you – was it perhaps long, long ago, or was it in the year that has just closed? – left you all too soon, and it was as if the sunshine were suddenly obliterated, and the music gone.

But will you think just once again of those shepherds? The Bethlehem angels did not just disappear into the unknown: it was God who recalled them when their work was done.

And if you have faith, so it is with your angel. God has recalled him, God has recalled her, into joy and light perpetual.

And better still, remember this: the angels, though now unseen, are still singing somewhere yonder. Listen on such a day as this. Listen when your heart is quiet ...

Angels of Jesus, angels of light,
Singing to welcome the pilgrims of the night.

And even though (as the Book of Revelation says) the choir of the Church Triumphant numbers ten thousand times ten thousand and thousands of thousands, you will hear some echo of one dear familiar voice, the voice you loved the best on earth, singing yonder of the love that guided and the heart that planned and the grace that was sufficient. And then the angel music will blend and mingle with the trumpet-notes of your own holy faith: 'Christ is risen! He has abolished death. He has led captivity captive. As in Adam all die, even so in Christ shall all be made alive.'

These things are true. I *know* they are true. The very character and honour of Christ are bound up with their being true. And because they are true, glory to God in the highest!

They are not lost, those dear ones on the immortal side of death, those angels in the realms of glory – they are our daily comrades still, and we are going to see them again by and by.

Paul once tried to describe it – but he threw down his pen in despair. 'It won't describe,' he said. 'No eye has seen, no ear has heard, no heart of man has ever imagined or conceived' – the thrill of life in the full sunshine of eternity.

But you have Christ's guarantee for it. That is why I said the very character and honour of Christ are bound up with its being true. Therefore, indeed and indeed, Glory to God in the highest! And may Christ, the dear Saviour of us all, bring us home – at last – for ever.

CHAPTER 20

Religion and Social Passion

Bartholomew (Nathanael) and Simon Zelotes.

~ St Luke 6: 14–15 ~

THERE are two conflicting moods or attitudes which are setting up a serious tension in many minds today. There is, on the one hand, the mood in which the only thing that matters is to find rest to our souls in the calm and peace of God; and there is the other mood in which nothing matters except to get to grips with the urgent, clamant actualities of life beating up around our very doors. There is, to put it briefly, the other-worldly attitude; and there is the this-worldly attitude. And we all know the inward tension to which these conflicting moods give rise.

We believe, on the one hand, that here we have no continuing city, and that our citizenship is in heaven; but we cannot forget, on the other hand, that we are also citizens of this world: if we are heirs of the hereafter, we are also children of the here and now, with all the immensely intricate relationships which that involves. We believe, with the Catechism, that 'man's chief end is to glorify God, and to enjoy Him for ever'; but we are also sure that this does not for a moment relieve us of our duty to history, or of our responsibility for the world that now is. We keep the windows of our devotional nature open towards the unseen Jerusalem, and with Bernard of Cluny we pray:

> O sweet and blessed country,
>   The home of God's elect,
> O sweet and blessed country
>   That eager hearts expect.

But over against that stands the other mood, when with William Blake we cry: 'I will not cease from mental fight/Nor will my sword sleep in my hand,/Till we have built Jerusalem ...' *here,* here and now, in this actual situation which is the setting of our lives.

These are the two conflicting moods or attitudes which in our hearts come into collision. Their rival claims set up a tension. And the question is – How are we to resolve it?

Are we to resolve it, as some people do, going all out for one attitude to the virtual exclusion of the other; by adopting, that is to say, either a thoroughgoing other-worldliness or else a thoroughgoing this-world-liness? Is that the right way to settle the conflict? Or is there a better way, some higher synthesis of the two moods that will resolve the tension?

This brings me to the two men of our text – Bartholomew (or, to give him his more familiar name, Nathanael) and Simon the Zealot. I want you to notice how these two men – in the days before Jesus called them – represented precisely the two contrasted attitudes we are concerned with now.

Here is Nathanael. What is your mental picture of Nathanael? Three things we are told about him. He was a man of prayer, with a secret devotional life: 'When thou wast under the fig tree, I saw thee.' He was a man of a rather narrow individualistic religion: 'Can any good thing come out of Nazareth?' He was a man of blameless character: 'Behold, an Israelite indeed, in whom is no guile.' These facts are in the record; and I think they justify us in taking Nathanael as a type of the predominantly other-worldly man – the man who tacitly assumes that religion is solely concerned with the beyond, who regards the faith rather as the ground-work of a personal piety than as a revolutionary force for the welter of this present earth.

Over against him stands Simon the Zealot. That label, the 'Zealot', gives us the man. For the Zealots were a recognised party. They were the political agitators of the day. They were men whose souls were boiling within them at the sight of contemporary conditions; men pledged to bring in a new social order for the downtrodden, half-starving peasants, even if it meant a revolution that would risk the wrath of Rome. Simon the Zealot stands as a type of the predominantly this-worldly attitude. I have no doubt his main interest in Jesus, when Jesus first appeared, was to use Jesus in the interests of his own party programme, to get Jesus entangled in a secular partisan movement. He was not troubling about the beyond. He was desperately concerned with the here and now.

There then are the two men, the two attitudes. Suppose they had met each other before either of them had met Christ – what do you imagine Nathanael would have said to Simon? He would have looked at the Zealot and said:

'What is the use of trying to make a new world, if you leave out God? All your short-cuts to the ideal society will lead only to futility and disillusionment,

if you neglect the basic problem − which is the heart of man himself. You think you can organise a kingdom of heaven upon the earth. You think your vociferous clamour and your violence will bring it into existence. You are desperately mistaken. Without God you can do nothing! "The Lord is in His holy temple: let all the earth keep silence before Him!"'

So Nathanael might have spoken to Simon the Zealot. But let us picture Simon speaking to Nathanael:

'You and your religion! Can't you see, man, that in a world like this, religion is just a sentimental irrelevance? What is the use of talking of the bread of life, if you are not giving men bread for their bodies? All your grand synagogues and temples are a downright offence, as long as there are slums and starving people and unemployment. Until you face these facts and deal with them, all your worship is an unethical hypocrisy!'

So Simon and Nathanael might have spoken, if they had met each other before either of them met Christ.

Of course we do not need to go to Palestine for these two men. They are with us still. Let us look at their modern counterparts. Let us look at their best and noblest representatives today.

Nathanael today, Nathanael at his best, is a man of vital spirituality. He dwells in the secret place of the Most High. He cultivates his devotional life. He strives after personal holiness. He walks with God as a pilgrim and sojourner here. He looks beyond this transitory life to the bliss of life eternal. He is a great and worthy soul − Nathanael at his noblest.

Take Simon the Zealot. Simon today, Simon at his best, is a man with the passion of a crusader. He does not care much perhaps for creeds and dogmas, but he does care mightily for men and women. Wherever there are wrongs to be put right, he will be there, never thinking of personal comfort or leisure, always going the extra mile. The easy toleration of unjust and demoralising conditions he brands as callous, unchristian cruelty. His main interest in the Christian faith is that it once turned the world upside down, and he is convinced that it ought to be doing the same today. He is a fine, self-sacrificing gallant soul − Simon at his noblest.

The trouble is, they are not always so noble as that. Not always do Nathanael and Simon follow their separate ways on that high level.

Nathanael sometimes *locks himself up* in the secret place of the Most High. He stands aloof, self-centred, defiantly individualistic in his religion.

He practises a holiness which takes no cognisance of the agonies that other men and women are facing and the vast miseries of the world. He always has a stained-glass window between him and the common light of day. He is quite sure he possesses a monopoly of Jesus' favour and vested rights in God. In Martin Luther's scathing phrase, 'he sits down and enjoys God all by himself in a corner'. And he doesn't see – poor, blind, self-deluded soul – he doesn't see Jesus turning on him, with eyes like a flame of fire; he doesn't hear the voice of Jesus crying – 'Woe unto you, who tithe mint and anise and cumin, and neglect the weightier matters of the law, justice and mercy! Woe unto you who devour widows' houses, and make long prayers! I will have mercy and not sacrifice!' 'A man,' says F. R. Davey, 'may be drenched in religious experience, and yet incarcerated in a prison-house of self-centredness.'

But if Nathanael is not always the noble character he might be, neither is Simon. Simon sometimes flaunts his irreligion. He scoffs at spiritual values. He says in his heart, There is no God! And God being obliterated, he sells his soul to Satan. And he doesn't see, he *can't* see, Jesus standing there and crying over the secular, God-denying civilisation that Simon and his like have built – 'Behold, your house is left unto you desolate!'

But come back to Nathanael and Simon as we meet them in their nobler representatives today. I ask you now to notice this, that each of these men – the man who has settled the conflict and tension by adopting a thoroughgoing other-worldliness, and his brother who has settled it by a thoroughgoing this-worldliness – each of them is sometimes visited by secret misgivings about his own position.

Nathanael – it is characteristic of Nathanael that he loves to sing:

Drop Thy still dews of quietness,
  Till all our strivings cease;
Take from our souls the strain and stress,
  And let our ordered lives confess the beauty of Thy peace.

~ Hymn 76: *CH3* ~

But why is there that shadow in Nathanael's eyes even as he sings it? It is the shadow of all the world's suffering, and injustice, and force, and oppression creeping up around the sanctuaries of Nathanael's soul, and haunting him with the thought that he will never really know 'the beauty of God's peace' until he is out fighting that encompassing darkness as Jesus fought it.

And Simon – it is characteristic of Simon that he is pledged to toil and labour and sacrifice for a better world. But why is there sometimes, even in the midst of that thrilling crusade, a shadow over Simon's soul? It is the shadow of the fear that the best economic Paradise may not be enough. It is the restless, haunting longing for something better than improved communities and garden cities. It is the cry for 'a city that hath foundations, whose builder and maker is God'.

There, then, are the two men – as they were in the Gospels, and as they are today, with their opposed attitudes to life, their contrasted convictions, criticisms, misgivings. But the decisive thing is this: Jesus called them both to His discipleship. That is mightily significant.

I think I can hear Jesus speaking in private to Nathanael:

> *'You are right, Nathanael, to emphasise the devotional life. You are right in believing that the one thing needful is to possess God. But you were wrong in thinking that social conditions are irrelevant. You are wrong in not seeing that the facts of this present world are the raw materials of God's eternal purpose. By all means, hold on to your devotional emphasis: but let that devotion out into action in the world!'*

So Christ speaks to our Nathanaels today. It *is* the one thing needful, to possess God. But it is a false deduction to say that therefore the evils of this present world don't matter. Do you remember what stands written in Exodus about the Israelites in Egypt to whom Moses was sent to preach? 'They hearkened not unto Moses for anguish of spirit, and for cruel bondage.' In other words, they could not respond to a religious appeal because the appalling, drab and dreary conditions under which they had to live had simply deadened their spirit. And Moses did not say, 'What matter their bondage, as long as I speak to them of God?' He *did* say, 'If their desperate conditions are disabling them from responding to God's appeal; if their bondage is having that effect – then their bondage must be broken!' And break it he did. And Jesus speaks to our Nathanaels today and says, 'Go and do ye likewise!'

I think I can also hear Jesus speaking in private to Simon the Zealot:

> *'You are right, Simon, to bear the world's injustices and oppressions upon your soul. You are right to dedicate your life to their removal. But you are wrong to think you can even begin to do it without God to brace your heart and nerve your arm. You are wrong to disregard the one true source of all effective power and poise and peace. By all means hold on to your social passion: but get your own soul rooted on the rock of ages!'*

So Jesus speaks to our Simons today.

Now we have got our answer to the question from which we started. We asked – what are we to do about the two conflicting moods or attitudes that set up a tension in our minds – the other-worldly and the this-worldly? How are we to resolve the tension? We see Christ's answer now. He does not say we are to resolve it by going all out for one attitude to the exclusion of the other. He does say we are to resolve the tension by a higher synthesis. That is His command – that there be in us *both* Nathanael *and* the Zealot!

Is that possible? It has been *done!* I have quoted that lovely Nathanael hymn – 'Drop Thy still dews of quietness.' But I would have you remember that the man who wrote it, Whittier, was also one of the world's greatest fighters against the slave trade. He was Nathanael *and* the Zealot. That's the synthesis! F. D. Maurice and Charles Kingsley were two of the most revolutionary social reformers our land has seen: but all their inspiration, every atom of it, came from God. That's the synthesis.

'For their sakes,' said Jesus once, 'I sanctify Myself.' Do you see? 'I sanctify Myself' – there's the Nathanael attitude; there's the secret place of the Most High; there's the devotional life and the quest for holiness. 'For their sakes' – there's the very spirit of the Zealot; there's the motive of the great world's need; there's the drive of social passion. 'For their sakes I sanctify Myself.' That's the synthesis! And that is what Christ looks for from you and me.

And that is the challenge that comes to us today, in the name of One who was both divine and human, the Word and the flesh, the fusing in one personality of God above and man beneath; One whose Face revealed as no other the glory of God, yet whose Face was marred as no other by the conflict with the wrongs and sorrows of this tragic earth; One whose Cross stands towering with its head to heaven, and with its shaft right down into Hell, and with its two arms reaching out to embrace the whole earth bursting with sin and sorrow; One whose central Sacrament was bread, the symbol at once of God's everlasting gift and man's most desperate social needs and struggles; One whose will is to be done, as in Heaven, so in earth. It is in His name that the challenge comes that we should be – not Nathanael, not the Zealot – but both in one, with one hand up to God in worship, and the other out to our brother man in service.

> *Bread of Thy Body give me for my fighting,*
> *Give me to drink Thy Sacred Blood for wine,*
> *While there are wrongs that need me for the righting,*
> *While there is warfare splendid and divine.*

That is the synthesis. God help us to achieve it.

CHAPTER 21

Learning from the Enemy

The children of this world are in their generation wiser than the children of light.

~ St Luke 16: 8 ~

THIS might well be called 'the problem parable'. At first sight it simply bristles with difficulties. It upsets so many preconceived ideas. It is apparently a panegyric on worldly prudence: but isn't that terribly unlike Jesus? Isn't it very strange that this rogue of a man in the story should be held up for eulogy? Can we conceive such a commendation of evil coming from Christ? In the attempt to get over the difficulty, scores of ingenious interpretations have been suggested. One German critic has actually tried to cut the knot by declaring that it can't be an authentic parable of Jesus at all.

The trouble of course is that Jesus, when He chose, could be so daring in His originality. Some of the commentators, not noticeable for originality themselves, become quite flustered when it thrusts itself into their path, as it does here. Clothe old truths in new and unaccustomed phraseology, and there will always be some who will grow uneasy, and suspect doctrinal unsoundness. Well, Jesus was not afraid of that. Let us be clear about this: you can't get Jesus to talk platitudes. The one thing He will *not* do is be dull and trite and obvious. You never know what He is going to say next. He electrifies with His dramatic unexpectedness.

Take this parable. Here is how it ought to have ended, in verse 8: 'And the Lord condemned the unjust steward to outer darkness.' That is what all the audience were sure was coming. And here is what did come – the very opposite – 'the Lord commended the unjust steward, because he had done shrewdly.' That's startling! And the thought in many minds is, 'That is not what Jesus ought to have said!' In fact, this whole picture is not the kind of picture He ought to have used – it is too motley in its characters, too lively in its keen-humoured wit, too unorthodox in its way of pointing a moral. *Can* this be Jesus?

If we experience that difficulty, may it not be that in a perfectly sin-cere but mistaken kind of reverence we have been allowing our mental picture of Jesus to become too formal, too stilted, too conventionalised in the halo that it wears? Of course this is Jesus! The very daring of it is the surest sign and seal of the Master's authentic touch.

Just look at it again. You will get the sense of it best if you re-translate these words 'the lord' and 'the steward' as 'the laird' and 'the factor': for that is exactly what it means. Here was this factor administering the laird's estate. He began (as we would say) to 'feather his own nest'. He began to juggle with the accounts. Then one day his embezzlements were dis-covered. Dismissal, ruin, stared him in the face. But swiftly his astute mind went to work. 'What shall I do when I am turned out of house and home, thrown out on to the streets? I can't dig: I haven't the physique for that. I can't beg: for I won't demean myself to that. But here's an idea! Why shouldn't I make friends of all the laird's tenants! Suppose I halve their rents!'

And it was no sooner thought of than done. 'How much do you owe the laird? Fifty pounds? Take your voucher and write down twenty-five!' And so he went right round. And when it was finished, 'Ha! now,' he said, 'when I'm thrown out, there will be plenty open doors to welcome me! I won't lack a bed or a meal!' And, says the story, the laird commended – please notice, it is the laird who commends him, not Jesus the teller of the story – the laird commended his unjust factor – not meaning, of course, that he approved the man's morals (we'd have to be painfully solemn literalists to interpret it like that), but meaning that he couldn't help admiring the fellow's sheer impudent resourcefulness and effrontery!

'My word,' he said, 'you *are* an astute and daring rascal! For barefaced coolness, you have got us all beaten hollow!' And there, abruptly, the story ends.

Now, once again, I beg you to remember the basic principle for interpreting all the parables of Jesus. It is this: each parable, unlike an allegory, was meant by Jesus to convey one cardinal truth, and that there-fore it is essential in every case to disentangle this salient truth in Jesus' mind from the details of the story, the picturesque ornament and drapery in which the story is clothed.

So here in the story before us. Half our trouble comes from persisting in asking – quite gratuitously – who do these characters – the laird, the factor, the tenants – represent? The answer is: They don't represent any-one – except three sets of people such as might be encountered in Galilee or anywhere else. The biggest mistake of all is the one we persist in making the most – our tacit assumption that the laird – the lord, as the story calls him – must stand for God. It is safe to say that nothing was further from Jesus' intention. The laird is *not* God: he is just any easy-going, slightly cynical man of the world – nothing else.

And do let me emphasise again that it is not the factor's morals or his methods that are being approved – but only the man's resourcefulness, foresight and acumen. That is the one highlight of the whole story.

In other words, here is what Christ is fixing on, here is the one salient truth He is after: *God's people might well take an occasional lesson from God's enemies – the saint has something to learn from the sinner.* For the children of this world are sometimes wiser in their generation – more resourceful and far-seeing and inventive and purposeful – than the children of light are for theirs. Or, to put it differently, if all God's people would bring to the service of God's Kingdom the superb, magnificent concentration, determination and resourcefulness that are so often given to the affairs of this world, what strides that Kingdom would make! That, then, is the challenge; and we dare not pass it by.

So, now, we've got to ask this question. In what respects are Christ's people to take a lesson from those outside? The parable itself suggests three.

For one thing, the children of this world might teach the children of light something about *definiteness of aim*.

Take this factor in the story. He knew exactly what he was after. Money, comfort, security – that was his all-absorbing quest. He saw his goal, and bent all his energies towards it. He could have said, quite sincerely, 'This one thing I do'.

That is characteristic of the children of this world. They work to plan. They see their goal, and go 'all out' to reach it. We have witnessed an illustration of that on a gigantic scale in our generation. Think of the people who are simply possessed, in body, mind and soul, by the total-itarian idea – the glorification of the state. *They* have no vagueness in their creed. *They* know what they are after, and what they mean to get.

Have we anything like that definiteness of aim in our service of Christ? Take the Church. Isn't there a danger of the Church getting side-tracked into non-essentials, frittering away on secondary things the time and strength that ought to be given to the one thing that justifies the Church's existence – namely, the bringing of men and women into a saving relationship to God through Jesus Christ? Take the evidence of history. The great days of the Church, the days when the tides of the evangel rose to the flood and swept the world and broke through the barricades, have always been days when the Church has gone crusading with one thought in her mind – the all-sufficient Saviourhood of Christ; and one passion in her heart – the passion for the souls of men.

Men and women, we want to recapture that definiteness of aim. We are not a society existing to carry on a score of unrelated activities. We are not a debating-club for the discussion of anything that happens to be topical at the moment. We are not a device for the multiplication of meetings and machinery. We are the community of Christ, charged with one commission – the winning of the world for God.

And I beg you to make no mistake about this, that in this day of rampant new religions, Caesarisms and Communisms and deified materialisms, creeds that are absolutely definite in their aims and categorical about the path that they pursue, it is no use playing about with a religion that is vague and nebulous and woolly and not quite sure of what it is after. The worldly-minded materialist believes the world to be of great importance: do we Christians give the impression of believing that the Kingdom of God is as commandingly important? It is no use setting up a 'C3' Christianity to meet an 'A1' paganism. 'The children of this world are wiser in their generation than the children of light.'

But if the Church can recapture that decisiveness of touch that has always been hers in her greatest days – or rather, let me put it like this (for I don't want to speak of the Church as an abstract thing, seeing that the Church is just the men and women who compose it), if you and I as Christians can live the dedicated life, in which the interests of God's Kingdom matter more than any personal interests, in which those truly terrific truths – the sovereignty of God, the eternity of right, the Redeemership of Christ – have gripped us like a passion, then, then only, we can beat the world at its own game; and even through the darkness of these days, God's Kingdom will go marching on.

Can't we learn a lesson from the children of the world? They pursue the trivial as though it were eternal; the Christian too often pursues the eternal as though it were quite trivial.

I've known a man keen enough on golf to spend hours correcting a slice or practising with a putter; absolutely absorbed in it – as he is quite right to be, if he wants to. But just compare that absorbed devotion to something which in the long run is utterly trivial, with our lackadaisical Christian attitude to things that matter as supremely as the Bible, and prayer, and the knowledge of God! A man will steep himself in Stock Exchange statistics, and if that is his job he is entitled to concentrate on it. But the searching question is – Are we Christians as keen to *steep* ourselves in the things of God?

That is one challenge to us of this parable. May the Holy Spirit give to us, as Christians, such clear definiteness of aim.

I pass to another thing. Don't you think the children of this world can sometimes teach the children of light a lesson about *inventiveness and resource?*

Take this factor in the story. He may have been defective in morals, but he certainly had plenty of wits. How fertile his imagination! How prolific his plans! Why, even the master he defrauded couldn't help congratulating him on his ingenuity!

The question is – Have we anything like that enterprising spirit, that ingenious resourcefulness, in our service of Christ? There was a characteristic prayer that Professor A. B. Bruce often used at the opening of his classes in New College: 'Lord, give us a fearless inventiveness in Thy service.' Have we got that, when we take counsel together concerning the things of the Kingdom – a fearless inventiveness in the service of Jesus?

What does it mean? Listen to what it meant for Paul the Apostle: 'I have become all things to all men, that I might by all means save some.' There obviously was a man you simply couldn't confine in any ecclesiastical rut! There was a man who refused to jog along the beaten tracks of precedent and tradition. 'I am become all things to all men.' Of course, he was criticised for it, and furiously misunderstood. But what matter? Christ blessed that fearless inventiveness of Paul's, that consecrated fertility of resource. And He waits to bless it still.

Surely, of all people, the children of light should be wide awake! Surely they, the sons of the morning, ought to have nothing to learn from the sons of night about the exhilaration of the spirit of adventure! It is a thoroughly bad idea that when a man comes to Jesus, he is supposed to leave his imagination at home. It is a thoroughly mischievous notion which suggests that to 'get religion' means to have all his individual excrescences smoothed out, to be cut to a standard stereotyped pattern, and to be doomed to walk in a groove for the rest of his days. If there *is* a religion like that, it is not *Christ's* religion.

Was there ever a mind so fearlessly inventive, so daringly creative, as the mind of Jesus? And are we not to pray?

Let that mind which was in Christ be also in us? Lord, give us the spirit of enterprise and discovery, and the spirit of the pioneer who strikes out into the unknown. Don't let it be said of the children of light that they were less resourceful for Christ's ends than the children of darkness are for the Devil's ends. Give us a fearless inventiveness in Thy service!

I pass to the final thing. I have spoken of definiteness of aim, and inventiveness of resource. But don't you think the children of this world can also teach the children of light something about *foresight and vision for the future?*

Take this factor in the story. When he saw his fortunes threatening to tumble about him like a house of cards, what did he do? He might have thrust disturbing thoughts of a possible dismissal away. He might have said, 'Why worry myself with what hasn't yet happened? The present is good enough for me!' But no! His one thought was – 'I must look ahead. I must devise means not to be left homeless and penniless when the crash comes. There's not a moment to lose. The time is short. If I act now, I may *just* manage it. Now is the accepted time!'

Well, what of the children of light? Stretching away in front of us the vast expanses of eternity – have we as much thought for that, as much foresight envisaging that, as the children of this world have for the narrow little sphere of this hectic earthly existence? In short, do we believe in our infinitely greater tomorrow as vividly and intensely as the world believes in the tomorrows for which it hopes and plans?

Mark you, I am not suggesting that religion ought to operate with prudential motives. I am not preaching that a man ought to give his life to God, simply to secure a blissful hereafter: that kind of spiritual feathering of our nest would be a travesty of the Gospel of Christ. But I *am* saying that if the basic assertions of our Christian faith are true; if you and I are really immortal with God's own immortality; if this world *is* a passing show, and only the spiritual things have any permanent validity; if weak things like beauty, truth, goodness, love, are destined to go lasting on when mighty things like the proud tyrannies of today are levelled in the dust and their very names forgotten; if these brief transient years on earth are big for us with eternal issues; if our true citizenship *is* in Heaven – if all that is true (and Christ is the guarantee that it *is* true), then isn't it lamentable that any who profess a faith like that should simply drift through life with loins ungirt and lamps unlit and slumber in their souls? The children of this world are wiser in their generation – they have more foresight, look further ahead – than the children of light!

But this is the Advent season. And ringing down the years comes Christ's Advent challenge to our souls – 'Behold, I come quickly! Behold, the years are hastening on! Behold your swift days are drawing ever nearer to the goal! Pause and consider. O make room in your life for thought, for prayer, for the incorruptible eternal things, for the living breath of God. You who are an immortal spirit, don't scorn your immortality!'

That is Christ's own Advent summons to all the children of men.

He hath sounded forth the trumpet that shall never call retreat;
He is sifting out the hearts of men before His judgment seat;
O, be swift my soul to answer Him; be jubilant, my feet!
Our God is marching on.   ~ Hymn 318: *CH3* ~

CHAPTER 22

What do we ask of Him?

And the two disciples heard [John] speak, and they followed Jesus. Then Jesus turned, and saw them following, and saith unto them, 'What seek ye?'

~ St John 1: 37-38 ~

HERE were these two young men, lingering uncertainly in the vicinity of Jesus. He turns and asks them, 'What seek ye?' – or, as it might be translated, 'What do you want? What are you looking for? Have you lost something? What are you after?'

That is Christ's question still to this bewildered generation. It is our lot to be living in an age of revolution – social, moral, technological, intellectual. Those demonstrations and protests we so often read about, marches and counter-marches, occasionally erupting into violence – they are all symptomatic of the revolution of the times. Even in the Church, for better or worse, it is a time of very considerable revolution – Protestant and Catholic Churches alike. And Christ's question is: 'What are you *wanting?* You are obviously seeking something, but what is it you are after? What is the aim and object of your quest? What is your real demand on life?'

Let us look at that question now, remembering it is Christ's question to us all. And let us listen to some of the answers forthcoming today.

There can be no doubt about one answer. 'What are you wanting? We want *Reality.* We have had enough of shams and conventions, shibboleths and sentimentalisms. Let us at all costs be realistic! We have no use for anything that is not real.'

Now I am sure that this was in the minds of Andrew and John, here in the story. They had seen the Pharisees praying at the street-corners, had heard them debating tiresome legalistic controversies quite irrelevant to life; and something in them said – 'That's not real.' They had some experience of a religion that could propound intricate theological conundrums, but was dumb about social injustice, 'straining at a gnat and swallowing a camel'; and something said – 'That's not real.' *And so they turned to Jesus.*

'We want reality' – that is one great dominant demand. Let us face it frankly. Where and how does unreality come in? It comes in wherever you get a hiatus between piety and practice. Thus, when men divorce the sacred from the secular, as though the life of politics and the secular city could never be any concern of the Church; or when I sing hymns about the sweetness of the divine Presence, and fail to consider whether there aren't things in my life which that Presence would burn to shreds – that is being unreal, in fact, just insidious trifling.

But now, look! over against all that there is one tremendous fact to set – *the sheer realism of Christ.* How starkly realistic Jesus was, and is! *He* never 'begs the question'. He never talks about unreal problems in an unreal way. And that is because He *is* Reality – all-penetrating and all-compelling.

It beats me to see why we should allow agnosticism or secular humanism to monopolise such fine words as realism and rationalism and claim them as their own! For the life of Jesus is far and away *the* most rational fact this mad world has ever seen. And for sheer startling realism, is there anything that can compare for a moment with the Cross? You are wanting reality? Then seek it and find it in Jesus, for it is shining and blazing there. And it is as we conform to His standards and share His life that He can make us real persons, with real motives, and a real work to do in the world.

Let us move on to something else. If one answer to Christ's question 'What seek ye? What are you wanting from life?' is 'We want Reality', another would be this – 'We want *Liberty!* We want the right to decide our own destiny. I want to be free to carve out my self-identity, to create an authentic existence of my own.'

Now here again, I am sure something of this must have been in the minds of Andrew and John in the original story. It was a rather narrow, provincial little place, Bethsaida, limited in its outlook, suspicious of new ways and ideas. These two young men, 'cribbed and cabined and confined' there, had begun to chafe at their bondage, begun to feel an urge towards self-expression. *And so they turned to Jesus.*

'We want liberty!' That is the second great dominant demand. And in its own way, it is a perfectly right and healthy instinct. 'I want the making of my own life! I want the fashioning of my own personality. I want, untrammeled by other people's notions of what is fitting and proper, unencumbered by the cramping inhibitions of an archaic outmoded ethic, I want to steer my own ship. I want to be absolutely free!'

A natural instinct, yes, certainly. But now, look, this is the important thing: it is not quite as simple as it sounds. What does it *mean* – 'absolutely free'? Is there such a thing? Has there ever been, or can there ever be? Is the truth not rather this, that if you want to be free there must first be a fixed point of bondage somewhere? Our very freedom to go on living at all in this world is dependent on our consenting to being bound by law, God's Highway Code for the pilgrimage of life.

The fact is – the gospel of absolute freedom (and that includes all the new permissive moralities) needs no elaborate refutation from the side of ethics or psychology or religion. The basic indictment is that it just doesn't work; it can't deliver the goods that it sets out to deliver. That you can have liberty without law is the primeval lie; and sooner or later that lie comes home to roost. The nemesis of that kind of freedom can be pathetic – nausea, self-loathing, despair.

No, it is the law of life: if you want to be really free, there must be that point of bondage somewhere. The Indian mystic Rabindranath Tagore once illustrated that beautifully: 'Here is a violin-string,' he said, 'lying on my table. In a sense, lying there, it is quite free. Only – it is not free to sing. But look! I take that string, and fix it into my violin. I tighten it up. Now it is *bound*. It is not free any longer. But now, for the first time, it really *is* free – because it is free to sing!'

That is a parable – and it means something mightily important about your soul and mine and Jesus Christ. And do remember this – that the man in the New Testament, St Paul, who on almost every page could call himself 'servant of Christ', 'bondslave of Christ', was the same man who was for ever singing about 'the glorious liberty of the children of God'. The 'bondslave', the 'glorious liberty', think of that! And then try to pray the words of that fine hymn:

> *Holy Spirit, Right Divine,*
> *King within my conscience reign;*
> Be my law, *and I shall be*
> Firmly bound, for ever free! ~ Hymn 106: *CH3* ~

The Bible does *not* say – 'Where you are your own master, there is liberty.' It says – 'Where the Spirit of the Lord is, there is liberty.' That is the Magna Carta of every Christian's life.

Let us move on again. We want Reality. We want Liberty. There is a third element in this generation's total demand on life, especially with the younger generation. 'What are you wanting?' We want *Adventure*. We want life delivered from tameness, with some zest and thrill about it. We want to be captured by a cause, something big and dynamic to live for.

So it was, I feel sure, with Andrew and John in the story. They couldn't bear the safe and sheltered existence of compromise and drift and suffocating, unheroic mediocrity. They wanted to stand up and live! *And so they turned to Jesus.*

And so today – and always. Man is by nature an adventurer – you might even say (in one sense at any rate) a born gambler. 'His interest,' said Robert Browning, 'is on the dangerous edge of things.' He doesn't want a dead certainty. A dead certainty is precisely that – it's dead. No! From Abraham with the morning in his eyes, setting out on his enormous pilgrimage; or from twelve men in an upper room in Jerusalem proposing to turn the world upside down – from that, right down across the centuries and the ages, to Albert Schweitzer in his African forest, or (shall I say?) to a group of cosmonauts navigating space and celebrating the Christian Sacrament of Communion on the moon (as in point of fact they did) – all that way the passion for adventure has haunted the human heart.

The danger, of course, is that if it cannot find a worthy outlet, it may find an unworthy one. It can even engender the arrogant aggressiveness that lands the world in war. Or it can lead to the mammoth gambling craze that saps a nation's morale. It can lead to intemperance and drug-addiction; yes, and to the so-called experimental moralities, those reckless parodies of love. It is the passion for adventure – deteriorated and gone wrong – that underlies them all.

And so we turn to Christ. The passion for adventure? Here is One who has been the moving Spirit of more desperate adventure than any other leader who has ever lived. Think of the Cross. There were gamblers at its foot – the Roman soldiers with their dice. Nowhere else? There come back to me some lines of that fine Christian soldier-poet Geoffrey Studdert-Kennedy:

> *He was a gambler too,*
> *My Christ,*
> *He took His life and threw*
> *It for a world redeemed.*
> *And e'er His agony was done,*
> *Before the westering sun went down,*
> *Crowning that day with its crimson crown,*
> *He knew That He had won.*   ~ 'He was a Gambler too' ~

You may approve that way of putting it, or you may disapprove. But the essential meaning is clear: He *was* a gambler, my Christ – and yonder in Galilee and Judea, at Gethsemane and Calvary, He took His life, and threw it for a world redeemed.

And that is the Leader we are supposed to be following. Oh, but we have diluted the high heroism of Jesus, watered down His radical demands, sometimes even offered people inducements – nice little cheap inducements – to come in and join our fellowship. And then we wonder why Christianity is not winning the world!

'The Kingdom of Heaven,' cried James Denney once, 'is not for the well-meaning. It is for the desperate!' There was a fine answer General Armstrong, of the American Civil War, gave when someone at a meeting criticised his plan for ending race-conflict as being quite impossible. In an instant the General was on his feet. 'Sir,' he blazed, 'and what are Christ's men put into the world for, but *to do the impossible* in the strength of God?'

You want adventure? Son of man, stand upon your feet and Christ will speak with you!

Well now, we have seen three answers to Christ's 'What seek ye? What do you want?' – Reality, Liberty, Adventure. But is there not something deeper still? Is there not this in our generation's quest? – 'I want *God*. My heart is restless till it rest in Him.'

I am sure that was the way of it with Andrew and John when they turned to Jesus. And I am certain that is the way of it with multitudes of people today. They would perhaps never put their feelings about these things into words; but they have a haunting intuition that this visible secular world is not the totality of existence – a craving for something, Someone transcendent, to give meaning to the jumble of their lives.

Yes, this human nature of ours must have God – and it knows it. Man must have something to fill what Julian Huxley called 'the God-shaped blank in his heart'. And if some of the thousands who are unhappy and restless today, with life drained of energy and meaning, if they could diagnose their own deep malady, you would hear them saying this: 'I must have God! This life is too dull for anything, without God. I resist Him, and yet I thirst for Him. I can't help it. In His will is my peace!'

Do you know what I should like to say to anyone wanting God like that today? I'd like to say – 'Friend, be of good cheer, for there is a fact prior to your wanting God. It is this, that *God also is wanting you.*'

Think of it like this. An artist wants beauty. He pursues beauty. But no! He wouldn't put it like that. He knows better. He would say that beauty was pursuing him. He doesn't concoct or create beauty in his studio or his brain. He doesn't find beauty. It is beauty that finds him.

So with the scientist. The scientist wants truth. He pursues truth. But he wouldn't put it like that. He knows better. He would say that truth is pursuing him. There's something *alive* – outside him, independent of him, eternally valid apart from him. He doesn't create or find truth. Truth finds him.

It is exactly the same with the greatest quest of all. We want God. We pursue God. Believe me – the deeper fact is that God wants us. God pursues us. God through His Spirit comes to us, *before* ever we can go to Him. Isn't that the profound meaning of the parable of the Good Shepherd, and indeed of the whole ministry of Jesus? Religion is not a matter of our petty devising. It is not something we have been clever enough to find out. No! It is God Himself who initiates our quest for Him. There's something alive coming after us. There's Someone tracking us down.

This is no imagination. It is the basic fact of life – of your life and mine. At every instant the eternal is interwoven with the temporal, the supernatural penetrating the natural, the absolute irradiating and giving meaning to the ebb and flow of circumstance.

And if ever you should get tired of religious argument and discussion, weary of the quest – perhaps then out of the shadows there will come a Figure, born of a woman, a Man of sorrows for ever speaking about His joy, despised and rejected yet ineffable in His strong serenity, with a strange light on His face that gives those who see it a swift, excited feeling that the transcendent world has come penetratingly near; One who goes marching at last through the blaze of a world's hatred to the Cross, dying there so that no poor wretched sinner should ever doubt God again. It is not that I find God at the Cross. It is that God at the Cross finds me.

And by far the best result of this service would be that someone here should go home, and perhaps tonight, when the house is quiet and this service is just a memory, should open his Gospel at the story of the passion of Jesus, and then kneel down and let God from that Cross have His way with him. Perhaps it is not necessary to wait to go home for that. Perhaps it could happen in a great hymn of the Cross we are just about to sing. Perhaps it could happen now.

Will it? Perhaps. Perhaps not. But I guarantee this: that if it *should* happen – this invasion of the divine and the eternal, this intervention of the very Life of God – you, I, anyone, could go forth from this Church with new life blossoming out of the ashes of disillusionment and defeat, a new song ringing and singing in the heart, and the whole world full of God's glory.

May the dear Lord grant it, for His love's sake.

CHAPTER 23

Drawing Living Water from the Deep Wells of God

Thou hast nothing to draw with, and the well is deep.

~ St John 4: 11 ~

With joy shall ye draw water out of the wells of salvation.

~ Isaiah 12: 3 ~

THERE is a famous story about Robert Southey, author of the *Life of Nelson*, and poet-laureate at the beginning of the nineteenth century. It was one of Southey's ambitions to write a life of John Wesley. He went to consult an old Methodist saint, who in his younger days had known Wesley intimately and had much valuable information about the great evangelist. But it was a disconcerting reception that he met. To the old Methodist it seemed incongruous, almost sacrilege, that a man like Southey, whose gifts were purely literary, should attempt to be the biographer of a man so spiritual as John Wesley. What equipment had Southey for a task like that? The old man looked at him searchingly, and then exclaimed, 'Sir, thou hast nothing to draw with, and the well is deep'. A devastating and memorable rebuke!

These words were originally spoken by the Samaritan woman to Jesus; and her statement was strictly accurate. Jesus, in the literal sense, *had* nothing to draw with, and Jacob's well *was* deep. But when you think of that other water of which Jesus went on to tell – the water of life – and when you remember the woman's dim, confused ideas about religion, might not Jesus have taken her own words and turned them round upon herself? '*Thou* hast nothing to draw with, and the well is deep.'

I think you will feel these words have lost none of their point or force today. Whenever the natural man endeavours to explore and pronounce upon the things of the spirit; whenever the finite human mind presumes to scan and comprehend the mind of the eternal; whenever a student, having read a few books of scientific rationalism, proceeds to dismiss religion as being an outmoded convention; whenever a literary critic tries to take the measure of the Bible, like the young man in Zechariah going out with his wretched foot-rule to measure Jerusalem; whenever a Mr H. G. Wells endeavours to give an account of the origins and history of the Christian faith; whenever a man of the world criticises some humble soul whose life is hid with Christ in God – there with perfect right you may use this text again: 'Sir, thou hast nothing to draw with, and the well is deep.'

There are men who will stand in the presence of the profoundest mysteries without a trace of awe or wonder, will talk jauntily of their emancipation from the ethics of Christ, and smile patronisingly at the prayers of the saints, and look pityingly at those who still frequent the worship and Sacraments of the Church. They have got a rationalistic explanation ready for every phenomenon of the religious life. Prayer, they will tell you, is auto-suggestion; conscience is just a utilitarian social contract; the doctrine of immortality is flagrant wishful-thinking; the idea of God is a projection of the human mind; in fact the whole structure of religion is a survival of childish credulity. How often one has heard all that 'weary, flat, stale and unprofitable' jargon of scepticism repeated! And how odd the idea that anyone should imagine that this immature mixture of bad psychology and half-baked rationalism should cancel out the witness of the Christian centuries or be the dynamite to destroy the Rock of Ages! Sincere and humble questionings and perplexities we can understand and appreciate and value as faith in the making; but to the man who, in the self-confidence of intellectual enlightenment, rejects the Christian revelation, what can we say but this – the words that the old Methodist used to Robert Southey who was proposing to write the spiritual pilgrimage of John Wesley – 'Sir, thou hast nothing to draw with, and the well is deep.'

Let me try to illustrate the truth that meets us here. I want you to think with me of some of those deep wells of mystery that surround us in this world, and of the vessels which we require to have in our possession if we are to draw the living water from their depths.

Think first of the mystery of *Nature*. Some people, in this strange, lovely world, continue to be extraordinarily matter-of-fact, stolid, imperturbable.

A primrose by a river's brim
A yellow primrose was to him,
And it was nothing more.   ~ William Wordsworth: 'Personal Talk' ~

Just as the music which to one man is an ineffable rapture may be to another a tiresome noise, so the beauty of nature which thrills one soul with awe and reverence may pass another by completely. Ask him about the sunrise and sunset and the evening star, and he will give you the mathematics of them more easily than the poetry. Mention a rainbow, and he will tell you of the spectrum and the laws of refraction of light. 'That's all there is to it,' he will say. 'Earth's crammed with heaven,' and he never sees it. He goes through the world like those people Paul spoke of, with a veil upon his heart. He has nothing to draw with and the well is deep.

What is the vessel the soul needs to draw with here, at this deep well of nature's mystery? Is it not a sensitised imagination, a quality of spiritual awareness, a sixth sense that apprehends nature as the garment of the unseen woven here upon the loom of time?

> *The poem hangs on the berry-bush*
> *Till comes the poet's eye;*
> *And the whole street is a masquerade*
> *When Shakespeare passes by.*

The primrose by the river's brim is more than a yellow primrose then. The 'flower in the crannied wall' is more than a weed of the wayside. It is a sacrament. It is a mystic symbol of the unseen and eternal: 'To me the meanest flower that blows can give/Thoughts that do often lie too deep for tears' (Wordsworth: 'Intimations of Immortality').

Let us take another of those deep wells of mystery that surround us in this world – the mystery of *human personality*. What is your estimate of human nature? Well, the Bible's estimate is this: 'Thou hast made man only a little lower than the angels: Thou hast crowned him with glory and honour.' It says that the poorest, loneliest creature that walks this earth is made in the image of God, and that whatever you do to one of the least of these you do to Christ. The Bible puts down the mighty from their seat: 'Dearer to God are the prayers of the poor!'

Does our estimate tally with that? Do we really see the essential glory in our brother man? We may see perhaps that he is intellectually un-distinguished and socially negligible; we notice his threadbare coat, his faulty grammar and irritating ways; we think his existence a deadly dull, monotonous, commonplace affair, unlit by any flash of colour or spark of heroism; we pity him perhaps in a superior way for his narrow horizons, his uncultured tastes, his shallow and provincial little soul. And we don't see – when we judge our brother man like that – it is *we* who are being shallow. It is *our* estimate of the human personality that is short-sighted and superficial. 'Thou hast nothing to draw with, and the well is deep.'

What is the faculty we need to draw with here, at this deep well of human personality? Is it not the insight born of sympathy, understanding, love? That was what made Jesus the most marvellous discoverer of the living waters of goodness, courage and spirituality in the least likely places.

Where the superficial observer saw nothing but worldliness, materialism, pettiness and squalor, Jesus went deeper, and found divinity. It was this love for those men and women that did that. And love is still the only vessel that can plumb the depths of this mysterious well. It is this insight born of sympathy that we need. That, and that alone, will disclose to us the hidden glories of humanity and the greatness of our brother man. It will reveal the amazing heroisms of life's common ways, the sweetness of unnumbered chivalries, and the sublimity of plain, ordinary folk who walk their ways of drudgery in high communion with the living God.

I pass on to a third deep well of mystery that meets us in this world – the mystery of *the Word of God*. What is our attitude to the Bible? Well, we are all glad, as Christian people, to know that this Book holds its place against every other as the world's best-seller: but that is not the question. We keep it in every home; we take one in our suitcase on holiday; we send copies to the troops; we like to hear of all the thousand languages and dialects into which it has been translated – but that is not the question. The question is – Is God speaking here, in this book, *to us?*

I ask one man that question, and he proceeds to tell me what the Bible is to him. Such marvellous literature, he declares. Such a fascinating compendium of poetry, history, prophecy, drama. Has not Quiller-Couch said there have been two miracles in English literature, one in verse, the other in prose: the one in verse being Shakespeare, the one in prose the Authorised Version of the Bible? 'Is that all?' I ask him. 'Yes,' he tells me, 'that is all.'

I go to another man, and ask him about the Bible. He tells me he has studied the Bible scientifically. He points out (which is perfectly true) that it is not just one book, but a whole library of books. He has discovered many interesting facts about the authorship of the Psalms. He can tell me all the theories as to who wrote Hebrews. He knows all about the complex inter-relation of the four Gospels. 'Is that all?' I ask him. 'Yes,' he tells me, 'what more do you want? That is all.'

I go to another man, and ask him about the Bible. He tells me frankly that my question does not interest him. The Bible, he says, was spoilt for him as a child. He had to learn the kings of Israel and the missionary journeys of St Paul. He has an objection to a book bound in sombre black covers, with small print, and double columns, all chopped up into verses. And when I say, 'Well, my friend, I have a lot of sympathy with these criticisms, I think the Bible has been unnecessarily spoiled for many people: but is that all?' – 'No, there's this,' he answers, 'I don't feel there is anything here in the least relevant to life. I certainly have no inclination, when reading it, to say, "This concerns me!" That's all!'

But *is* that all? Is there not another story to tell – of all the broken hearts this Book has healed, of all the shining valiant fortitude it has inspired, of all the saints it has created, of all the conversions it has achieved, of all the tears it has dried, of all the daybreak after midnight it has brought to the seeking souls of men?

A man may have the finest literary judgment, and the most sensitive critical acumen, and the most faultless canons of taste; but if that is all he can bring to the Bible, if that is how he is going to test and measure the Book, what can we say to him but this – 'Thou hast nothing to draw with, and the well is deep.'

Years ago, Thomas Huxley demonstrated scientifically that there are sounds our ears cannot hear, and whole ranges of colour that our eyes cannot see. 'The wonderful noonday silence of a tropical forest,' he wrote, 'is after all due only to the dullness of our hearing; and could our ears catch the murmurs of these tiny maelstroms as they whirl in the innumerable myriads of living cells which constitute each tier, we should be stunned as with the roar of a great city.' And if it is a scientific truth that there are sound-waves our ears can't catch, and colour-rays our eyes can't see, is it not equally true that there are spiritual overtones in the Bible we may miss completely through not being tuned in to them, not possessing the organ of spiritual radio-location?

> *The angels keep their ancient places;*
> *Turn but a stone, and start a wing!*
> *'Tis ye, 'tis your estrangèd faces,*
> *That miss the many-splendoured thing.*
>
> ~ Francis Thompson: 'The Kingdom of God' ~

It is not the Word of God that is on trial: it is the man who reads it. And if he can't find God speaking there, it is not the Bible he is judging: it is himself. He has nothing to draw with, and the well is deep.

What is the vessel that we need, to draw water at this deep well? It is a reverent and devotional spirit. It is a pure heart, and a surrendered will. 'Put off thy shoes from thy feet, for this is holy ground!' And Jesus never said – 'Blessed are the critics, for they shall find God in the Bible.' He said, 'Blessed are the pure in heart, for they shall see God' there. 'The Spirit,' declared Paul, 'searcheth all things, yea, the deep things of God.' And when we have that Spirit, then with joy can we draw water from the wells of salvation. Then, in the pages of the Bible, we meet God face to face.

> *O that we, discerning*
> *Its most holy learning,*
> *Lord, may love and fear Thee,*
> *Evermore be near Thee!*
>
> ~ Hymn 130: *CH3* ~

I have spoken of these deep wells of mystery – Nature, human personality, the Word of God – and of the vessels we require to have, to draw the living water from their depths. One final mystery let me mention – the mystery of *the Cross of Christ*. How many theologians have expounded the Cross, and reduced its meaning to some compact, tidy formula! How many sects of Christians have arisen, waving as banners their own particular dogmatic interpretations, and looking askance at those who differ! How many people have worked out to their own satisfaction a perfectly neat and logical 'plan of salvation', with everything cut-and-dried, no loose ends anywhere! And that – just imagine! – that is the line with which they propose to fathom the everlasting mystery of the Cross! Run and tell them – 'You have nothing to draw with, and the well is deep!'

On the other side, there are those who frankly declare that the Cross, to them, says nothing. A brave death, yes indeed: but has not many a martyr died as bravely? 'Why all this talk about atonement?' such a man may ask. 'I don't see the need of it. If I lead a decent life, if I am a loyal, respectable, hard-working citizen, what need have I of any atoning? That Cross to me looks remote, impersonal, irrelevant. I can't pretend it thrills me, when it doesn't.'

Ah, if that is my attitude, then the word peals forth again – 'Thou hast nothing to draw with, and the well is deep!' To the man who is satisfied, self-approving, consciously righteous, the Cross has indeed nothing to say – for the Man who died there came not to call the righteous and self-approving, but sinners and the broken-hearted, to repentance.

There is a vessel we must have, to draw from this deep well the living water – a sense of need. When I see John Bunyan's pilgrim hirpling along with a great burden on his back, I know 'there's a man to whom the Cross will speak'. When I watch Augustine growing restless and utterly disenchanted with the misery of a divided life, I say, 'there's a man who will apprehend the message of the Cross'. When I myself have tasted the frustration of broken hopes and the grief of guilty shame, then I need no text book of theology, nor manual of Church doctrine, to elucidate the meaning of Calvary. 'He died for me! Bless the Lord, O my soul; and all that is within me, bless His holy name! He died in love for me.' That is the living water of salvation.

Come, thirsty soul! The well is deep, deepest of all the thousand wells of God: but thou *hast* something to draw with. Come, take the water of life freely!

CHAPTER 24

Harvest
Thanksgiving

Say not ye, 'There are yet four months, and then cometh harvest'?
behold, I say unto you, 'Lift up your eyes, and look on the fields; for
they are white already to harvest'.   ~ St John 4: 35 ~

IT is good, in times like the present, when faith and hope are daunted by
the chaos of the world, and Cassandra voices prophesy civilisation's doom,
it is good to confront ourselves deliberately with this royal, resolute faith
of Jesus. 'Don't say, "There are months and months till harvest comes!"
Don't say nothing is happening to the soul of humanity – that the world
drags drearily from one catastrophe to another, while God sits idle, doing
nothing! Don't let that bleak doleful disillusionment paralyse your faith
or chill your soul to apathy. Your proverb says, "There are yet four long
months, and then the reaping". That depressing adage is more than half
a lie. Lift up your eyes, and look on the fields; for they are white already
to harvest!'
Let us get the context of this saying clear. Jesus was seated by Jacob's
well. The immortal conversation with the woman of Samaria was just
finished. He had seen this poor lost soul coming out of her darkness and
blindness into light and full salvation. He had seen this sudden dramatic
harvest of his toil. He had witnessed again the eternal miracle – a human
heart reborn. No wonder the Master's soul was deeply moved and stirred:
'I thank Thee, Father, Lord of heaven and earth.'
And just then came those blundering, obtuse disciples, breaking in
upon the Master's mood of rapture. 'They marvelled that He talked with
the woman.' Just think of it! 'Friend of sinners' – they should have *known*
by this time that He was Friend of sinners: every thing about Him should
have told them that; yet all they could do – dull tedious creatures – was
to marvel that He spoke to her. And then their next inept remark: 'Master,
eat.' For they had never noticed, so blind they were, the rapt expression of
His countenance. 'Master, what about some food?'

'I have meat to eat,' said Jesus, 'that ye know not of': as though to say, 'To see the glory dawning in a human soul, as I have just seen it now – that's meat enough for Me!' And then those disciples, in a perfect climax of bathos and ineptitude, 'What does He mean – "meat to eat that ye know not of"? Has someone perhaps brought Him food while we have been away?'

Then comes this dramatic message of our text. It was just as if, behind this lesser harvest of His labour, this woman who had found the light, Jesus had seen in a vision the whole of Samaria, the whole land, the whole world reaching out hands for the gift of God. If only these disciples of His could see what He saw! If only their faith in God could shake itself free from the blight of conventional half-belief, and become really live and passionate expectancy! If only men, instead of frustrating heaven's grace by the poverty of their hopes and the scepticism of their very prayers, would realise intensely that when the living God goes into action on the human scene, all things become possible! Here was a living illustration of it – this unlikeliest of creatures who had found the Kingdom, this hardened soul, this stony ground. Here was a living illustration. 'And yet you say,' went on Jesus, 'you say in the words of your proverb – "Yet four months" – that there is no hope of seeing results for ages yet to come. Nay, lift up your eyes, and look on the fields; for they are white already to harvest!'

And even as Christ said it, there occurred a kind of dramatic corroboration. The road leading out from the city to the well became suddenly full of people. The woman had carried her tidings to the market-place: 'I have found a Man who told me all that ever I did. Is not this the Messiah?' And they all came flocking out to see – to investigate this exciting piece of news for themselves, half hoping that, though incredible, it might be true, hurrying out to the well where the Master sat and watched their coming. And as He watched, 'Lift up your eyes!' He cried to His disciples, 'See what is happening! Never say that God is not working! Lift up your eyes! Look at the fields. They are white to harvest *now!*'

And today, in these troubled and chaotic times when, in many Christian souls even, faith burns dim, and hope feels crushed and baffled, today he says it still to you and me. 'Men and women, trust in the Lord! Be done with that dismal reckoning, "Yet four months, yet four years, yet four millenniums, and then perhaps God will return to a world He has deserted!" That's rank blasphemy. For God is alive, and God's Spirit mightily at work. Lift up your eyes, and look: for the fields are white already to the harvest!'

And indeed if God could bring such a sudden harvest out of the unpromising soil of this woman's wasted life; and if God could then go further and use her conversion as the starting-point of a religious movement that shook a whole neighbourhood and took a whole community by storm – do not we today, no less than those disciples, stand rebuked? What *is* our faith, when all is said and done, a vague conventional half-belief, a tame and formal assent that masks a latent scepticism – or is it, as Christ would have it, the very basis of our being and our thinking and our planning, an intense and vigorous and passionate conviction of God's grace and God's sufficiency?

There was, of course, an element of truth in this proverb the disciples quoted. Four months? Yes, four lifetimes may not see our dreams for this distracted world fulfilled. And the human heart gets restless and fidgety with the strain of waiting – waiting for achievements that will never happen in our generation, and for triumphs of brotherhood that our eyes may never see. And that strain produces scepticism, and blinds us as to what God is doing now.

It is this mood Christ here challenges, calling us to a revolutionary vitalising of our lame and languid faith. 'Lift up your eyes – and look!'

You know the prevalent mood. 'This is no time,' it says, 'to be looking for spiritual victories! This is the worst time possible for dreams of world victories! This is the worst time possible for dreams of world evangelism. This is Christianity's unpropitious hour, and all those harvest dreams are mad, and will lead to nothing but fiasco!'

Well, they have often said it. They began saying it away back at Calvary. And certainly on *that* day it sounded terribly true. There He was, a poor broken-down thing, dead on a Cross – all His followers scurrying away into their bunk-holes, and all His dreams in ruin! They didn't know. They couldn't tell that in the hour of death those eyes of Jesus were lifted up looking on the fields white to the furthest horizons with the harvests of God. Yes, and just a few days later, the first stroke of the Gospel sickle – Peter's sermon on the day of Pentecost – was to reap three thousand sheaves!

Or read a little further in the story. What an unpropitious day it seemed for the whole Christian enterprise when Saul of Tarsus, his soul seared and scalded and blistered with hatred and venom, set himself to wreck the Church's hope. No hint of harvest about that! But look at this. Acts chapter 9 begins, 'breathing out threatenings and slaughter'. Acts 9 chapter 11: 'behold, he prayeth.' Who said God couldn't bring sudden harvests? Lift up your eyes, and look! Verse 1 – 'breathing out slaughter'. Verse 11 – 'Behold, he prayeth.' Nine short verses – what a harvest-home!

Or, because the Book of Acts isn't done, come down the centuries. Because the Book of Acts is a serial story, running on and on across the ages, one thrilling instalment after another, volume upon volume of it – come down to the sixteenth century. An unpropitious time for Christians, yes – dead, barren fields, just stones and rocks. I could tell you of Martin Luther, but let me tell you of another – Francis Xavier, the first member of the Society of Jesus in the University of Paris, one of the greatest pioneer missionaries the world has ever known, driven by the love of Christ across the vast oceans to India, to Malaya, to the East Indies, to Japan, dying at last on an island at the mouth of the Canton River in China. People were saying then – 'Yet four centuries, and then cometh harvest!' Xavier said – 'The fields are white now' – and that faith led to the greatest expansion of Christians the world has ever seen since the age of the Apostles.

Or take down another volume of the Book of Acts, the close of the eighteenth century, and read there how a little group of men, meeting in a back parlour at Kettering, decided – in defiance of the stifling scepticism of the age – to found a new society to win the earth for Christ. The initial capital with which they set out to convert the world was thirteen pounds two shillings and sixpence. As if to emphasise the absurdity of the project, the next year other men, across in France, were tearing down the Cross from the top of Notre Dame Cathedral, to *show* that God was dead and Christ had ceased to count. An unpropitious day indeed! Yes. BUT – on the very day when Europe trampled on the Cross, William Carey from that back-room in Kettering set foot in India, and a new tremendous reaping was begun.

And so it goes – volume after volume of the story down the centuries, until we reach today. And perhaps we think – 'Oh, yes, God was visibly at work in ages past, but where's the sign of it now? No doubt there were great harvests once to be reaped, and may conceivably be again: but we are in a depressing interregnum between.'

I know what Christ would say to that mood. He would say, 'Lift up your eyes, and look! Never in any age have God's signs been written so clear. Lift up your eyes!'

There was a day in 1933 when an angry strident voice blared out in Europe. 'I promise you,' it said, 'I could destroy the Church in a few years. It is hollow and false and rotten through and through. One push and the whole structure will collapse. Its day is done.' That was Hitler in 1933. He tried to do it in Holland, among other places. He tried to kill the Church, and by a queer irony of fate he did the very opposite. Listen to this testimony by a leader of the Dutch Church: 'God has sent His breath on the dry bones, and we have once more a Mother Church which gives us guidance and consolation, and which holds up our hands in the struggle.'

Hitler tried to do it again in Prague. And last Sunday morning in this pulpit Dr Bednar of Prague, after six awful years at close quarters with this beastly thing, stood and told us – like a modern Apostle – that 'experience worketh hope', and that today the gates of the Divinity Faculty of the University of Prague are being besieged by three times as many applicants for the ministry as they can deal with. 'Lift up your eyes, and look on the fields!'

Indeed, the expansion of Christianity in the last quarter century, between the two World Missionary Conferences of 1910 and 1938, has been quite startling. Here is a significant thing: at the first Conference, there was just a handful of delegates from the younger Churches of Africa and the Orient, a mere sprinkling among the great mass of delegates from Europe and the West. By 1938, so great was the expansion of the younger Churches of the East, that their representatives were more than half the total. No sign of God today? Why, never have God's mighty acts been so clear! Lift up your eyes, and look! – and don't say, 'Tomorrow, and tomorrow, and tomorrow'. For the harvest is waiting now!

I wonder if, in closing, I can bring this nearer home. I wonder if I can bring it right home to your own life and mine. I wonder if God's plan for us is all in the far future tense; or if there isn't a chance of a harvest now – today.

'I have chosen you,' said Christ to His first disciples, 'that you may bring forth fruit, and that your fruit may remain.' And suddenly Christ turns from Peter, James and John, and looks full at you and me. 'I have chosen *you* to bear fruit, you to bear My harvest!' Whereupon – 'But, Christ,' we protest, 'you know me better than that! You surely know my ordinary type of nature too well to expect any striking results from me! My character was fixed and grooved and settled long ago.'

I wonder if to someone here there will come through this service the still small voice of Jesus, saying – 'Friend, God's power is nearer than you think. There are fields – in *your* life – white to harvest now. Lift up your eyes and look!' Let me leave with you the words of one who had the great experience:

> O Christ who holds the open gate,
> O Christ who drives the furrow straight,
> O Christ, the plough, O Christ, the laughter
> Of holy white birds flying after,
> Lo, all my heart's field red and torn,
> And Thou wilt bring the young green corn,
> The young green corn divinely springing,
> The young green corn for ever singing;
> And when the field is fresh and fair
> Thy blessed feet shall glitter there.
> And we will walk the weeded field,

And tell the golden harvest's yield,
The corn that makes the holy bread
By which the soul of man is fed,
The holy bread, the food unpriced,
Thy everlasting mercy, Christ.

~ John Masefield: *'The Everlasting Mercy* ~

CHAPTER 25

The Crown Rights of Jesus

'*Behold the Man!*' (St John 19: 5)
'*Behold the Lamb!*' (St John 1: 36)
'*Behold your King!*' (St John 19: 14)
'*Behold your God!*' (Isaiah 40: 9)

HERE, in these four texts, we have a special pilgrim's progress of many a soul in its spiritual apprehension of the fact of Christ. '*Behold the Man!*' That, for many of us, is the first step to Christian faith: when we are gripped by the sheer manliness of Jesus. Then, in the soul's experience, that first step has led on to a second – '*Behold the Lamb of God!*' That has come next: they have been moved to the depths by the meaning of the sacrifice of Jesus. And then, these first and second steps together have led on to a third – '*Behold your King!*' That has been the third step: they have acknowledged the sovereign rights of Jesus. And then these three steps together have led on to a fourth – '*Behold your God!*' That has been the final step: they have the Man, the Lamb, the King, the God Incarnate – that has been the pilgrim's progress of many a soul in relation to the fact of Christ. It is the road that most young folk who are out-and-out for Christ today have travelled. It is the road that many who are just feeling their way in religion are travelling now – some of them quite slowly, held back by doubts and difficulties, and refusing (all honour to them for their refusal) to be hurried or stampeded into faith, or to take their religion at second hand. It is the road the first disciples went. And it is the road that the Church now exists to point out to pilgrim souls. Let us follow this road in thought tonight.

I

Here, to begin with, was Pilate – proud, cold, haughty Roman; and on the balcony beside him this Jew from Nazareth, standing there with His hands bound with thongs, and the purple robe of mockery flung over His shoulders, and the blood from the crown of thorns streaming all over His face, and that mad mob in the street desperate to lynch Him – 'Give us Him, give us Him! We'll rend and trample on Him!' – and the Prisoner, through it all, motionless, silent, with His eyes right up to God! And suddenly Pilate, flinging out his right arm and pointing – 'Behold!' he cries, shouting above the clamour of the crowd, *'Behold the Man!'* Ah, Pilate, truer word you never spoke – *'the Man!'*

Reading recently in *Lawrence of Arabia* – that great and fascinating story – I came upon this sentence: 'No man,' it said, 'could lead the Arabs unless he ate the rank's food, wore their clothes, lived level with them, and yet appeared better in himself.' To that tonight, I should like to add this: No one could lead the hosts of humanity unless he mingled with the rank and file, wore their human frame – bone of their bone, flesh of their flesh – living level with them all the time, and yet somehow beating them at their own game, beating them for sheer downright manliness! Isn't that the Christ?

Do you remember Alfred Lord Tennyson? 'Strong Son of God!' he begins, and goes on … 'Thou seemest human and divine,/The highest, holiest *manhood* Thou!'

The French critic, Renan, said something different. 'In Jesus,' he said, 'tenderness of heart was transformed into infinite sweetness, vague poetry, universal charm.' What a travesty of the truth! Behold not the soft, sweet, sentimental dreamer, not the vague ineffective romanticist – behold the Man!

I wonder – could we characterise this essential manliness of Jesus in a single phrase? Suppose we try. Suppose we say it was the manliness of *a chainless soul*. You remember Emily Brontë's cry as her sad, chequered life was running out towards its end:

> *Yea, as my swift days near their goal,*
> *   'Tis all that I implore:*
> *In life and death a chainless soul,*
> *   With courage to endure.*

A chainless soul! A fearless conscience! That was Christ.

There was a day when the devil came. 'If you bow down to me, Jesus,' he said, 'if you'll consent to make a bargain with me, I'll see that the kingdoms of the world and the glory of them are yours tomorrow. But if not – if not …' (and the shadow of the Cross suddenly blackened the sky) 'if not, then …. '

'Stop!' cried Jesus, and there was God's thunder in His voice, 'Stop! I know you! I defy you! I'll die sooner than consent!' Chainless, fearless soul of Christ – that we might learn of Thee!

Have you ever thought of this? That dramatic picture Jesus once drew – the rains descending, and the floods rolling in from the sea, and the winds blowing and beating upon a house: that house was – what? *The soul of Christ Himself,* bashed and battered by the storm, swept by whirlwinds of human hate, blown and beaten upon by every subtle wind that ever blew from hell's wide open mouth, and – the end of the story? The house fell not, for it was founded upon rock! What a chainless soul was Christ's!

No wonder George Matheson, the blind poet-preacher, author of 'O love that wilt not let me go' – no wonder he could say: 'Son of Man, whenever I doubt of life, I think of Thee!'

'Behold the Man!' cried Pilate, and his words have come echoing down the centuries, have been taken up by soul after soul, have been cried aloud by the spirit of youth, catching sight of Jesus from afar, have swelled into a mighty volume of adoring praise – 'Behold the Man!' And that discovery is the first step to full faith in the Redeemer.

II

After that first stage of the road there comes a second. 'Behold the Lamb of God!' said John the Baptist. This is going deeper. This is more than manliness. This is sacrifice. This is suffering for others. This is love sweating blood. This is love confronting all the world's sorrow, shame and sin, and taking it upon itself. *'Behold the Lamb of God!'*

What is love? You can't define it. It has never by any poet or prophet or lover been defined. But if you ask me what is its central characteristic, I should say that it is *its readiness to take things upon itself.*

When Charles Dickens' fine old Yarmouth fisherman went out after his erring child in her shame, his Emily who had been the light of his life, went out searching for her, murmuring all the time, 'I'll go till I drop dead to find her' – what is it that you read on that drawn, haggard face? It is this – 'He is bearing her sin: he is *taking it upon himself.*'

When General Booth in his young days first felt the call of the slums, and the underworld and all life's pitiful wreckage; when he wrote, describing his feelings then, 'I hungered for Hell, I pushed into the very midst of it, I loved it because of the souls I saw' – what do the gallant words mean but this – he was *taking it on himself?*

When Mildred Cable goes out carrying the Cross into the wilds of the Gobi desert, when out of love for those souls in darkness she lives with them and makes their lot her own, when she comes back and stands in this pulpit (as she stood one day two years ago) and declares that she and her friends could never have endured it unless they had sung each day this prayer –

> Guide me, O Thou great Jehovah,
>   Pilgrim through this barren land;
> I am weak, but Thou art mighty;
>   Hold me with Thy powerful hand –   ~ Hymn 89: CH3 ~

when you see a soul like that, is not your first thought this she is bearing humanity's burden, she is *taking it upon herself?*

And when now our thoughts rise beyond all those sacrificial spirits of this earth, when our eyes pass beyond that host of gallant vicarious souls to Him who marches at their head, when we see Jesus making our burden His burden, our uttermost disgrace His disgrace, our deadly doom His doom, when we see (in Frederick Myers' words) the 'Desperate tides of the whole great world's anguish/Forced through the channels of a single heart', what can we do then but cry adoringly, 'Oh Christ, our Christ, Thou hast *taken it upon thyself! Behold the Lamb of God!'*

What would you say is the finest passage in the whole range of English literature? The late Professor Saintsbury was once asked that question, and he gave his decision immediately. He chose the passage in the Song of Solomon (8: 6-7): 'Set me as a seal upon thine heart, and as a seal upon thine arm: for love is strong as death; many waters cannot quench love, neither can the floods drown it.' The finest bit of the English language? Ah, but infinitely more than that! It is God's great beating heart made bare in Christ – love stronger than death, unquenched by floods of sin, undrowned by torrents of wildest agony!

'Oh,' cried old John Duncan, thinking of the price Christ had to pay, 'oh, it was terrible, it was terrible, *it was damnation! And – He took it lovingly!'*

I think I can understand why it was that Denney, staunch rigid Protestant as he was, could yet declare, speaking one day to his students about the newer theology that was trying to construct a bloodless Gospel, and the newer theologians who were forgetting the Cross, could declare, 'If I had to choose between being such a one, and being a Roman priest holding up a crucifix to the eyes of a dying man and saying "God loves like that", I had rather be the priest – every time!'

Yes, indeed! For what I see in the Cross, and what you see in the Cross, is not only Someone summoning us to play the man in this hard, difficult world: it is Someone caring enough for us to take everything on to Himself, and to sink His very life in the cause of our happiness and peace. 'Behold the Man' – yes, manhood to perfection, manliness incarnate: but more, but deeper, but far more moving and subduing – Behold the sacrifice! Behold love's willing agony! 'Behold the Lamb of God!' It is the second stage on the road to full faith in the Redeemer.

III

Now I am going to put this to you. If a man has taken the first step, and if he has then gone on and taken the second step, then he is bound in honour – sooner or later – to take the third step. If he has been fascinated by the sheer manliness of Jesus, and if he has been moved to the depths by the sacrifice of Jesus, then (if he is in earnest about this thing) he is bound to go on, and surrender to the sovereign rights of Jesus. 'Behold the Man!' 'Behold the Lamb of God!' What then? Add these two things together and they produce the most terrific challenge on this earth – *'Behold your King!'*

The writer to the Hebrews one day had a great vision, and he took up his pen and wrote the vision down. 'We see Jesus,' he wrote, 'crowned with glory and honour!' I am going to ask you tonight – *do* we? 'We see Jesus crowned' – do we? If He were really crowned in the heart and affection of the world, would there be any war? Would there be any slums? Would there be any running after salacious plays and films and novels? 'We see Jesus crowned' – look into your own heart, and then tell God: Is it *true?*

There is a strange story from long ago which says that when Henry V, that gallant, well-loved monarch of England, was ill and near his end, he awoke from sleep one day to see his boy – Henry VI who was to be – trying on the crown. And the dying man raised himself and said, 'Wait a little, son! Wait until I am dead. While I live, that crown is mine!' A strange, pathetic little story – yes; but here is a King who never dies, here is the deathless King of the ages; and I say to you young folk here tonight – while Jesus lives, let the crown be His!

And you know what that means. It is not just a form of words. You know what it works out at, down in the real arena of life – some temptation that has got to be broken, some slackness there to be taken in hand, some friendship to be radically altered, some difficult decision to be made, some strenuous, sacrificial service accepted. You know what it works out at in terms of your own life.

And you know that whatever your difficulties about religion may be; whatever your criticisms (many of them perfectly justified, I know) about us blundering folk who profess Christ in this world, and misrepresent

Him; whatever your dislike of the slow, sometimes painfully slow, machinery of the Church that bears His name, and of its delays in giving His will effect – whatever your feelings on all these matters may be, here is one challenge that none of these things touch, one challenge that remains and will remain through everything: *What about Christ and your own life?* Has He yet got the throne? Are you prepared to take the final step, the step of a soul's bounden honour? 'Behold the Man! Behold the Lamb of God! And therefore, soul of mine, *behold your King!'*

Tennyson has given us a wonderful picture of England long ago, waking from its pagan darkness and horrible nightmare dreams at the trumpet summons of King Arthur. Down all the roads of the land they came, flocking to Arthur's standard; and the song of their march was this:

> *Blow trumpet! He will lift us from the dust.*
> *Blow trumpet! Live the strength and die the lust!*
> *Blow through the living world – 'Let the King reign.'*
>
> ~ Morte d'Arthur' ~

Have we the will and the grace to make *that* our attitude to Jesus?

They knew, those men of Arthur's, what it might cost them. They knew that, if they once swore their fealty, he would hold them to it forever. And yet their song was this –

> *Strike for the King and die! And if thou diest,*
> *The king is King, and ever wills the highest.*
> *Blow through the living world – 'Let the King reign.'*

Have we vision enough to see that whatever conscience and Christ may cost us, whatever the shrinking of our hearts from full surrender, this settles it – 'The King is King, and ever wills the highest.' He has a claim on you. By His perfect manhood, by His sacrificial suffering, He has a claim on you. Behold the Man! Behold the Lamb of God! And therefore (soul of mine – stand to attention!) *behold your King!*

IV

Last of all and most of all – 'Behold your God!'

What is this Christianity I have been speaking of tonight? It is not just loving your neighbour, or observing the Golden Rule, or living decently and respectably. It is the message that God has come right down into human life. God has broken through. God has acted. God has come.

Did you think Christ might have His day and cease to be? Is there a chance that Nazi Germany might root out Christ's religion? Yes, if Christ is just another voice appealing to us to love one another. But no, if He is God in action!

Don't be too obsessed by the human actors in this drama. Get your eyes right off Hitler and Mussolini occasionally. 'Say unto the cities of Judah, "Behold your God!"'

God has come! God is here! At any moment, He may break through again. That is the world's hope tonight. That is *the* hope of every contrite heart, the joy of all the meek'. 'Behold the Man! Behold the Lamb! Behold your King! Behold your God!' Let Him hear you say it now in the secret of your heart – 'O Jesus, forever I adore Thee! My Lord and my God!'

CHAPTER 26

Our Spiritual Pilgrimage

I am not ashamed of the gospel of Christ: for it is the power of God unto salvation.

~ Romans 1: 16 ~

THAT fine man of letters G. K. Chesterton, who in his time bulked largely – both physically and intellectually – on the literary scene, was once asked by an agnostic critic: 'Aren't you ashamed in this modern world to go on being a Christian? Ashamed of the outmoded absurdities of belief?'

'Ashamed?' Chesterton flamed back, 'my good sir, let me tell you this: so far from being ashamed, *I'm positively prancing with belief!*'

A lovely phrase, isn't it? – 'prancing with belief!'

At any rate, it points right at the heart of a most vital issue for all of us who are Christians today: *our right to believe,* our right to be Christians unabashed.

Let me in a word outline the path for our thoughts to travel. Quite briefly, it is this. Our encounter with Christianity, our spiritual pilgrimage in matters of belief, tends to follow certain clearly marked phases, and to pass through more or less definite stages.

I

First, there often comes a stage of *acquiescent acceptance:* the religion of our early years. Many of you here today have probably known the name of Jesus almost as long as you have known your own. We have been born in a country which has had a long-accumulated heritage of Christian teaching, and therefore still – thank God – has something of Christ in its life, something of Christ's Spirit in the atmosphere and climate of its thought. We heard the Gospel stories before we ever learnt to read. We sang in Church and Sunday School some of the most stupendous doctrines of the faith – as in those lines of 'Once in royal David's city': 'He came down to earth from heaven/Who is God and Lord of all' – not realising the sheer dynamite in such a statement. In the shelter of our early homes, we took these things for granted. They were just there – part of our inheritance – accepted on authority. That is often the first phase of an encounter with the faith: acquiescent acceptance.

II

But now upon that first phase there is apt to supervene a second. We go out into the world. The faith we have inherited is subjected to various strains and stresses. Life batters our acquiescence, besieges our assurance, tears down our spiritual equanimity. And you know what often happens then: that distressingly familiar phase distrustful of all inherited religion, uncertain of the relevance of the faith, *ashamed of the Gospel.*

There are three distinct factors in this experience. One is *emotional:* a mood of reaction, a kind of mild revolt, an almost instinctive breakaway from everything established and traditional. At this stage, the very fact that a thing is traditional biases the mind against it; it must be dull, we assume, tedious, respectable. The whole set-up of the thing irritates us, and an iconoclastic passion begins to smoulder. The Church, just because it is the organised Church, becomes an easy target for our criticism; the Christian faith, because it is reputed to be dogmatic, inflames the forces of revolt. Far be it from me to disparage or denounce this rebel mood: I believe – in fact I know – that very often the Spirit of God is at work in it. But sometimes it does end in this: ashamed of the Gospel.

The second factor in this developing experience is *intellectual.* Out from the shelter of home you meet all kinds of people with a vast variety of beliefs. You are thrust daily into contact with people whose beliefs differ strenuously from your own. There opens up before you the world of science, with its passion to prove everything, to believe nothing except on proof; and perhaps the question rises – Can I maintain at once my scientific rectitude and my religious faith? You become increasingly aware of the existence of great systems of thought diametrically opposed to Christianity. Above all, there confronts you the contrast – the glaring, shouting contrast – between the immense material forces of history on the one hand and the pathetic-looking weakness of the resources of Jesus Christ on the other. 'What a credibility gap!'

That was the nerve of the problem for Paul himself. He was writing here to Rome. We know something about first century Rome – its learning, art and wealth, its intellectual sophistication, its superb magnificent organisation, its glamour of world-conquest, its high imperial disdain. 'What have I to set against that?' Paul may have wondered. 'Is it not quite mad, preposterous, to go campaigning there? How they will scoff at this penniless Jew with his new religion! And what a religion! A Man upon a Cross – think of it, a Cross – in the eyes of those Romans the last symbol of utter degradation. And a Resurrection – can't you just hear, Paul, the shouts of amused derision?'

Whether or not it occurred to Paul – that momentary doubt, that shadow of hesitation, that temptation to be ashamed – it certainly occurs to us. It is *the* problem today for multitudes. And now that man's scientific ingenuity controls incalculable power, it is more the problem than ever. The contrast – the terrific, shattering contrast – between the might of the forces of secularism and the weakness of the enterprise of Christ. How can we believe, men ask, that this Cross on a Judean hill is the hope of the future? How can we believe that the coming of the Kingdom by an act of God is any more than a pleasing fiction? How can we believe that Christ is risen and has abolished death and brought life and immortality to light? 'They have taken away my Lord, and I know not where they have laid Him.'

> Comes faint and far Thy voice
>   From vales of Galilee;
> Thy vision fades in ancient shades;
>   How should we follow Thee?

Credibility gap indeed! Sadly and reluctantly they have come to that: ashamed of the Gospel.

We have seen, then, two factors in this developing experience – emotional and intellectual. But there is a third factor that enters into it – the *moral* factor.

You don't need to have travelled very far through life before encountering the disillusionment of experience. No doubt, to begin with, we are sure we are capable of making life full and rich and wonderful, a big, clean chivalrous game. And indeed life has its thrilling splendours, its marvellous good times, its generous idealisms and ample satisfactions. But the years pass, and we are not so sure. Things go wrong with the plan. The shadow of disenchantment falls. The whole world seems to be a hideous moral tangle, and we feel oppressed by our futility to do anything at all about it.

And the matter is more personal than that. For if it is true, as William Wordsworth dreamt, that we come at the first 'trailing clouds of glory from God who is our home', the tragedy is that so often the glory gets trailed in the dust of moral mediocrity and in the mire of real defeat. Things happen, and leave a mark, and we know they ought never to have been. And then, because that mood of disenchantment has laid hold of us, we grow slack about our prayers; and because we have grown slack about prayer, the sense of God grows dim within our souls; and because the sense of God is dimmed, we find it harder to believe; and because belief loses grip, we drift towards doubt and denial; and we end up ashamed of the Gospel.

Let us see the point we have reached. We have been analysing a spiritual pilgrimage in relation to the Christian faith, and have distinguished two phases that often (not invariably, of course, but quite often) mark that pilgrimage: the first, a stage of acquiescent acceptance; the second, a stage where in some degree we are ashamed of faith – and this (as we have now seen) may be either emotionally, intellectually or morally conditioned.

III

But now, will you notice this? Upon that second stage there may supervene – and very often in the providence of God there does supervene – a third. There comes a point where we are suddenly *ashamed of being ashamed*. Where once we revolted against our religion, we now revolt against our irreligion. We are disillusioned of our own disillusionment. We are 'visited [as G. K. Chesterton said happened to himself] by the first wild doubts of doubt'. We look at the sceptic and the self-styled realist who have discarded the unseen and eternal from their thinking. We suddenly realise that whoever may have found the secret of existence, they have not. We wonder how we could ever have toyed with a view of life so callow and boring and dull. We can't bear to be identified with it any longer. We are ashamed of being ashamed.

Now it is interesting and exciting to observe how the same three factors we have already met reappear in this stage of experience.

There is the *emotional* factor. I may discard the faith of my fathers, may tell myself – 'I am going to live on a frankly secular basis.' But what am I to do if one day, when I have settled down in my confident impregnable secularism, there happens to me what Robert Browning described in 'Bishop Blougram's Apology'?

Just when we are safest, there's a sunset-touch,
A fancy from a flower-bell, someone's death ....
And that's enough for fifty hopes and fears ....
To rap and knock and enter in the soul.

What am I to do if there rises to confront me the reproachful, loving face of Christ Himself? Mark you, in a world where Christ is risen and alive, that is always liable to happen – I am speaking what I know. What am I to do if one day across the path of my apostasy and rebellion there falls the shadow of a Cross, and I hear a voice saying, 'This have I done for you: what have you done for Me?'

What *can* I do then but cry, 'O God, forgive me! I have been ashamed of that. I have been living and thinking and acting as if that glory of Thine on the face of Jesus were a common thing, and not the fairest among ten thousand. O God, forgive me – I'm ashamed of being ashamed!'

But if there is an emotional factor in this experience, there is also an *intellectual*. Suppose that, finding faith difficult, I react into scepticism. Have I then got rid of my difficulties? By no means. On the contrary, I have added to them. I have actually made them worse. For consider the alternatives. Man, says faith, is a child of God. Nothing of the kind, says materialism, he is the product of blind chance. Human life, says faith, is under the directive control of the loving purpose of an eternal Father. What nonsense, says the secularist. It is 'the outcome of accidental collocations of atoms'. These are the precise words of one of our leading secularists. Now just think! The psalms of David, the confessions of Augustine, the music of Beethoven, the prayers of my mother, the love in the eyes of my own child, 'the outcome of accidental collocations of atoms'!? Tell me – which view makes sense and rationality? Is it Christ's, when He assures me that life is ultimately spiritual and the training-ground for immortality; or that secularist's, who would have me believe there is nothing here but physical circumstance, and the Kingdom of God is a myth, and we die like dogs in the end? One of them is *wrong* – Christ or that critic. One is mistaken. *Which?* Not Christ, my soul, not Christ! It is Christ who interprets the universe; it is Jesus who is the most rational fact this mad earth has ever seen. And when I see that, it is the end of all my callow scepticism; and I cry – 'O God, forgive me; I'm ashamed of having been ashamed!'

We have seen the emotional and intellectual factors in this experience. What of the *moral* factor? One thing is clear: for Paul himself this was the decisive factor. For look what he says: 'I am not ashamed of the Gospel.' Why? *'Because it is the power of God.'* It does things. It goes to work, changes lives. It can change the world.

And with that, I think, Paul turned and looked at Rome again. If for a moment Rome, with its magnificence and sophistication and disdain, had threatened to daunt and paralyse him, he was past that now. In a flash he saw the truth. There was a dynamism in the Gospel which Rome with all its might knew nothing about. What could Rome do to change men's lives? To deliver them from the sin that rots the soul and imperils its eternity? To keep them sane and steady and serene amid the crash of empires and the wrecks and ruins of the world? Nothing. And Paul found a force that could do all these things. 'I am not ashamed of the Gospel, ,for it is the illimitable energy of the divine erupting into human history: 'It is the power of God!'

I beg you today – don't be put off Christianity because it is a still small voice compared with the shouting and the tumult of the raucous ideologies which bestride the world. And don't be put off it because some Christians are unworthy; or some church services dull; or some unimaginative blunderers have domesticated the living spirit of religion, and tamed the lyrical elation out of it, till nothing is left but the quintessence of formalism. Get to the real issue, the marrow of the Gospel. It is good news, not good advice. It is the very news that you who are discouraged, or defeated, or at the end of your tether, are needing most of all today. Its characteristic words are power, strength, victory.

> O Love of God! O sin of man!
> In this dread act your strength is tried:
> And victory remains with Love.   ~ Hymn 243: *CH3* ~

Paul in one place, not content with the verb 'to conquer', goes on to coin a new word: 'to more than conquer.' 'We are more than conquerors through Him who loved us.' That is characteristic Christianity. And when it breaks on me, it is the end of being shamefaced or browbeaten by a scoffing world. Ashamed of the Gospel? God forgive me. I'm ashamed of being ashamed.

IV

Let me finish with this. We have distinguished those three attitudes to faith: acquiescent acceptance; ashamed of the Gospel; and then, ashamed of being ashamed. Have I been describing the spiritual pilgrimage of someone here today? I would urge you to follow the logic of your position one step further – the fourth and final stage – *an ambassador unashamed!*

> Saviour, if of Zion city
>   I through grace a member am,
> Let the world deride or pity,
>   I will glory in Thy name!
>
>   ~ Hymn 421: *CH3* ~

I am not suggesting we should go about thrusting our personal religion at people. But I *am* saying there is something wrong if you and I can go upon our way day after day and no one ever 'take knowledge of us that we have been with Jesus'. There is something far wrong if we who are His followers are so indistinguishable that it never even occurs to the world to taunt or reproach us with His Name. The real problem for Christ today is not the hardened sinner or the charming pagan or the blazing red-hot atheist – it is the apathetic Christian. Surely to live at a time like this and never give any inkling that in Christ we have found the secret – that is what crucifies the Son of God afresh. The Gospels say that 'Jesus wept'. Sometimes I can almost hear Him weeping still today. Why? Has He not got over the death of Lazarus yet? No – He is weeping for those who will not stand with Him in the light. It is no time this for timid, apologetic discipleship, incoherent, inarticulate – 'Son of man, stand upon thy feet!'

The great slogans of today are revolution and revolt. If only some of those who are loudest with such slogans would realise that the greatest revolution that ever takes place is when a human being revolts against the dictatorship of self, and surrenders to the Mastership of Christ!

I may be tempted often enough to dim down the light of faith and play for the safety of a dumb conventional religion. But, thank heaven, there is a Voice that won't ever let me forget – You are Christ's man, and that is *the one great fact*. Let the world deride or pity. I will glory in His Name!

So let Isaac Watts, whom our text inspired to write one of his greatest hymns, sum it all up for us in his familiar, challenging lines:

Jesus, my Lord! I know His Name,
His Name is all my boast;
Nor will He put my soul to shame,
Nor let my hope be lost.

I know that safe with Him remains,
Protected by His power,
What I've committed to His trust,
Till the decisive hour. ~ Hymn 591: *CH3* ~

And to His dear redeeming Name be all the glory.

CHAPTER 27

The Story of Two Refugees

Greet Priscilla and Aquila my helpers in Christ Jesus: Who have for my life laid down their own necks ... likewise greet the Church that is in their house.
~ Romans 16: 3-5 ~

THE refugee problem is no new development. It was particularly acute at the beginning of the Christian era. Here is a sentence – a deeply significant sentence – from the Latin historian Suetonius, which contains incidentally one of the earliest references to Jesus of Nazareth to be found in secular literature: 'The Emperor Claudius expelled the Jews from Rome, because they were persistently making disturbances, a certain Christus being the moving spirit.' There you have the great historian's account of the first stirrings of Christianity in the Jewish ghetto of the Imperial City, and the consequent aggravation of the problem of refugees.

Now turn to the Book of Acts 18:1-3, and see how the sacred writer and the pagan historian corroborate each other. Here is St Luke, the writer of the Acts, speaking:

After these things Paul departed from Athens, and came to Corinth; And found a certain Jew named Aquila, born in Pontus, lately come from Italy, with his wife Priscilla; (because that Claudius had commanded all Jews to depart from Rome:) and came unto them. And because he was of the same craft, he abode with them, and wrought: for by their occupation they were tent-makers.

Here, then, were these two Jewish refugees in Corinth, banished by the racial decrees of a first century Fascist government. But God – who is in a very special sense the God of all exiled, lonely creatures – God in His Providence caused their wandering road and the road of the great Gentile Apostle to intersect; and from that moment their destiny was secured, and their future career settled. So I want you to look at this godly couple this morning: I think the subject will repay our study.

I

First, I would ask you to notice this – *how Providence can use the most trivial circumstances of our life for the most far-reaching results.*

What brought Aquila and St Paul together in the first instance was not the fact that they were both interested in religion – nothing so central as that – it was simply the fact that they both happened to be tent-makers. If it hadn't been for that apparently irrelevant detail, they would probably never have met at all. Aquila and his wife had set up in Corinth in a small way in the tent-making line; and Paul, whose custom it was on his journeyings to support himself by manual labour, had gone into their shop one day seeking a job, asking if they had room for an extra hand. And it was that 'chance' meeting, as we would call it, that purely commercial relationship, that changed the world for these two refugees, and eventually was to write their names imperishably in the records of the Church and the scriptures of the Word of God.

See, then, how the details of life can be used by Providence for mighty results. Indeed, I sometimes wonder whether, from God's point of view, *anything* is a detail? I fancy most of us would be ready enough to see God's hand in the great events of our lives – we believe that in a general sort of way and on large-scale issues God does guide us; but perhaps we are inclined to feel that the great mass of trivial occurrences that make up our ordinary days are really devoid of any spiritual significance, and too small to be within the interest or even cognisance of God. I wonder? You get a postcard one day, a printed invitation with a penny stamp, asking you to a gathering of some kind, and you throw it aside and forget all about it – a mere detail. Some days later you are clearing out your desk, and the postcard turns up: you are just on the point of dropping it into the waste-paper basket when you notice the date – the gathering you have been invited to is that very day. 'Oh well,' you say, 'I've nothing better to do: perhaps I *will* go after all – anyway, it's a mere detail', and into the wastepaper basket the postcard goes. But you go to the gathering; and there perhaps you meet someone who is going to be the biggest fact in your life ever after. Is anything a detail? If we could see life from God's side, might we not perhaps discover that there are no such things?

You know, so many men and women feel that the whole of life is made up of details – writing letters, catching buses, adding up figures, running a house, mending clothes, cooking meals – nothing but wearisome details all the time. But what if, from God's side of things, nothing is a detail? Then doesn't life become suddenly packed with meaning?

Suppose you get someone to come to church one Sunday. Well, there is nothing dramatic or out of the ordinary about that. But suppose in that service God speaks to the friend you have brought, suppose that years afterwards he marries and has a son, suppose he teaches his son religion, suppose the son grows up and becomes a missionary, or a great Christian statesman, or a Christian industrial leader with a vast influence for good – and it all started from what seems so trivial, your chance invitation to someone, one Sabbath years before!

So I repeat, you'll be using language wrongly, in a world where God reigns and where all the threads of cause and effect are worked together so elaborately, you'll be using language wrongly if you call anything a detail. Was it a detail that Aquila and Priscilla were tent-makers to trade? Was it a detail that Paul, when he reached Corinth, was hard up and out of a job? Was it a detail that, on that very morning, perhaps they had just had the sign outside their shop painted? Was it a detail that Paul went for a walk down that street? Ah, God can use the trivial circumstances of life for the most far-reaching results.

II

The second truth I find in the story of these two refugees is this: *no human love is so rich and strong as that which has a spiritual basis.* Here were a husband and wife utterly at one in the Lord. Aquila and Priscilla were at one about the great central realities. They were at one in their sense of the unseen and eternal. They were at one in their vision of God. They had taken each other as a gift out of God's good hand. God gave their mutual love significance.

Isn't this a matter that needs emphasising today, when the basic spiritual realities are so widely ignored, and when it is considered so much more important to be able to talk cleverly and to live pleasurably than to do justly and to love mercy and to walk very, very humbly before God?

I have seen young people setting out in life together, starting a home together, with no spiritual foundation to it, no acknowledgment of the things that pre-eminently matter, no settling of their love against a conscious background of God. And the tragedy of that is not only the risk and precariousness of the adventure they are embarking on: the tragedy is what they are losing without knowing it. They know something of the thrill of having found one another: but they don't know that there could be twice that thrill in that love of theirs, if only they could see God in the heart of it. Leslie Stephen the agnostic, after his wife's death, was writing about her to a friend: 'I thank,' he wrote, and then suddenly remembering that being an agnostic he had no God to thank, he drew a dash on the paper. 'I thank —— that I have ever known her!' How terribly much love stands to lose by that! How gloriously much it gains by being founded on the eternal spiritual realities! St Bernard said that 'the love of Jesus, what it is, none but His loved ones know'. Might we not add that the love of two people for each other, what *that* is, and what that can be, none can ever know except those who love each other, as Aquila and Priscilla did, *in the Lord?* Those of us whom some kind Providence has blessed with a love like that ought indeed to rejoice in the Lord, and to remember that 'unto whomsoever much is given, of them shall be much required'.

III

The third truth I find in the story of these two refugees is this – *that woman-hood has a very special vocation in the work of the Kingdom*. It cannot fail to strike you as significant that, throughout the New Testament references to this godly couple, Priscilla is nearly always mentioned first: Priscilla, an endearing diminutive of Prisca. That suggests – doesn't it? – that hers was the more outstanding intellect, real ability, the stronger character, the deeper spiritual insight. There is a theory, widely held amongst competent New Testament investigators, that the Epistle to the Hebrews, which stands anonymously in our Bible, was written by Priscilla. I can't go into the arguments for that just now, but it is good to know that one of the great documents of the New Testament is quite possibly from a woman's hand. In any case, her story reminds us, not only of what womanhood has owed to the Christian Gospel, but also of what the Christian Gospel has owed to womanhood.

Again and again during Jesus' ministry, the men on whom He might have counted failed Him. But you'll search the Gospels in vain for any record of a woman who ever failed Him – there wasn't one. When the disciples were all cowering behind bolted doors, the women were last at the cross, and first at the tomb. And it wasn't only in courage that they surpassed the twelve: their spiritual insight, their understanding of what Jesus was trying to do – that, too, was deeper. What a sorry figure the men cut that day when Mary came with her alabaster box! How much nearer to the Kingdom of God was Pilate's wife than Pilate himself! Or pass to the Acts and the Epistles: it was a woman, Lydia of Philippi, who was the first Christian convert in Europe; it was her house that was the first European Church. Most of the martyrs' names on the tombs in the Roman catacombs are women's names. And all through the centuries, through the pieties of the Middle Ages, and the struggles of the Reformation, and the desperate heroisms of the Covenanters, right down to the present day – where would the Church have been without its women, who, like their forerunners of Gospel days, have companied with Jesus and 'ministered to Him of their substance'? Qualities like sacrifice, and sensitivity, and spiritual insight, and steadfastness – if they mean anything, womanhood's vocation in the Kingdom of God stands sure forever.

IV

The fourth truth I find in the story of these refugees is this – *the urgency and honour of Christian service*. See how the great Apostle describes them here in Romans: 'my helpers in Christ Jesus', or, as the Revised Version has it, 'my fellow-workers in Christ'. Priscilla and Aquila were lay people, but not passive Christians, leaving the main Christian issues to be the province of a few enthusiasts. They weren't a dead-weight for the Church to carry: they carried the Church. They were workers.

Is our personal religion like that? Are we putting ourselves into it? Are we, by zeal and wholehearted co-operation, giving the whole thing a lift? I don't only mean, are we taking part in Church activities? It is so much wider than that. But are we remembering our duty to those of whom Jesus said, 'Inasmuch as ye do it unto one of the least of these, ye do it unto Me'? Are we active in Christian witness? Are we working at prayer? That is a thing we don't always realise – prayer is work, real strenuous work that makes a draught in a man's spiritual vitality. Prayer does things. Are we active in that? Are we workers?

And notice what Paul says: 'My fellow-workers in Christ.' Don't you think it must have inspired these two refugees enormously, to be called 'fellow-workers' with the great Apostle? It's one of the constant inspirations of our Christian calling – the society, the fellowship, we enter in this business of the Christian life – apostles, heroes, martyrs, the Columbas, the Luthers, the Latimers, the Livingstones, the Chalmers – fellow-workers with them! Are we earning our right to stand in that great succession?

Above all, there is this – 'Fellow-workers *in Christ.*' 'Share *with Me*,' says Jesus. And I'm sure that if ever the Christian adventure were to lose its zest and savour, if ever the burden and the sweat of it were beginning to feel sheer drudgery and weariness – I am sure that this would pull me up and set things right: 'Fellow-workers *with Christ.*' 'Partners with Me,' says Jesus. The urgency and the honour of the humblest Christian service! 'Your labour is not in vain *in the Lord.*'

Still another truth emerges from the story of these refugees and it is *the necessity of living dangerously for Christ*. 'Greet Priscilla and Aquila, who have for my life laid down their own necks' – Paul's vivid way of saying that at some critical moment, perhaps during the riots at Ephesus, his two friends had risked their lives for him. Years after, Paul looking back before execution, saw the scenes of his life again. There were one or two to whom he waved a final greeting – among them Priscilla and Aquila. Tradition has it that they were ultimately beheaded. Certainly they had the martyr's spirit.

I don't think we should assume that the days of living dangerously for Christ are ended. And, in other subtler ways, the hazard of the faith of Jesus is with us still. It *is* a hazardous thing believing in God enough to gamble your whole philosophy of life upon Him against all appearances. It *is* a hazardous thing trying to run your life by Christ's spiritual standards in an unspiritual world. Devotion to Christ for St Francis, the most fastidious young man in Assisi, meant kissing a leper. For Shaftesbury, it meant risking an illustrious career. For a young man today, it may mean speaking out where he would much rather keep silent. For another, it may mean losing the goodwill of some who were once his friends. For another, it may mean the surrender of a life of ease, and instead toiling terribly, and life being burnt up in the consuming fire of God. Not 'safety first', but 'Christ first', is the true Christian's motto; and in the twentieth century, no less than in the first, it can be a dangerous thing – dangerous to comfort, and tranquillity, and self-regard – being friends with Jesus Christ. 'Who for My sake – for Christ's sake – have laid down their own necks.' Have we the spirit to hazard things for Christ?

V

One final truth I find in the story of our two refugees, and it is this – *the essential unity of the Church and the home, the altar and the hearth.* 'Greet Priscilla and Aquila – likewise greet *the Church that is in their house.'* That striking phrase reminds us that the early Church had no buildings like this to meet in: persecution and poverty made the provision of separate buildings for worship quite impossible; and for generations the Christian Church consisted of groups of Christians meeting in private houses. Aquila and Priscilla, having returned to Rome on the expiry of the decree of banishment, put a room of their house at the disposal of the Christians there: hence Paul sends greetings to 'the Church that is in their house'.

But don't you feel that this phrase is symbolic of a deeper truth? 'The Church that is in their house' – could that be said of us? Are the two things – church and home, the altar and the hearth, sacred and secular, worship and work – are they so unified in our experience? Or is it not a fact that these two aspects of life, which Scripture always persists in regarding as one, too often today have a real cleft between them, and seem to belong to different worlds?

We speak about 'going to church'. We enter the doors of a church building on a Sunday morning, and hear the familiar words – 'This is none other than the House of God, and the gate of heaven.' We go there, it may be, seeking refuge from the burden and heat of the day, a brief hour's escape from the toil and moil of ordinary living. We go to the sanctuary to meet God. But believe me, the only question that ultimately matters is this – when we leave the sanctuary, do we take God with us?

This little world of spiritual fellowship here, and that other great complex world that is waiting for us just beyond the threshold of the sanctuary – are these, for us, a radical antithesis; or are they, as the men of Scripture saw them, essentially one? Can we, turning from the altar to the hearth, pause there and say, 'This, too, is the House of God; this is the gate of heaven'?

We have spent this hour together here; and now our worship is finished, and we go our several ways again. But let us go rejoicing and gladly confident in this – that, whatever the toils and tasks of the days ahead, the Christ who has met us here will be with us there – that Christ whose dear companionship can make the street a shrine, and the hearth an altar, and the home a church. 'The Church that is in *their* house.' God grant it for us all!

CHAPTER 28

Foreground
and Background

*We look not at the things which are seen, but at the things which are
not seen: for the things which are seen are temporal; but the things
which are not seen are eternal.*

~ II Corinthians 4: 18 ~

I

THIS is the difference between life's foreground and life's background.
'The things which are seen' – the foreground. 'The things which are not
seen' – the background.

Life's foreground today is certainly disquieting and terrifying enough:
this world of fierce economic pressures and political uncertainty, of
violence and vandalism, of international conflicts generating who knows
what potential catastrophes. We begin to wonder – Can we really go on
coping with the world indefinitely? Can we ever come to terms with
these vast impersonal systems in which we feel ourselves imprisoned?

The trouble is that so often we see *only* the foreground, things
beautiful or ugly right there in front of us, presented to us by the media
– newspapers and television – constantly, persistently, daily. We are seeing
that. And we forget that to all that foreground there is a *background*, a
divine eternal background which alone gives meaning to this strange,
confused, ambiguous existence, and which matters more than all the
rest.

The fact is, as Paul here reminds us, *we inhabit two worlds, not one,* two
worlds intermingling all the time – the foreground world of the seen and
temporal, and the background world of the unseen and the eternal; the
foreground of our immediate historical perspectives, and the background
of the everlasting plan and purpose of God.

For example, take your own life. Each event of your life happens in this space-and-time conditioned world. Yet each event is directly linked with God. This two-foldness goes right through our experience.

II

But let us be clear just what we mean by this, and what Paul means in our text.

First, to remove misunderstanding, observe what is *not* meant. We are not to think (as unfortunately many do think) of the secular and the sacred sides of life, the material and the spiritual, *standing over against each other in radical opposition* – contradictories, cancelling each other out.

Christians should be the last people to denigrate or minimise the natural, material order in which our lives are set, retreating from it into a self-cultivating spirituality, a beguiling pietistic other-worldliness. Any such compartmentalising of life – into the common and the holy, the secular and the religious – would manifestly be untrue to the Christian revelation, which *centres precisely in an act of incarnation,* as down-to-earth as the stable at Bethlehem and the workshop of Nazareth. Christianity does not despise matter: it consecrates it. It does not scorn the secular: it proposes to transfigure it.

That being so, the Church of today should be not less, but actually *more* involved than it is in the seen and temporal, *more* concerned with this troubled, chaotic, God-forgetting world which in love and pity Christ died to redeem.

III

That is true. *But it is not the whole truth.* That is the foreground. But don't let us forget the background.

If the Church exists to help christianise the foreground, as it does, *it exists even more to remind us of the background.* And any church service that does *not* do that – that does not renew the awareness of the dimension of the transcendent – is a failure utterly. And any church service that *does* that – that renews the sense of the transcendent – is a real gift of God in heaven to men and women on this earthly pilgrimage.

To remember the background means to recognise that there is *an element of 'beyond-ness' in the midst of life. Beyond* the everyday world of on-going secular history, with its sinister and frightening possibilities, there is another world of supra-sensible reality – which keeps haunting the conscience of history, which is the mainspring of the universe, the environment of every day's existence, and the true home of your life and mine at this moment.

IV

Do you remember that day when Elisha and his young servant found themselves surrounded by hordes of Syrians out to kill? 'Master,' cried the young man, 'what shall we do?' And Elisha's answer was a prayer. 'O Lord, open his eyes, that he may see.' And we are told, 'The Lord opened the eyes of the young man, and he saw: and behold, *the mountain was full of horses and chariots of fire round about Elisha'*.

This is our situation – foreground and background, the foreground of the immediate appearance of things, the background of an encompassing *reality* beyond.

But so often we are just like Elisha's servant. We can see nothing but the foreground – nothing but the hills round Dothan and the Syrians camping in the valley. We are needing some sixth sense to awaken us to the total reality of things: God's ring of fire round the mountain, and round our mortal weakness, rank upon serried rank of the shining hosts of heaven.

They are there at this moment for someone in this congregation who has been feeling hemmed in by problems, lost in the labyrinth of life's enigmas, and unable to cope. I assure you they are there now – God's strengthening angels in the unseen. How glad I'd be if I could convince someone of this today!

V

Do you remember how Francis Thompson put it?

> *O world invisible, we view thee,*
> *O world intangible, we touch thee,*
> *O world unknowable, we know thee,*
> *Inapprehensible, we clutch thee.*

That was not just a poet romanticising. He was being strictly realistic and his logic was as hard as nails.

For this world *has* a background – more real and abiding than all the confusion and turmoil of the foreground. And it is only when seen against that background that life becomes meaningful. Only against that background does what we do here in church make sense, and touch the very heart of heaven. Only against that background can our souls find hope and courage and serenity and faith triumphant over death.

But now, having to belong to two worlds at once is not easy. It is liable to create a tension: the pull of earth and the demand of heaven. And *it is precisely this tension between two worlds that is man's glory and tragedy.*

Here we are, as it were, living a double life: at home in these fleeting earthly surroundings, yet not fully at home; torn between the two worlds, confined within the seen and temporal and yet living on the borderland, the frontiers of the unseen and eternal.

If only I could forget the one or the other, I might secure some sort of peace. But if I try to settle down in the present world, the world invisible is going to haunt me. And if I try to live for that higher world, the present keeps dragging me down.

Sometimes men have tried to ease and resolve that tension by their own efforts. They have endeavoured to pierce the veil of the eternal *from the human side,* 'climbing up,' as Martin Luther disdainfully expressed it, 'climbing up to the majesty on high' – as though we could somehow capture the dimension of eternity in the poor little temporal net of our own logic or imagination. It can't be done – not in ten thousand years.

Only one thing can resolve the tension. We can't climb up to that invisible realm. Therefore – *it must reach down to us,* and lift us up. It must invade the visible.

VI

The Gospel says this is precisely what has happened. Once and for all, in Jesus Christ, the world unseen and eternal has broken right through. It has penetrated the seen and temporal, not with a fitful flickering gleam, but with a great shaft of heavenly light that has changed the whole history of the human race. *Christ bridges the gulf.*

And you can see why. It is because He – He alone – *belongs perfectly to both worlds.* He is bone of our bone, flesh of our flesh, in true solidarity with our humanity. But He can also say – 'I and the Father are one.' In other words, this is *God acting to reveal Himself,* the love that came to us at Bethlehem and Calvary and the empty tomb; the love which through the Holy Spirit is for ever coming to us still, new every morning; the love divine all loves excelling which is in fact coming to us at this very moment – God loving you not in some aloof, impersonal way, but passionately and eagerly, longing to take you by the hand and recreate your courage and your hope, and send you on your way rejoicing.

In Jesus Christ, Son of Man, Son of God, *time and eternity are fused;* so that we are now for ever linked to that overwhelming Reality which overarches our existence and is our true essential home. *The one thing needful is to possess Christ, and be united to Him by faith.*

VII

In such a union, what do we discover? Two stupendous discoveries, and with these I close.

We discover, on the one hand, that *we can begin to live – even here on earth – the life of the eternal world.*

It is a tremendous thing to claim, with change and decay around us and within – the remorseless years going on, time running its inexorable, irreversible course, life's brief pageant soon over, the outward man perishing. But the New Testament unequivocally declares that eternal life is *not* to be regarded as something beginning only on the further side of death. It begins, for those who belong to Christ, who are incorporated into Christ, *here and now.*

There are in fact men and women here in this church today who can testify to this from their own experience. They are still pilgrims and strangers and sojourners as all their fathers were; but in Christ, through vital association with Christ, that other unseen world has begun *to take control* – eternal life in the midst of time, a foretaste, a first instalment, an anticipatory sample now and here of what is to be looked for hereafter, when God's Kingdom comes and human destiny is complete. That is the one discovery: eternal life a *present possession.*

VIII

And the other discovery we make is this: *the validity of the resurrection hope.* For in Christ we have been joined to the immortality of God, and that by God's own act. And clearly if you are joined to the immortality of God you cannot die. What we call death is simply a bridge over which one day we pass into the fulness of the life eternal – the 'sweet and blessed country, the home of God's elect'.

How sad, how utterly tragic that the Church should sometimes seem to soft-pedal the resurrection note, perhaps thinking thereby to rehabilitate itself in the eyes of secular man! It is the most pathetic of mistakes. For what is the sense of the journey, if you don't know where the road is leading?

I tell you now: this horizon of the hereafter is no dubious or super-fluous adjunct to Christian belief. It is no conjecture. *It is the very heart and essence and climax of the faith.* And the Church that fails to proclaim and celebrate it is throwing away the most precious thing it possesses, and trivialising the Gospel disastrously.

IX

Let us today at this anniversary – when we look back across the years and think of the generations gone before, including dear ones of our own – let us today rejoice and glory in it, that the God who made you at the first is one day going to *re-make* you after the pattern of the very image of Christ.

What an astounding promise, the miracle to crown all miracles, incredible but true! 'When He appears,' wrote St John, '*we shall be like Him*, seeing Him as He is.' *We – like Christ!* 'Sweet and blessed country' indeed!

Like Christ! Don't ask me to explain it. I can't explain it. No one can. It is far beyond comprehension. Only God can explain it – whose judg-ments are unsearchable and His ways past finding out. But I'm sure of the fact. I can only speak of what I know. And I know this stands on the word of God the Father, God the Son, and God the Holy Spirit.

Like Christ! That is the purpose of God, and He is working at it even now: and *God does not drop a work He has begun.*

In the meantime, I have Christ's word to rely on. I know (for didn't He say it Himself?) He is going to be with me always, even to the end of the world, and even to my last short hour on earth. Therefore: 'Lord, into Thy hands I commend my spirit.' Into those hands of unfathomable loving-kindness, with quietness and expectancy, I commend my spirit every day I live.

And at the end? 'Lord, now lettest Thou Thy servant depart in peace, for mine eyes have seen Thy salvation.'

Therefore, to the dear Saviour to whom we owe it all – to Him be all praise and glory given, now and for ever.

CHAPTER 29

Life's Handicaps

And lest I should be exalted above measure through the abundance of the revelations, there was given to me a thorn in the flesh ...

~ II Corinthians 12: 7ff ~

THE subject I want to speak about this morning is 'Life's Handicaps, and how to manage them'. The world is full of people labouring under one or other of the many different kinds of handicap that life imposes. Almost everyone of us, indeed, feels himself or herself to be handicapped, limited, in some particular direction. And as so many people have to run life's race under these conditions *through no fault of their own*, the problem raised is a very real one, and the sense of injustice is sometimes not far away.

Sometimes, for instance, the handicap is ill-health, that wearing drag upon the spirit. Sometimes it is poverty, and financial worry. Sometimes it is the fact of being born into a home which, to be quite honest, was not the kind of home you would have chosen. Sometimes it is the tragedy of being condemned to distasteful work, because other people chose your career for you and you had to go 'into the business', and now you feel like a galley-slave. Sometimes it is a lack of social gifts, that awkwardness and shyness which win few friends, and which leave life a very lonely thing, stranded in a backwater. Sometimes it is a mistaken, perhaps too impetuous, decision, long ago, which is going to cause you to go on a broken wing all your days. Sometimes it is the oppression of being saddled with people's selfishness. Sometimes it is a broken heart. There is no end to them – the handicaps of life.

Well, let us take this striking passage of apostolic autobiography. It is a thing we are apt to forget – that this great soul Paul was one the most badly handicapped of men. You might have thought that when God was searching for a likely man to carry Christ and commend the Gospel to the wide, waiting world, He would have chosen a man of fine, handsome, commanding presence and unimpaired health and vigour and physique:

but the reality was very different. The man God actually hit upon, the man who far more than any John Wesley did, 'took the whole world for his parish'; whose tracks could be found across the lonely moorlands and heights of Asia, and in the great, uproarious commercial cities of pagan Europe; who has left the impress of his personality on the civilisation and the religion of the whole world – the man who achieved such astonishing results was a man (as the tradition tells us) little and undistinguished in stature, plain and even ugly in appearance, often prostrated with bodily weakness, and sometimes quite desperately ill. Paul's mighty achievement was carried through in the face of a terrible handicap.

What the 'thorn in the flesh' was, he has not told us explicitly. Various guesses have been hazarded, some of them certainly wide of the mark. Thus, for example, the early Christian fathers took it to mean the rankling of some unconquered sensual sin. St Chrysostom, looking in another direction, found in it a reference to the perpetual pinpricks Paul had to endure from men like Hymenaeus and Alexander the coppersmith. John Calvin thought it meant all the worries and cares of ecclesiastical life, the problems of the ministry. But the truth is, Paul's 'thorn' was something definitely physical. According to one line of evidence, it may have been epilepsy – a trouble from which other men so distinguished as Julius Caesar, Napoleon and Peter the Great are known to have suffered. According to another line, it may have been ophthalmia. According to still another – and this the most likely – it may have been malaria. Whatever it was, it was something recurrent, and humiliating, and prostrating; and that is all we need to know. Indeed, the very vagueness of it is all to the good; for it makes it easier for us to get this thing applied to ourselves, to read our own case in this great passage, to see what it has to say about *our* handicap, *our* limitation, whatever that may be, whether it is physical or social or spiritual. And, of course, *that* is what we are after.

Well, you will observe that, while Paul was by no means explicit about the thorn itself, he was perfectly explicit about why it was sent to him. Look at his words again. *'Lest I should be exalted above measure by the abundance of the revelations,* there was given to me a thorn in the flesh.' In other words, he says – 'In case my spiritual experiences by their very number and vividness, should produce in me a kind of spiritual self-confidence, this thing was sent to keep me humble.' Now that is worth pondering. Here is the Apostle saying that any spiritual experience that comes to you and me may (unless we are careful) turn into a temp-tation. Here is a man, a saint if ever there was one, pointing out to us that one of the subtlest dangers in the world – subtle because so often it is never guessed and never realised – is the danger that springs from a man's very goodness. Here is Paul confessing that he himself, so great were his spiritual convictions and assurances, might easily have succumbed to the temptation of a kind of spiritual superiority, would certainly have succumbed to it, if God hadn't sent this humiliating thing to remind him that he himself was nothing. 'Lest I should be exalted through the abundance of the revelations', this thing happened to me.

Let us be grateful to Paul for being so frank about it! Certainly we can see his point. After all, these others – these Corinthians to whom he was writing – *they* hadn't been arrested outside Damascus by a flash that had dazzled the noonday. *They* hadn't all been caught up into Paradise, or spoken to God in the third heaven. *They* hadn't all been taken so deep into the mystic intimacies of Christ. And, says Paul, it took the pitiless pressure of God's humbling hand, this thorn in the flesh, this life-handicap I had to endure – it took that to keep me right.

Doesn't that cast light on all life's handicaps? I am not raising the question now as to whether those thorns in the flesh are directly sent to us by God. I think it is reasonably clear that we can't *always* say '*God* sent this thing to me'. But the point I am concerned to make is this: that *any* handicap which we can't break through but have to endure, any thorn whether it is sent to us by God or not, may, instead of being a negative affliction, become a positive divine safeguard for the soul – God's device to keep the edge of conscience keen; God's way of saving us from the danger of self-confidence. Yes, that is indeed the truth of it: 'lest I should be exalted above measure.' For if there is one thing more than any other we need saving from, one thing which though often not found in the category of sins at all was nevertheless in Jesus' view far more ruinous than any hot passion of the flesh – it is precisely that thing which Paul thanked God for guarding him against, the blight of a soul's self-confidence. Anything that holds a man right *there* is most abundantly worthwhile; any hard handicap that will remind him of his creaturely weakness, that will save him from the blight of spiritual self-satisfaction, and take him again and again to his knees, crying 'God be merciful to me a sinner!'

But looking at the passage again, you will observe that this reason for his 'thorn' did not dawn upon the Apostle's mind at once. His first impulse, he tells us, was to beg God to take it away. '*For this thing I besought the Lord thrice, that it might depart from me.*' Now that is always the first impulse. And in a way it is a perfectly right impulse. For you see, there are two types of handicap – those which cannot be altered, and those which can. If your handicap is of the latter kind – one that *can* be broken through – then, in God's name, up and break it! For God doesn't always counsel submission: sometimes He says, Fight!

'I prayed the Lord,' says Paul, 'that it might depart!' And in Paul's case, there was a genuinely noble and unselfish motive behind the impulse. It was the Lord's work he was thinking of. He was thinking – 'If only this handicap were lifted, how much faster I could go on Jesus' service! If only these irksome limitations were removed, how much more Gospel influence I could wield! It is not myself I am thinking about, I'm not afraid of pain: but I can't understand why Christ's work should suffer, why so many things I'd like to do for Him have perforce to remain undone, why there should be this perpetual feeling of being thwarted and frustrated and held back by my own infirmity.' *That* was Paul's problem.

But it is the problem of many a Christian man and woman today, who is thinking – 'If only the handicap were gone! If only I had more strength, more leisure! If only I moved in a wider circle! If only my influence were stronger, my words more persuasive – what a much finer, more serviceable life I could live than now!'

That is the thought. In Paul's case, as it happened, it was mistaken; but at least it was perfectly understandable. And it is natural – perhaps it's right – to do what Paul did, when he besought the Lord that the thorn might depart from him, the handicap be eliminated. But God knows best; and I want to say now that it is often when that prayer seems utterly unanswered that it is being answered most gloriously.

Look at it like this. There are two possible ways of helping a man with the burden he has to carry in this world, two ways to lighten the load. One is to diminish the actual weight of the thing, to level down the handicap to suit the soul's resources. The other is to level up the soul's resources to match the handicap. Again and again the first can't happen: for some reason, the lightening of the load is excluded. What does happen is that God takes the second way: levels up the soul's resources to meet the need.

And He chose that way with His own Son Christ. 'Father,' prayed Jesus in the agony of Gethsemane, praying it three times like His own great disciple here, 'Father, if it be possible, let this cup pass!' But it didn't pass. And yet the prayer was answered. For God gave Christ the strength to drink the cup. So it was with Paul. 'I besought the Lord thrice that this thorn in the flesh might go!' But it didn't go. And yet the prayer was triumphantly answered. For God gave His servant a spirit to match the need. 'My grace is sufficient for thee!'

And you who have prayed God once, twice, thrice, a score of times, to remove some handicap and give you a decent chance in life, and yet for all your praying nothing seems to be happening, listen – is that not God's voice still, 'My grace sufficient for thee'? In other words, may not God be seeking to answer you, not by reducing the burden (which might not be a compliment to a man at all, but simply an indulgence to his weakness), but rather by letting the thing stay, and keying up your strength to it (which is the way God treats His heroes)?

I think these words, 'My grace is sufficient for thee', should be written in letters of gold and flame right across our life's horizon. For it is no abstract theology they give us, but life's greatest, most practical reality. Where would some of us be today if Christ's grace hadn't proved sufficient? Can't you remember some hour when you would most certainly have broken down, if Christ hadn't come in and given you just the added bit of strength you needed? Or some period of your life when everything seemed going against you, and the only consolation was that there was One at your right hand – Christ? Or some heavy cross you had to carry, and you wouldn't have carried it long, would just have sat down and wept beneath its weight, and nothing in yourself or anyone else would have held you to it or brought you through with honour – and then, at the critical moment, the marvel happened, and Christ somehow got into you, actually into your soul and body, and weakness, self-pity, self-consciousness, defeat, all fled before that mighty reinforcement? 'My grace is sufficient for thee' – bind that great word about your heart!

'For,' went on the voice to Paul, '*for My strength is made perfect in weakness.*' Have you thought of that? – it is a most wonderful thing – Christ, so far from being frustrated by the weakness of us who are His instruments, actually using that weakness to His glory! Do you see what it means? It means that as long as a man is self-assured, and strong, and independent and conscious of no need, he is really living in a terribly narrow world, limited by his own human strength and natural resources. But as soon as you have got that same man with his self-assurance gone, and conscious of nothing so much as that he is a poor, broken reed, then God can come in with the limitless reserves of the supernatural.

Hadn't Paul's own experience proved that? Once he had been almost defiantly determined to be master of his own fate and captain of his own soul, felt himself sufficient to any calls life might make on him, would have ridiculed the idea that in religion or anywhere else, he, Paul, couldn't see things through for himself without any power from the beyond to help him. As long as *that* was his nature, the man was simply playing at life, wasting time, useless to God – an impediment to God. But when one day life got him down, with every shred of the old assurance gone, and nothing but a cry – 'I'm finished, I can do no more. You'll need to take things now into your hands, Christ' – from that moment God began to use him mightily. Through his very brokenness, God's power came into play; and God's strength was made perfect in his weakness.

And what Paul found, ten thousand others have found. 'We have this treasure in earthen vessels.' There's nothing like self-trust for keeping the supernatural out of your life: there's nothing like having your self-trust broken to pieces for letting supernatural power come in. And that is true, whether you think of it on the world-wide or on the scale of your own soul. On the scale of world events, it means that as long as we imagine we can patch up some solution of our present troubles by our own ingenuity, we are merely pottering and trifling and sure to sink deeper and deeper in the mire; but from the moment when at last, in sheer despair, our world flings itself on God, we'll begin to rise. And on the scale of our own life it means this – that before any of us can function with maximum efficiency and really secure God and our generation, somehow we have got to touch rock bottom, to have our souls stripped of every relic of self and self-trust and left absolutely bare and naked, so that it has simply *got* to be God then, or he is done! It is the men who, out of that despair, have flung themselves on Christ for help, on whom the energising Spirit of Christ comes like a passion. It is when a soul, beaten and broken down into helplessness, has made its utter God-surrender, that it rises into the power of an endless life. And whatever burden or handicap it is that bears you down, it is a *blessed* thing, if it casts you into the arms of God.

And so this intimate, self-revealing passage that began with tears ends with doxology. 'Most gladly therefore will I glory in mine infirmities, that the power of God may rest upon me.' 'Most gladly will I glory' – in my handicap. That's the real Paul. That's the real Christian spirit in every age. Do you remember John Masefield's lines?

> Men in desert places, men
>   Abandoned, broken, sick with fears,
> Rose singing, swung their swords again,
>   And laughed and died among the spears.

'Most gladly will I glory.' Will your soul rise to that when life is hard? Can your soul sing like that, in the Valley of Humiliation? In Bunyan's story, *Pilgrim's Progress,* the Guide, leading the pilgrims down into the Valley of Humiliation, asked them to notice how green the Valley was, and how beautiful with Lilies; and he told them that men had been known to meet angels there, and that the Lord Himself had once had there His country-house. And as they went through the Valley, they heard the sound of music. It was a shepherd-lad, who carried in his bosom the herb called Heart's Ease; and this is what he sang

> He that is down need fear no Fall,
>   He that is low, no Pride;
> He that is humble ever shall
>   Have God to be His Guide.

It is the hearts that have learnt that song who hold the key of the Kingdom.

CHAPTER 30

Faith and the Strain of Life

The life which I now live in the flesh I live by the faith of the Son of God, who loved me, and gave Himself for me.

~ Galatians 2: 20 ~

'THE life which I now live, I live by faith.'

'Yes,' retorts the world, 'that is precisely what you Christians do! That is the whole point of our case against you. You have hit the nail on the head. It is faith, faith all the time with you – instead of rationality, realism, commonsense. You are always harping on the same string, babbling about this discreditable and discredited attitude. The life which you live, you live by faith. That's just it. You have put our case against you in a nutshell.'

So speaks the world. And what does the Christian do? Does he hang his head before that criticism? Does he feel ashamed? Does he retreat in confusion? On the contrary. He stands his ground. He is completely unabashed. He is not in the least apologetic about his emphasis on faith. A recent biographer has made the significant remark about Mr Bernard Shaw: 'All his life he has suffered under a handicap, which is that he is shy of using the name of God, yet cannot find any proper substitute.' The Christian is not shy of using the word 'faith'. He has no intention of looking for a substitute. He is quite frank and unequivocal about his world-outlook and his philosophy of life: 'The life which I now live in the flesh, I live by faith.'

In justification of this attitude of the Christian, let me draw attention to two facts which his critics have singularly overlooked. One is the fact that *faith is not only an integral part of religion – it is a necessity of science as well.* The whole corpus of scientific knowledge is (as it were) within brackets, with the sign of faith outside to qualify it. Before the scientist can get going at all, he has to postulate two tremendous hypotheses – one, the rationality of the universe he is investigating; the other, the reliability of the mental processes he is using. If you disallow either of these, you make science utterly impossible. The whole structure is built on them. And what are these twin postulates but just faith — faith at its most splendid and most daring? So I say, faith is a necessity of science. And what right has the critic to accept it tacitly in one field of activity, and then denounce it in another? That is not being scientific.

The second fact to underline is this — that *faith is a necessity of life*. Its most violent critics, if they only realised it, are using it all the time. In fact, the only way to stop using faith would be to stop living. We are dependent on it at every turn. When we rise in the morning, and face the untravelled road of a new day, when we make engagements for tomorrow or next week or next year, when we plan for the future of our children, when we make friends and trust them, when we engage in business, when we join a political party, when we go for a journey, when we lie down to sleep — it is all faith in action. And again I ask: Why should this quality be sanctioned in every other realm of life, and yet disallowed in religion? It is the critic, not the Christian, who is irrational.

Hence, the Christian Church gives its testimony without shame, knowing that it has right on its side. 'The life I now live, I live by faith.' And indeed, the world's criticism is largely due to a regrettable misunderstanding as to what religious faith really is. Let us try to get this clear.

For one thing, faith is not credulity. It is not a superstitious experience of the unintelligent.

'Now,' said the Queen to Alice in Lewis Carroll's story, 'I'll give you something to believe. I'm just one hundred and one, five months and a day.'

'I can't believe *that!*' said Alice.

'Can't you?' the Queen said in a pitying tone. 'Try again: draw a long breath, and shut your eyes.'

But faith is not like that. It is not, as the schoolboy is said to have defined it, 'Believing what you know isn't true'. The faith of the Christian is on a different level altogether. He lives by faith, because faith makes sense of the universe. Faith gives a satisfying interpretation of life. The fact is, that if it is to be a question of a charge of credulity, then irreligion lies far more open to the charge than does religion. The intellectual difficulties in the way of consistent scepticism and unbelief are far more serious and insurmountable than those in the way of faith. Eliminate the religious interpretation of life, and now you have got to believe that there is no directing mind or purpose at the back of things, that all the story of history, and all the struggles of humanity, and all the sacrifices of the souls of men for beauty, truth and goodness, and everything like conscience, and the magic of two hearts in love, and Beethoven's music, and the wizardry of Shakespeare, and the death of Captain Oates among the Antarctic snows, and the light in the eyes of children, and the valour of the saints – all that has no more ultimate significance than the dust that eddies down the street. I say, it is asking far more of the human intellect to accept *that* than to say 'I live by faith'. Talk of credulity!

It is *unbelief* that is the credulous thing, the ultimate irrationality.

Faith, then, is not credulity. A second point worth emphasising is that it is not sentimentality. That is another charge which is often heard. 'You Christians,' it is said, 'have created for yourselves a world of fantasy. You are wanting comfort and refuge from the stark facts of life; and so you have invented religion to be a kind of cushion between you and these facts. Your faith is nothing more nor less than what is technically known as "wishful thinking". You *wish* certain things were true; and so your mind, as it were, projects them upon the screen, and says they *are* true. It is just another instance of the working of a perfectly familiar psychological process – the human mind's inveterate tendency to believe what it wants to believe, and to assign objective validity to its own subjective desire. Faith is really a running away from the facts. It is sentimentality.'

Now, I am not going to maintain that this criticism is *never* cogent or legitimate. It is perfectly true that there has sometimes appeared an attitude to life calling itself religious, and yet consisting in just the kind of illusion, whether deliberate or unconscious, which this criticism describes. But surely we are to judge a phenomenon by the real thing, not by any deplorably degenerate imitations of it.

Well then, here is my answer to the criticism that identifies religion with fantasy, wishful thinking and sentiment: it is along two lines. One is that indulgence in fantasy, if carried beyond a certain point, inevitably weakens character and reduces efficiency for the battle of life; whereas the effect of religion is the exact reverse: it strengthens character, and stimulates efficiency. The other answer I give to the criticism is this – it is obviously nonsense to talk about men inventing religion to make life comfortable, and creating faith as a cushion: actually, times without number, religion has made life desperately *un*comfortable for those who have professed it. What about the martyrs? What about the heroes of the eleventh chapter of Hebrews? What about the thousands of people today for whom religion is obviously making life, not less, but far *more* difficult and dangerous than it would have been without it? The symbol of religion is not a cushion: it is a Cross. Whatever faith is, it is not sentimentality.

What is it, then? It is self-commitment. It is not credulity; it is not fantasy; and, perhaps I should add, it is not doctrine. You can subscribe a dozen doctrines, and yet know nothing about faith – a fact which the Apostle James gave us a devastatingly blunt reminder in the words, 'Thou believest that there is one God? Thou doest well! The demons also believe and tremble'. It is not doctrine; nothing theoretical. It is essentially practical.

It is doing something with your life. It is bridging the gulf between the seen and the unseen by putting one's own life into the gap. It is risking putting all the weight and strain of your soul on to the slender-looking rope that some divine Hand has let down from above into the fearful pit of our human troubles and distresses. It is, as Donald Hankey expressed it, 'betting your life that there is a God'. Faith is self-commitment.

Now notice this: for the Christian, as distinguished from other people, faith is specifically self-commitment to God revealed *in Jesus;* and more specifically still, self-commitment to God revealed in *the death of Jesus.* That is why Paul here, in the great confession of our text, exclaims 'the life I now live, I live by faith' – and then, defining it more clearly, 'faith in the Son of God' – and then, more clearly and precisely still, 'who loved me and gave Himself for me'. In short, Christian faith is self-commitment in the light of the Cross.

This sharpening of the definition is decisively important. And you will see why it is so important if you reflect on the terrible, perpetual challenge to which faith, in every age and in every individual soul, is subjected – the challenge of the mystery of evil. Faith has to be self-commitment *in the light of the Cross,* if it is to be adequate for that.

Now, I do want you to get this clear. The challenge to faith, the challenge of the mystery of evil, meets us in two forms – physical evil, *ie* suffering; and moral evil, *ie* sin.

How often the fact of suffering has proved ruinous to faith – specially the suffering of the innocent! And this earth is full of it; at any given moment, there is such appalling anguish in the world, so many of our fellow-creatures at the breaking-point; and sooner or later, the dark spectre of trouble – in one or other of its myriad forms – invades every life irresistibly. It is a terrible challenge to faith – this fact of suffering.

But there is the even grimmer challenge of sin. What are we to say of the radical twist in man's nature that baffles all the moral philosophers? What are we to say of his abominable crimes that have brought civilisation itself to the brink of the pit of extinction? What are we to say of his powerlessness to extricate himself from the chaos of his own contriving? What are we to say of our own rebellious, inconsistent hearts, oscillating so bewilderingly between dreams of perfect good and the magnetic, malignant lure of the world, the flesh and the devil? The fact of moral evil is shouting at us today from the international scene, shouting at us in the glaring headlines of our newspapers, daunting us in the secret places of our own hearts. What are we to say of sin?

That is the double challenge evil throws out to faith. That is why faith, if it is to survive and triumph, must be faith of a certain specific kind: not just faith in a general providence, not faith in a vague 'divinity that shapes our ends, rough hew them how we will', but faith in a God who has spoken once and for all time in the conquering death of Christ, faith in 'the Son of God who loved me, and gave Himself for me'. It must be self-commitment in the light of the Cross.

Why that? How is it that the Cross creates a faith more strong than the strongest challenge of the mystery of evil? I do want to get this clear: for so much Christian thinking about this is vague and hazy and inclined to miss the point. The point is this – the Cross creates faith, precisely because that Cross itself *was* the problem of evil at its worst, the most unpardonable, desperate deed that ever defaced the page of history, the most terrifying triumph of sheer, naked evil. And yet it was that – oh, don't you see the wonder of it? – it is precisely *that,* the very stuff of sin, which God has chosen to be the vehicle of His mightiest act of love. It is there, where sin has confidently proclaimed its supreme and final victory, that God has achieved sin's uttermost defeat. That is why Christian faith takes its stand at the Cross, and will always triumph there.

Think what was happening when Jesus died. Was there ever a worse miscarriage of justice in history? Did ever malevolence, self-interest, ruthless ambition, and all the petty passions of men, perpetrate a fouler deed than this? Was ever evil more concentrated in its malignity? 'Behold, and see if there be any sorrow like unto My sorrow!' In other words, the Cross *is* the problem of evil *at its intensest.* The Cross is the deadly challenge to faith at its deadliest. The Cross is the age-long, baffling mystery – the twin mystery of suffering and sin – in its most baffling and tragic and shattering form. Were there no more to be said, the Cross would not help or strengthen faith – it would kill it outright for ever.

But there *is* something more to be said. There is this (and you *must* see how it transforms the whole tragic situation, and floods it with sudden light) – that the Christ who died on that Cross as a victim of the mystery of evil, died even more as a victor. The principalities and powers that put him there fancied that they were masters of the situation: but all history today bears witness that there was only one master of that deadly hour – and that was not Pilate, or Caiaphas, or Annas, but the conquering soul of Christ. If they could have made Him on that Cross false to His own teaching (which was what they were trying to do); if, in the shame and torment of it, His love – even for a moment – had flickered and gone out, that would have been their victory. But it never came. They might break His body; His spirit they could not break. When I look at that Cross today, I *know* it is not defeat I am seeing. It is triumph like no other triumph in this world. It is not the language of pity and pathos that I need to express what meets me there: it is the language of victory, songs of a conqueror's march – such language as John Henry Newman's ...

O loving wisdom of our God,
  When all was sin and shame,
A second Adam to the fight
  And to the rescue came.   ~ Hymn 238: *CH3* ~

His was the controlling will, His the mastery of the situation, His the voice that cried at last, with the shout of a conqueror, 'It is finished!'

When you have seen that, you have seen God in action. You have seen God taking the worst that earth could do, and out of it fashioning the best that heaven could bestow. You have seen Him taking that very mystery of evil which is our own most terrible problem, and out of that – not out of something else, mark you, quite different from that, but precisely out of evil at its stubbornest and most absolute – bringing His noblest and sublimest gift for men. You have seen Him taking 'the hour and power of darkness', and making it victoriously the hour and power of light. After *that,* there can be no situation too difficult for God to handle, no irreparable disaster, no crown of thorns that He can't twist into a crown of glory.

That is what I mean when I say that if you want a faith that is adequate for life, a faith that can take the strain and the weight of life upon it, a faith that can confront the desperate challenge of the mystery of evil and remain undaunted – if you want that (and what else is worth having?), then you must get it at the Cross. If you have seen God triumphing there, and if to that conquering grace you have yielded up your soul in absolute, irrevocable, self-commitment, then every suffering you may have to bear is utterly transmuted, and every sin that tries to shackle you is broken and defeated; and bright against the dark background of the tragic mystery of evil, you see the glory of the kingdom that is to be.

For God raised Christ from the dead with power and glory; and all I have said today is ratified and sealed forever by the tremendous fact of which Easter and the Ascension speak. The measure of Christ's triumph over the mystery of evil is not any man-made human answer. It comes from beyond himself and beyond history. It is God's answer. 'I am He that liveth and was dead, and behold I am alive for evermore.'

This – nothing less – is Christianity. This is the faith the Church proclaims. This is God's answer to all mankind's predicament. This living Christ is God's sure word to you. And something you may ever need is here – hope when you are despairing, courage when you are terrified, light when you are in darkness, forgiveness when you have blundered, friendship when you are feeling lonely; and at the last, a wonderful welcome home, from the Lord of life eternal, when your day has run to sunset, and the dusk descends, and the evening star is in the sky.

The Books of James S. Stewart

*The Life and Teaching of Jesus Christ (1932).
A Man in Christ: The Vital Elements of St Paul's Religion (1935).
The Gates of New Life (1937).
The Strong Name (1940).
Heralds of God (1946).
A Faith to Proclaim (1953).
Thine is the Kingdom (1956).
The Wind of the Spirit (1968).
River of Life (1972).
King for Ever (1974).

Publisher's Note

While all reasonable attempts have been taken to trace the literary and biblical sources used by James S. Stewart in his Sermons, because of the nature of the original material some sources have been impossible to locate. Any information regarding the origins of some of the unreferenced quotations is welcomed and would be included in the next edition of this book.

The version of the Bible used by James S. Stewart, unless otherwise indicated, was the Authorised or King James Version.

*This book is currently available from Saint Andrew Press, Edinburgh.